Railroads and Rifles

Soldiers,
Technology,
and the Unification of Germany

RAILROADS
AND
RIFLES

Soldiers,
Technology,
and the Unification of Germany

Dennis E. Showalter

ARCHON
BOOKS

Library of Congress Cataloging in Publication Data

Showalter, Dennis E.
  Railroads and rifles

    Bibliography: p.
    Includes index.
      1. Germany—History, Military—19th century.
  2. Prussia—History, Military. 3. Railroads—
  Germany. 4. Germany—Defenses—History. 5. Krupp,
  Alfred, 1812–1887. I. Title.
  DD103.S54   335′.00943   75–17710
  ISBN 0–208–01505–1
  ISBN 0–208–02137–X (paperback)

© 1975 by Dennis E. Showalter
First published 1976 in a hardcover edition
and in paperback in 1986 as an Archon Book,
an imprint of The Shoe String Press, Inc.
Hamden, Connecticut 06514

Printed in the United States of America

Contents

Maps

Maps 3 and 4 by John Carnes are from *The Battle of Koniggratz*, by Gordon Craig, copyright © 1964 by Gordon A. Craig, and are reprinted with the permission of J. B. Lippincott Company.

Preface

The preparation and completion of this study furnished ample proof that no man is an island. The Woodrow Wilson Foundation, the Danforth Foundation, and the Fulbright Foundation supported the initial research on which the work is based. The Colorado College provided additional financial assistance at several critical times. The library staffs of The Colorado College, the University of Minnesota, and the university library of Freiburg and the staff of the *Militärgeschichtliches Forschungsamt* were consistently helpful beyond the call of duty, particularly in the matter of inter-library loans. Sections 1, 2, and 3 of chapter III are reprinted from *Military Affairs*, April 1974, pp. 62-67, with permission (copyright 1974 by the American Military Institute). I also wish to thank the publishers and editors of the following journals for permission to incorporate in altered form material originally appearing in their pages: *The Historian*, XXV (February, 1972); *European Studies Review*, IV (April, 1974); and *Studies in Modern European History and Culture*, Vol. I, (1975).

Turning to more personal acknowledgements, Professor Harold Deutsch took an interest in the project from its inception; his advice and suggestions merit special thanks. Two sets of parents, Mr. and Mrs. Edwin Showalter and Mr. and Mrs. John F. McKenna, lent encouragement when it was needed; and Mr. John Wheatley served by turns as critic and friend. The students of Colorado College and my departmental colleagues past and present have contributed to an atmosphere in which both scholarship and teaching are respected. I am particularly grateful to Professor Arthur Pettit, who adjusted his own demanding schedule to read the manuscript and make many valuable comments. Helen Foster not only turned pencilled hieroglyphics into legible typescript, but also brought to the project her impressive skills as an historian and editorial assistant. Without her the manuscript would have taken much longer to produce.

I owe a personal and professional debt beyond measure to two men. Professor J. F. Heininger, "Prof" to a generation of students at St. John's University, initiated me into the study of German history and provided an unforgettable example of scholarship and teaching. Professor Otto Pflanze first conceived the project and guided its initial development, pruning away errors and ambiguities, offering advice, opinions, and encouragement without stint. What merits this work may possess are due in large part to his labors as a *Doktorvater*; only the errors are the author's sole responsibility.

My wife, Clara Anne, has contributed to the research, writing, and completion of the book in so many ways that a detailed enumeration would amount to a definition of the concept of marriage. I dedicate it to her, with love.

D.E.S.

Introduction

Few issues in modern European history have attracted as much attention as the unification of Germany; fewer still have provoked as many acrimonious debates among scholars and the general public alike. The process itself, highlighted by three victorious wars and dominated by the enigmatic figure of Chancellor Otto von Bismarck, has much the same interest for Germans as the Civil War does for Americans. The half-century after the founding of the German Empire witnessed the publication of dozens of memoirs, novels, poems, and histories somehow related to the theme of unification. But the subsequent course of German history provided ample justification for keeping the *Reichsgründung* from becoming merely a topic of antiquarian interest. Twice in thirty years the state which was born at Versailles on January 18, 1871, challenged Europe and the world. Its double defeat has been more responsible, directly and indirectly, than any other single factor for the drastic changes in the political and economic balances which have characterized the twentieth century. Historians seeking the origins of the Third Reich are paying more and more attention to the nature of Bismarck's Germany.

The year 1866 marks the turning point in the establishment of Bismarckian Germany. Intellectually as well as politically it is an historical watershed between the Age of Metternich and the Age of Bismarck.[1] This watershed was crossed on the battlefield. Leo Tolstoy justifiably mocks those who believe that the destiny of Europe was irrevocably altered because Napoleon had a cold in his head on the day of Borodino. Nevertheless it represents no distortion of history to assert that Germany was in fact unified by the sword, that the aspirations of years and decades were realized through the victories of the Prussian army. Otto Pflanze has recently challenged the assertion that Königgrätz merely confirmed Prussia's earlier success in achieving economic hegemony in Germany by asking if the Second Empire would have come into being if the Austrian army had triumphed on July 3. Would Prussia's economic strength still have given her the leadership of Germany?[2] The same question can be asked with reference to Prussia's political history, whether domestic or foreign. The years between 1864 and 1867 have been described as Bismarck's years of triumph, years in which he laid the constitutional and diplomatic foundations of the German Empire. What name would they have borne if Austria and her German allies had won the war of 1866? The Prussian victory at Königgrätz left the Chancellor's foes in a shocked daze. Yet in spite of the impetus this triumph provided, July and August of 1866 were the most crucial months in Bismarck's career. Had Hapsburg triumphed over Hohenzollern, might not Bismarck have made good the resolution he expressed to the British ambassador on the outbreak of war, seeking death in battle rather than witness the collapse of his grand designs for Prussia and Germany?

Prussian-German military history has been the subject of more lectures, articles, and monographs than any other aspect of modern German historiography except, perhaps, Adolf Hitler. Modern scholarship, however, has primarily focused on the role of the military in the German catastrophe. The army's influence on society and its relationship to the state, the composition and attitudes of its officer corps, the growth of militarism—these are the themes of twentieth-century analysis. In the process the German army as a military instrument has been somewhat neglected. It is generally conceded, tacitly or explicitly, that among the factors making the greatest contribution to the dominant position of the army in the Second Reich was the heritage of victory from the Wars of Unification. The unification of Italy was also accomplished by force, yet after Custozza the Italian army had nothing like the influence of its Prussian counterpart on state and society. To repeat a question raised earlier, could the German

General Staff and the German officer corps have achieved the position which they did, a position surviving even the collapse of 1918, if Königgrätz had been a Prussian defeat? Would the army's critics in the *Landtag* have been as ready to end their attacks on the military budget and the military establishment if the Seven Weeks' War had ended with Austrian troops bivouacked on the outskirts of Berlin? Perhaps. From France in the early years of the Third Republic to the post-Bataan career of General Douglas MacArthur, modern history offers many examples of defeated armies and defeated generals maintaining, even increasing, their prestige by shifting the blame to a government or emphasizing their heroic struggle in a lost cause. But the stream of time which men call history is neither a laboratory nor a sound stage. The proportions of the compound cannot be altered, nor can the scene be reshot from a different angle with different players. If the unique position of the army in Bismarck's Germany was due even partly to its ability to win wars, then the reasons for this military superiority are at least as important to an understanding of the period as any specialized monograph on diplomacy, politics, or industry.

The lack of modern studies of the Prussian army as a military instrument results in part from the apparent difficulty of finding anything new to say about the subject. Universal conscription, Moltke's strategy, improved weaponry—all were extensively discussed in the nineteenth century, and the basic facts remain common property. The quality of the Prussian army is regarded as generally accepted, something to be discussed in an introductory chapter, repeating the basic outline which everyone *knows* to be correct.[3] Conflicts in interpretation are usually of the type historians prefer to leave to antiquarians and hobbyists, such as the wisdom of given strategies and the actual performance of certain generals or troops in battle. But in Leopold von Ranke's words, there are two possible ends for the historian. He can aim either at imparting new factual information or at presenting a new outlook on what is already known.[4] The present work pursues the latter goal.

The Industrial Revolution was above all an era of technological change, a period when machinery exercised direct and expanding influences on individuals and institutions. Armies were not exempt. In particular, the first half of the nineteenth century witnessed the beginning of a series of changes in military material "so rapid, so conscious, and so continuous that scientists have become as important in warfare as politicians or soldiers."[5] Yet technology and its influence remain among the significant fields neglected by military historians.

This neglect is selective. Military history has moved far from its traditional focal points. Modern scholars of the first rank, both European and American, prefer to interpret warfare in the context of military systems and military systems in the context of the socio-political structures to which they belong. The result has been an increasing number of studies in such areas as war's effect on scientific development or the genesis of various military-industrial complexes. On the other hand, battle history, the detailed study of who did what, where, and to whom, is distinctly unfashionable. As a corollary, studies of the direct application of technical innovation to tactics and strategy generally remain confined to the military and popular presses. This is not merely a question of professional emphasis. In his study, *Technics and Civilization*, Lewis Mumford summarizes a common academic opinion when he describes armies as strongholds of inferior minds, not only uninterested in the technical improvements stimulated by war, but actively resisting their incorporation into the military system.[6] From the proud refusal of the Swiss pikemen to abandon their traditional phalanx in the face of Spanish firearms to Lord Kitchener's dismissal of the tank as a pretty mechanical toy, modern military history offers ample corroborating evidence. This attitude, however, cannot be entirely explained by conjuring up the much-overworked image of Colonel Blimp, or by characterizing armies as strongholds of idealism and romanticism.

Military establishments, like all institutions with a continuing existence, face the necessity of constantly adjusting to changing circumstances. But their problem is magnified on one hand by the army's position as the ultimate source of security and survival for the state it represents and on the other by the difficulty of testing proposed innovations and determining their actual value for war under artificial conditions. It is possible to explain, if not always to justify, much of the conservatism often considered characteristic of military establishments as legitimate reluctance to trust the public safety to anything not thoroughly proved and tested.

Soldiers, in fact, are as likely to be accused of uncritical admiration for machinery as of technological illiteracy. In R. H. Tawney's acerbic words, "a general with a railway is like a monkey with a watch"[7]—fascinated by a new toy whose uses and potentialities he is incapable of understanding, emphasizing technical and material superiority at the expense of intangibles, those military and social virtues such as courage, morale, and leadership. The air power enthusiasts, the Alexander de Severskys and Guilio Douhets, have been discredited from Coventry to Haiphong. The notion that tanks alone could achieve decisive success in modern war did not survive Russia and the Western Desert. Most recently, the image of the computerized, mechanized, helicoptered American infantryman vainly lunging at his pajama-clad opponent armed only with a rifle and a cause has become an academic and a military cliché regardless of its validity.

The relationship between weapons and fighting is too obvious to require elaboration. Most standard definitions of the technique of war embody some form of recognition of weapons and their use.[8] One of the twentieth century's most distinguished military theorists, J. F. C. Fuller, has gone so far as to declare that ". . . weapons, if only the right ones can be discovered, form 99 per cent of victory . . . in modern wars, wars in which weapons change rapidly, one thing is certain, no army of 50 years before any date selected would stand 'a dog's chance' against the army existing at that date . . ." Napoleon, for example, would have been defeated by Lord Raglan because Raglan's army was equipped with Minié rifles, despite the fact that Napoleon was a far greater general. In the same way Moltke would have bested Raglan, not because he was a better soldier, but because of the needle gun.[9]

The conviction that machines, rather than men, are the decisive factor in modern warfare has grown even stronger in this age of the black box and the automated weapons system. On closer examination, however, some startling discrepancies emerge. In particular, soldiers and scholars agree that even in the wars of industrial societies, anything more than marginal technical advantages are rare. What is loosely described as technological superiority usually means either greater skill at employing roughly equivalent means, or simply greater numbers. Where it does exist, superiority in the quality of weapons and equipment in land warfare is marginal and ephemeral, seldom remaining long with any army.

13

Technology, moreover, has an essentially independent existence: successful innovations cannot be produced to order. When they are introduced to the battlefield, they seldom succeed a second time before an effective antidote is developed. Thereafter the new machinery is merely an additional strain on an enemy's resources and resourcefulness. The art of war again becomes "the optimum use of weapons governed by the traditional skills of general-ship."[10]

Given the above combination of factors, it is hardly surprising that the study of military technology in general, and its contribution to Prussia's military efficiency in particular, has remained peripheral. Yet the struggle for mastery in Germany was influenced in great part by the struggle of armies with technology. This work focuses on three aspects of this problem, each presenting a different set of challenges. Part One deals with the influence of steam on the thinking and practice of the German armies. Here military establishments were relating to developments they could influence marginally at best. Defense budgets were not elastic enough to subsidize construction of militarily desirable railway lines. If by 1866 Prussia had five railroads leading into the theater of war while Austria had one, this by itself said little about the response of either army to the industrial revolution. The key issues were rather how to make the best use of existing networks, how to integrate the railways into operational planning. In short, how well could German armies adjust to broad material changes in the societies of which they were a part?

Part Two moves from the greater to the lesser world by considering the effect of the technical revolution on infantry weapons, infantry training, and infantry tactics east of the Rhine. In the first half of the nineteenth century infantry remained the dominant branch of service, particularly in Prussia, where it was emphasized at the expense of cavalry and artillery. In a real sense the infantry *was* the army, and any changes made in its organization, training, or armament were far more likely to affect the overall efficiency of the military establishment than the same type of changes made in other branches of service. And in 1866, technical superiority made its first decisive appearance on a modern battlefield. The Prussian infantry carried breech-loading rifles into action; the Austrians and south Germans were armed with muzzle-loaders. Moreover, by the outbreak of war the contending armies had developed coherent, comprehensive doctrines for the use of their respective infantry weapons. They had had time to train their rank and file according to these doctrines. And they were confident that their armament and training would contribute to victory. The development of these divergent responses to weapons technology played a decisive role in the Seven Weeks' War.

That weapons technology is not mere gadgetry is clearly indicated in Part Three. This section evaluates the effect of the technical revolution on a technical arm: the artillery. This branch of service was as a rule more concerned with weapons development than any other in the German armies. Improved ammunition, new methods of construction and production, innovations in tactical doctrines, all made relatively early appearances in the artillery. The faint beginnings of a military-industrial complex are visible in the efforts of manufacturers like Alfred Krupp to sell their wares to the armies of Germany. Questions of cost-effectiveness arise in the debate over adopting cast steel cannon in place of the traditional bronze. But the problems of deciding just what the weapons of the future will be and the dangers of focusing on material to the exclusion of methods are also illustrated, particularly by the experiences of the Prussian artillery. Its breech-loading rifles were by no means as effective as those of the infantry in 1866—a significant indication of the limits of technical innovation.

The study is deliberately based on printed sources. Military technology, particularly in the area of weapons innovation, cannot remain an arcane mystery if it is to be effective. Regimental officers and noncommissioned officers, junior staff officers without access to high-level conferences, cadets and reservists, must have an idea of the nature and potential of the tools they are expected to use. Their impressions, the information made available to them, the terms of discussion in clubs and messes, are a better indication of the impact of military technology than any number of minutes and reports carefully embalmed in a war ministry's archives. Memoirs and diaries, unit histories, the contemporary military press, indicate the frames of reference of the German armies' response to the industrial revolution. The problem, for the historian as well as the soldier, remains the striking of a proper balance, the evaluating of the relative importance of material factors in a given situation. This study is an attempt at reaching such a balance for an army and a war of a century past— and determining the success or failure of the soldiers of Moltke's Germany in doing the same thing.

PART I

RAILROADS

The development of Germany's railway network during the first half of the nineteenth century was in no way a response to the demands of Germany's armies. Businessmen and promoters stressed the military advantages of steam-powered mobility, but this reflected their belief in the disproportionate political influence of the German Confederation's military establishments. Soldiers tended to remain skeptical, and their skepticism was initially justified in view of the limited carrying capacity of the early railroads. As this improved, so did the willingness of staff officers to integrate railroads into their operational planning, particularly in Prussia. After 1858 Helmuth von Moltke increasingly stressed the potential importance of the railway in buying time for a state without significant natural frontiers, yet surrounded by potential enemies. This process in turn had two results. It contributed to the development of military specialization and professionalism. Experience gained during the Olmütz crisis of 1850 and the Austro-French War of 1859 demonstrated the need for thorough mastery of the details of railway operation. Those traditional stereotypes of an officer, the hero and the clerk, began to share a place with the technician/bureaucrat, the man who could make the nonmilitary transportation network do what the military wished it to do. And as time grew more important in strategic planning, it became too important to waste. Initially the railroads had been expected to increase diplomatic as well as military flexibility by enabling troops and supplies to be moved immediately to counter any threat. In 1866 the structure and the efficiency of Prussia's railway network did in fact compensate for the government's reluctance to order mobilization and concentration against Austria. Yet paradoxically the delays engendered by that reluctance involved risks seeming so great that they overshadowed the final result in the minds of Moltke and his subordinates. Prussian-German military planning after 1866 increasingly stressed the need for making mobilization the real beginning of war—a process which had tragic results in 1914.

Chapter I

Movers and Shapers, 1815-1848

The development of the German railway system reflected and embodied a drastic change in the thinking of governments and businessmen alike. The first locomotive in Germany, built in 1815 by the royal foundry in Berlin, was displayed as a public curiosity. By the 1820s, however, industrialists and a few public officials were beginning to take seriously the suggestion that a comprehensive system of railways could do much more for Germany in general and Prussia in particular than merely expedite the movement of coal. Most of the early promoters were bankers and merchants—Friedrich Harkort, Ludolf Camphausen, David Hansemann, the brothers von der Heydt. Primarily interested in the railway's commercial aspects, yet finding it impossible to raise sufficient funds for large-scale construction from private investors preferring bonds or low-risk enterprises, they turned to the state for moral support and financial assistance. Specifically, they turned to the army. Over half of the Prussian budget was devoted to military spending. Military influences were strong at the court of Frederick William III. Former Chief of Staff Carl von Grolman had advocated a network of all-weather highways built to commercial and strategic requirements. If his successors could be convinced that railroads had the potential to perform some of the same functions, the entrepreneurs might have a useful ally in overcoming bureaucratic resistance to this proposed innovation.[1]

As early as March, 1833, Friedrich Harkort's pamphlet, *Die Eisenbahn von Minden nach Cöln*, argued that the proposed line would enable Prussia to reinforce her isolated provinces immediately in case of a surprise attack from France. David Hansemann, who had turned from insurance broker to railway promoter, was equally convinced that a Prussia sandwiched between powerful neighbors, her western provinces cut off from the rest of the state, dared not fall behind her powerful neighbors in the matter of railroad construction. Though a firm defender of private enterprise, Hansemann also believed that railroads should be regulated in the public interest, with the state building strategically or commercially important lines when private capital was not available. Future Minister of Commerce Ludolf Camphausen was somewhat more moderate in his recommendations. Advocating a railway between Cologne and Antwerp, he suggested that among other things spurs of the main line could be used to connect the Rhenish and Westphalian fortresses. Arrangements could also be made between the railroads and the government for the transporting of masses of troops in an emergency. Camphausen believed that Prussia's military organization was essentially defensive, since it depended on the Landwehr, the people in arms. Quick reaction to any threat was therefore vital, and a good railway network would make it possible to concentrate so rapidly that the active army could safely be reduced enough to finance at least part of the construction costs.[2]

Camphausen's simultaneous appeals to the Prussian liberals' dislike of large standing armies and their concern for economy were hardly calculated to win support from a military establishment already worried about curtailed budgets. In any event, neither Harkort, Camphausen, nor their contemporaries had made more than passing reference to the military potential of the railroads. Far more significant in this respect were the writings of Friedrich List. A native of Württemberg, exiled for political activity in 1825, he had made a remarkable career in the United States, returning as an American consul with the dream of a "new and greater Germany, unified by internal free trade, external protection, and a national system of ports and railways"—particularly railways.[3] For List the growing unity and cooperation among the individual states of the German Confederation had increased their importance, prosperity, and military potential.

The confederation as a political system rendered it "impossible" for Germany to wage aggressive wars. "Internal conflicts [were] in reality scarcely thinkable."[4] A nationwide network of railroads would reinforce both positions by increasing the risk of invading Germany, or any other country with a railway network.

List was convinced that the railways' netlike, concentric structure made it ten times easier to defend, ten times more difficult to attack. The further an aggressor pressed forward along one or two lines, the greater the risk of his encirclement by troops debouching from the others. Defending forces, on the other hand, could be concentrated at any threatened point in days or hours. They would be delivered fresh and eager from the mobilization centers to the battlefield; they would rest from the exertions of one struggle as the trains carried them to another. This overwhelming superiority of the defensive meant that wars would be confined to frontier areas, and once the nations of Europe discovered the impossibility of following up their victories, they would conclude that it would be better—and more profitable— for all to live in peace. Thus the railroad would be the instrument which destroyed war itself.

Best of all, List argued, the railway system making this possible would exist in ten years because its construction would be profitable. Strategically, Germany required north-south railroads along the Rhine and the Vistula, plus an interior network connecting these lateral lines with each other and the major military centers. Since the military centers were also centers of commerce and industry, it was to the advantage of both government and private enterprise to see that they were connected by railroads. This self-interest, List argued, would lead to cooperation in the national interest without coercion being necessary.

Traditionally the military establishment had been a drain on the state's resources of manpower and capital. Now the railroads offered a substantial improvement in military efficiency which would be profitable to the civilian economy as well. Transporting troops by rail was relatively inexpensive. To move a hundred thousand men would require a hundred locomotives and two thousand wagons costing at most a million thalers—only a tenth as much as a first-class fortress. Admittedly, the system would suffer some damage from an invading enemy in wartime, but most of this would be superficial. The right of way itself, which cost the most, would require as much time and effort to demolish as to construct. The costs of replacing ties, tracks, and fixtures could be amortized over several years. Part of it might well be assumed by the state, and the payment for troop movements would compensate tenfold for damages. All forms of property are subject to destruction in wartime, List argued. Why, then, should capitalists deem railroads a special case and be reluctant to invest in them? In any case,

> it is just as little left in our hands to determine whether we shall make use of [the railroads] as it was left to our fore-fathers to determine whether they should shoulder the musket instead of the bow and arrow. . . . Every mile of railroad which a neighboring nation has ready earlier than us, every mile more it possesses, gives it a strategic advantage over us.[5]

Given List's views on the importance of peace for Germany's economic welfare, his opinion that railroads would make war difficult or impossible may be interpreted as a case of the wish being father to the thought. He was not, however, alone in his opinion. In 1833 an article in the Leipzig *Sachsenzeitung* proclaimed that war would be obsolete when a nation could load its entire army onto trains one day and the next day unload it in battle order at a predetermined spot. A nation with a smaller army than its potential adversary could be sure of being weaker on the battlefield; the government would therefore refuse to declare war. The optimistic author did not address himself to the probable attitude of states with large armies. Similarly, a pamphlet declaring that railroads would revolutionize the art of war over the next quarter-century by multiplying the defensive strength of any nation loses some of its force, for the modern reader at least, by suggesting that these advantages could be achieved by the use of human muscle and horse power as well as steam.[6]

Neither rhetoric nor statistics could overcome the inertia of Germany's bureaucrats. If promoters hoped for state-subsidized railways, they depended on government permission to form private joint-stock construction companies and government approval of projected routes. Both came slowly. In Prussia, the death in 1830 of Finance Minister Friedrich von Motz removed the only senior official who believed railways might eventually play a significant role in the development of the state. Postmaster-General Karl von Nagler dismissed a projected Berlin-Potsdam line as a stupid idea and declared that no one would ride it. Minister of Commerce Christian von Rother, director of the *Seehandlung* and the National Debt Redemption Office, successful negotiator of the English loans which enabled Prussia to balance its budget, leading exponent of government intervention in business and industry, was deeply interested in improving the state's communications network. But while encouraging and in some cases subsidizing the construction and maintenance of roads and waterways, Rother doubted that railroads would ever carry enough freight to be a paying proposition. As late as 1835 he declared that

> no reason as yet exists why the central government should at its own expense provide railways to serve as routes of general commerce, why it should support such enterprises with comparatively large sums, or why it should make any other notable sacrifices on behalf of the new undertakings or grant them special privileges.[7]

Nagler and Rother modified their opposition to railroads by the end of the decade, but their initial attitudes were hardly likely to inspire confidence in the new development on the part of the military. The *Artillerie-Prüfungs-Kommission*, created in 1809 to determine the military potential of all inventions presented to it, was initially made responsible for studying the railways. However, the novelty of steam transportation made its military evaluation extremely difficult. Both the APK and the commission of General Staff officers subsequently created to consider the problem depended chiefly on information supplied by interested parties—which meant civilian experts. The increasing criticism of the standing army on ideological and financial grounds, combined with the army's own consciousness of itself as a bulwark of order, hardly predisposed the officers responsible for the army's equipment to listen to the liberal Rhenish industrialists who were the foremost advocates of railroad development. Nor were junior officers ready to take up steam engines as a hobby in the way that some of them were to sponsor the needle gun. Those who did were as likely to resign their commissions and seek a new career in the railway industry as to attempt to convince their superiors of its military potential. Under such circumstances it is scarcely surprising that the Prussian army's initial attitude towards the railways was anything but enthusiastic. The first recorded memorandum on the subject, submitted on July 16, 1834, was a detailed warning against neglecting highway construction in favor of railroads. *Chaussées*, argued Chief of Staff Johann von Krauseneck, were the only means of transportation suitable for all arms at all times and seasons, the only reliable basis for calculating the time and space required for mobilizations or campaigns. The APK did begin estimating the costs of moving a force of all arms by rail and studying the possibility of making some experimental transports. But since there were as yet no railways in Prussia, the problem remained theoretical.[8]

2

Since 1833 the indefatigable Friedrich List had been submitting proposal after proposal to various Prussian ministries describing the political, economic, and military advantages of projected railway lines in various parts of the kingdom. If he failed to obtain the concessions he sought, his repeated warnings that peace would not endure forever, and that in a future war a railway connecting the Rhineland with Prussia proper would be worth more than a victory, were not without effect. The War Ministry had also been considering the military value of a railroad from the Rhine to the Weser, and in January 1835 a special commission was appointed to study the issue. Its conclusions were sober, practical, and pedestrian. The commission agreed that railroads might be useful for transporting war material in the rear of an army, removing supplies from the path of an advancing enemy, or concentrating scattered troops at important points. But even for a widely extended state like Prussia their value was at best questionable. Since railroads were easier to destroy than to rebuild, it was highly uncertain how long they could be used in wartime. Operations based on this new and untried means of transportation were more likely to fail than to succeed, the commission declared; they would never replace highways. In January, 1836, Krauseneck informed the War Ministry that Prussia required an improved means of transporting troops. However, he also seemed convinced that the railroads would not make enough difference in the conduct of war to make their construction a military necessity—at least in the immediate future.

If this report proved convincing to the Prussian War Ministry and General Staff, events in the south German states followed a different pattern. Fear of a French attack had never completely abated after the war scare of 1830. When news of a projected Paris-Metz-Strasbourg railway became public, editors and politicians alike took fright. The popular press, conjuring up the specter of thousands of French troops transported overnight to the frontier, echoed the arguments of Friedrich List by advocating the construction of a German railroad network to counter the French threat. The scare was welcomed, if not fostered, by merchants, industrialists, and would-be promoters sensing possible profit. Temporarily at least, they had greater success than their Prussian counterparts. The Bavarian government in particular was sufficiently concerned at the prospect of a steam-powered French invasion to broach the subject of cooperative railway construction to the Prussian authorities. A mixed military-civilian commission replied to the Bavarian proposal by declaring again that railroads could only supplement highways. Their vulnerability, combined with the length of time required to load and unload troops and equipment, sharply restricted their use in wartime. More significantly, the commission declared that military value alone was not enough to keep a railroad operating at a profit, and military budgets were too small to permit subsidies. The armies of Germany would therefore have to make do with commercial, civilian lines.

This growing interest in the railways on the part of staffs and war ministries was not exactly reflected in the contemporary military press. Most of the early pamphlets and articles did not go beyond speculating on the increased superiority railroads conferred on the defense, or the possibility of obtaining state subsidies for constructing military lines.[9] These speculations also considered the limited carrying capacity of contemporary railways. Major du Vignau of the Prussian artillery declared that to be really effective in war, the railroads must be able to move a corps of 12,000 infantry, 700 cavalry, and 24 guns simultaneously. The track, the locomotives, and the rolling stock necessary for such a feat did not exist, nor were they likely to come into existence in the near future.[10] A pamphlet published in 1836 argued that under existing conditions a corps of twenty-four battalions, twenty-eight squadrons, and ninety-six guns would require twenty days to cover fifty-two German miles by rail—a distance the same force could cover afoot in sixteen. Even infantry alone, if carried in farm wagons on good roads, could cover ground at a rate only slightly slower than the railroads. Five years later the same author reasserted his opinion that using railroads to transport masses of troops would bring at best marginal gains of time at prohibitive expense. Despite the technical improvements made since 1836, he declared, railways were still better suited to transport supplies than men.[11]

The lack of enthusiasm reflected in these reports and articles cannot be explained entirely by blind conservatism or technological illiteracy. The civilians, Harkort, Camphausen, even List, saw the military possibilities of this new development, but ignored the details of implementing it. They were promoters and publicists, believing that the railroads would be good for business, for Prussia, for Germany as a whole, and willing to proclaim them a panacea for almost any problem in order to win support. That they would attempt to convince the army of the potential worth of railroads was inevitable, especially in Prussia. It was equally inevitable that initial zeal would fade when faceless men with pen and paper began calculating the actual and potential carrying capacity of the projected railroads and comparing it with the numbers of men in a modern army. Ninety years later the first suggestions that troops and supplies could be carried by air were nearly rejected out of hand because it was obvious that the wire and strut biplanes of the 1920s had payloads too small to make the scheme viable except in special cases. In the same way, German specialists in supply and transport argued that the flimsy carriages, the underpowered, spark-throwing locomotives, had a cost-effectiveness ratio too low to be acceptable at a time of curtailed military budgets. If this evaluation was short-sighted, it was also indisputably accurate. And such issues as strategic mobility, rapid mobilization, or prompt reinforcement of distant provinces were of secondary importance in states whose territory could be traversed afoot in a matter of days, and which expected to go to war only as part of a Confederation army or with powerful allies.

The states of Germany might not be under intensive pressure from their military establishments to build railways. The hope of economic gain, however, generated increasing willingness to allow entrepeneurs to risk their own money in such ventures— particularly if these speculators were willing to build their lines between cities specified by the government. Armies did not entirely ignore the resulting developments. Troops were moved for the first time on a German railroad in 1839, when eight thousand men of the Prussian Guard were transported from Potsdam to Berlin at the end of the September maneuvers. In 1840 a battalion of Saxon light infantry travelled to Dresden for a review via the Leipzig-Dresden railway. In 1846, two companies of the Bavarian *Leib-Regiment* went from Munich to Stockhausen and back, while seven battalions were shuttled from Munich to Augsburg during the fall maneuvers. These operations, however, bore the stamp of the promoter rather than the staff officer. They were essentially spectacles carried out with bands playing and colors flying, public shows designed to attract attention and investment capital. As training exercises their value was marginal, while neither the cost nor the time element were particularly encouraging to economy-minded cabinets. Transporting the guardsmen the few kilometers from Potsdam to Berlin, for example, required ten trains and cost a thousand thalers.[12] The Prussian railways remained in private hands. And if those of the smaller German states were subject to increasing public control, this reflected a shortage of private capital as much as it did positive decisions. In Saxony and Bavaria, governments intervened when promoters exhausted their funds. Even where state railway systems existed from the beginning, ministries and parliaments were often reluctant to grant funds for construction or maintenance. The particularism which prevented contingents forming part of the same federal army corps from standardizing equipment and training together also militated against common action on the railway question. A mixed commission assembled in Munich in 1836 to study the communications systems of Bavaria and south Germany probably discussed the potential uses of railways, but issued neither recommendations nor reports.[13] No further gestures of unity would be made for twenty years.

3

The tests, studies, and maneuvers might not have influenced staffs and governments. However individual officers, analyzing their own experiences or evaluating those of other German armies, were becoming increasingly steam-conscious. The Saxon captain Karl Eduard Pönitz believed that railways would foster German unity militarily as the *Zollverein* had done politically, by creating an identity of interest and an awareness of common problems among staffs and high commands. But in order to clothe this dream with reality, it was necessary to determine the probable impact of this new invention on the art of war. Like most of his contemporaries, Pönitz was convinced that railroads conferred an overwhelming superiority on the defense. They made possible rapid movement of troops, supplies, and information. They could be used to reinforce both weak points in a defensive system and threatened or besieged fortresses. They could easily be damaged to deny access to an enemy, which increased the options available to military planners. But Pönitz considered the offensive as well as the defensive possibilities of the railroads. A railway running along the west bank of the Rhine, he suggested, would enable German troops to concentrate quickly at a single point, then thrust into France before the enemy could react. Even enemy railroads might prove useful, especially in a surprise attack. With an imagination unusual in that era, Pönitz spoke of trainloads of infantry and artillery rolling into the heart of the enemy's country along tracks captured by independent mobile task forces of cavalry and mounted infantry—a concept which can be described as visionary or farsighted with equal validity.

In his search for general principles Pönitz did not neglect specifics. His works include long and careful analyses of the use of railroads in every kind of contingency. Like most German officers, he was no friend of liberalism or capitalism. The railway service, he declared, was essentially military in its requirements. Order, discipline, and precision were as essential for the successful operation of a railroad as for the proper functioning of an army. Railways, therefore, should be militarized, staffed by military personnel, and integrated into the military establishment. Officers and men of other arms must have the opportunity to become acquainted with the demands of the railway service; every regiment should be able to produce trained railroaders from its ranks in an emergency. While some lines still used horses for switching, Pönitz wrote of the need for double tracks, for more powerful locomotives, for carriages with improved brakes, for yard facilities extensive enough to keep the heaviest military traffic rolling smoothly. At a time when thinking on the subject of troop movement by rail had scarcely advanced beyond the concept of loading everyone onto trains at one end of the line and unloading them at the other, Pönitz presented a sophisticated analysis of the use of transport echelons as the only way to move the masses of men necessary for modern war.[14] His guidelines for organizing and controlling military traffic subsequently influenced the official regulations of several German states, including Prussia. In the context of the 1840s, however, they were at best portents for the future—especially since their author served a small state.

Particularly in Prussia, economics was more important than ideology in stimulating awareness of railways. An increasing number of officers became aware that principle and profit might well join hands where this new invention was concerned. In an era of profound peace and blocked promotions, a junior officer's pay was small, his prospects slim. On the other hand, the promoters and financiers desperately angling for railway concessions welcomed the opportunity to obtain access to circles often closed to them. An officer of noble birth, good connections, and reasonable industry and intelligence was a prize to be wooed with flattery and stock options. As early as 1840, for example, the promoters of the Berlin-Hamburg railroad listed a Guards officer, Captain E. A. von Witzleben, among the leading Berlin bankers who formed part of the committee.[15] The next year another military man joined the project—a major on the Prussian General Staff named Helmuth von Moltke.

Moltke was initially surprised when he was offered a post on the board of directors. He was not particularly well-acquainted with either the men or the idea. He had spent the years from 1835 to 1839 as a military adviser in Turkey, and was out of touch with recent events in Germany. But the promoters knew their man. Moltke had served on the General Staff for twelve years, earning a reputation as a conscientious officer of exceptional talent and an author good enough to supplement his salary by regular contributions to the civilian press. What he did not know about railroads, he could learn. Even more important, the projected Berlin-Hamburg line would have to cross the territory of two other states—Mecklenburg and Danish Lauenburg. A nobleman wearing the crimson stripes of the Prussian General Staff would be a vaulable asset in negotiating for concessions in conservative Mecklenburg, and Moltke was Danish by birth, with influential connections in Denmark. It was an ideal combination.

Moltke was by no means a hired hand converted to the cause of railways by a generous retainer. He was sufficiently convinced of both the financial prospects and the ultimate value of railroads in general, and the Berlin-Hamburg line in particular, to sink most of his assets into company stock. Moreover, in his first year on the board at least, he seems to have received no fixed salary. This sizable personal stake in the success of the enterprise further reinforced Moltke's characteristic zeal and energy. During the three years he served as a director, his desk was constantly full of articles, papers, and memoranda on railroads. He studied the projected right of way, inspected the site of the Berlin terminal, talked with surveyors and engineers. He participated in the successful negotiations with Mecklenburg and Denmark. He composed numerous reports and memoranda, some of which formed the nuclei of the essays on railway construction and policy which he published in such periodicals as the *Deutsches Vierteljahrsschrift* and the *Augsburger Allgemeine Zeitung*.

For Moltke the Berlin-Hamburg railway represented something more than the linking of two great cities, something more than rapid transportation to his family and his bride in Holstein. Moltke's experiences and observations in Turkey and the Balkans, and his own status as an "outsider" whose family included Danish citizens, had shown him that the German states were faced with a choice between cooperation or insignificance. This did not mean that Moltke advocated furthering German unity by war, either civil or international. Rather he hoped the industrial, economic, and technical progress rendered possible by railroads would bring Germany together and eventually make all wars unlikely. It was an echo of Friedrich List, and a far cry from Moltke's own subsequent thoughts on the function of war in society.

Moltke's work paralleled that of List in other respects as well. While recognizing the railway's potential value for military operations, he did not address himself to the technical problems involved. Nor did he advocate the construction of railroads for purely military purposes. Military requirements must of course be considered along with economic and national-political demands. In general, however, the main commercial arteries were almost certain to be the major lines of operation in wartime. The military's needs could be met by such measures as taking extra precautions in frontier zones, routing lines through fortresses wherever possible, and providing means for demolition in the event of invasion.

Moltke did not accept unequivocally the principle of a privately-owned and operated railway system. Railroads were far too important for the development of the Prussian state and the German nation to be left in the hands of financiers and promoters. Most of the existing lines, he argued, had been built with an eye to quick profits and nothing else. For this reason they had been concentrated in the most prosperous areas and devoted primarily to passenger traffic. Private enterprise, with its stock manipulations, its greed for gain, its internal conflicts, could not be trusted to build a true *network* of railroads, with less profitable lines sustained by the others. Apart from any other considerations, the initial costs of roadbeds and rolling stock able to carry heavy freight were too high, the risks were too great, to tempt private companies with their limited capital. Moltke strongly favored the use of government funds to make up the difference. Only state ownership or state control, he declared, would guarantee the centralized economic planning and construction necessary if Prussia were to reap the full benefit of the new development.[16]

4

The pressure of Moltke's military duties combined with a routine transfer to Coblenz led him to resign from the board of the Berlin-Hamburg line in 1844; for the next four years his primary association with railroads was as a passenger. His arguments produced no drastic conversions. In 1848 soldiers still described railways as a useful means of long-distance communication which might make marginal and unspecified contributions to defensive operations. The engineer corps, whose high percentage of technically trained officers made it, theoretically at least, a natural patron of the sciences, regarded steam engines with indifference or hostility. Since 1815 the attention of Prussia's engineers had been focused on the design, construction, and maintenance of barracks and fortresses. It was work calculated to produce artisans and nothing else, an attitude personified in the Inspector-General of the corps, General von Alster. An aloof, methodical, businesslike officer with little formal education, he distrusted intellectuals in uniform and had little use for theoretical speculation. Above all he feared the potential effect of railroad lines on Prussia's carefully planned fortresses. If by 1848, the railway network included all of the corps and divisional headquarters and most of the larger garrison towns, in many instances this represented a victory over the adamant opposition of military governors and commandants. The image of a hostile army rolling through the gates of Magdeburg or Coblenz may have been unrealistic, but it was sufficiently vivid to inspire demands that the tracks be laid as far as possible from defense works, or at least that their construction be tailored to military requirements regardless of expense. It was an attitude provoking bitter conflicts, not only with the directors of the railroads, but often with the merchants and businessmen of the cities involved, who were willing to accept the supposed risks at which the military balked.[17]

Enlightenment appeared little greater at higher levels. King Frederick William IV, with his facile enthusiasm for the new and different, believed in the railways' military potential without doing anything to transform it to reality. Most of the treaties involving the construction and control of railways crossing more than one state were initiated under pressure from promoters. Developments outside of Germany were not ignored. Thus an evaluation of French views on the military importance of railroads was published in 1845 as a supplement to Prussia's foremost military journal, the *Militär-Wochenblatt*. Nevertheless, Hermann von Boyen, the hero of the Era of Reform reappointed War Minister in 1841, found it difficult to adjust his thinking to the demands of a new age. He particularly failed to understand the revolutionary impact railroads could have on mobilization and deployment—a failure encouraged by his belief that wide-

spread use of railroads might make mobilization plans dangerously rigid and mechanical. Boyen's memories of the successful
improvisations of 1813 and 1814, combined with his recognition
of the importance of flexibility, led him to argue the folly of
assuming that peacetime preparations could be executed without
change in war.[18] The result of this conviction was that as late
as 1848 troop trains were run as specials, sandwiched into the
regular service, moving from station to station as the right of
way cleared ahead.

Boyen's skepticism also reflected the fact that the ability of
railroads to support large-scale military operations remained
limited. Germany's railway system had expanded geometrically,
from 469 kilometers of track in 1840 to 5,856 kilometers by 1850
—a rate of growth over twice that of France.[19] The 1840s were
years of economic expansion in Germany and the railway boom
did much to shape the nature and direction of that expansion.
But for military purposes, the network was still thin. Most lines
were single-tracked. Railway companies, public or private, lacked
experience in large-scale, rapid movement of men and freight.
Connections and switches were primitive, roadbeds inadequate
to support heavy traffic. Managers, stationmasters, engineers,
mechanics were still learning their trades. Specialized, systematic
training for railwaymen was a decade away. Some government-
owned lines in south Germany even included officials transferred
from the postal service for no better reason than their availability.[20] Standardized gauges and equipment were still a debat-
able issue. It was obvious to anyone able to compare the strength
of a modern army with the carrying capacity of existing and
projected railroads that to move and supply a significant number
of troops it would be necessary to draw engines and carriages
from other lines than the ones immediately in use. The state of
Baden, however, had adopted a wider gauge than that used by
the other German states—or by France. It was a defensive measure, an effort to delay, at least, French occupation of the duchy.
In such states as Württemberg and Hesse-Darmstadt, where
railways still existed only on paper, there was some temptation
in military circles to favor the Baden gauge for the same reason.
Pönitz did his best to convince the doubters that the advantages
offered by this decision were illusory, while the crippling effect
it would have on the German railway network was all too real.[21]

But if Baden remained the only state in Germany with a wide-gauge railway network, the credit rested primarily not with the soldiers, but with businessmen and industrailists who preferred the concrete economic advantages of standard gauge to security against a possible future invasion.

In the face of these facts, how is it possible to speak of the genesis of a relationship between soldiers and steam during this period? Nothing like a common doctrine, a generally accepted set of principles for the conduct of railway warfare had yet emerged. Pönitz and Moltke were just two more theorists whose ideas remained unproved. Speculation on the military potential of railroads had involved generalizations, not specifics. Even the generalizations were often inaccurate. The hypothesis, for example, that railroads favored only defensive operations was to be thoroughly discredited in 1866 and 1870. But the reports, articles, and monographs advocating the integration of railroads into military operations had provoked controversy. The indifference of the 1830s was giving way to an awareness of railways and the claims made for them. The awareness often focused on present limitations rather than future possibilities, emphasizing the gap between military requirements and existing facilities. This, however, represented accurate observation rather than inflexible conservatism. Technical and administrative improvements might well be expected to change the terms of the debate.

If armies had refused responsibility for planning and constructing railroads, they could ride the coattails of those who accepted it. The Union of German Railway Administrators, formed in 1847, was attacking such problems as the transfer of freight and passengers from one line to another. Factories were beginning to produce standardized rolling stock. Track mileage and volume of freight carried were increasing consistently. Even the government control advocated by List and Moltke had begun to emerge under pressure from nonmilitary bureaucrats. For example the Prussian Railway Law of 1838 prescribed in oppressive detail the procedures for building and administering railroads. It also authorized state purchase of lines whose concessions had expired or been voided. The permanent Railway Fund, created in 1843, offered a subtler method of influencing railway development. By making direct loans, by purchasing shares in joint-stock companies, and by guaranteeing the interest rates of railroad stocks, the fund and similar subsidies were intended to encourage the construction of lines deemed economically desirable, yet not promising enough profit to attract investment capital. Some Prussian officials, particularly the future Minister of Commerce August von der Heydt, openly advocated the nationalization of existing railroads, with new ones to be constructed entirely from public funds. This policy would become official after 1848, opening the door to increased military involvement in railway affairs—assuming that the military was interested.[22]

And the military was interested. Even Boyen, despite his fears of inflexibility, initiated extensive theoretical studies of the time and material required to move a given number of men a fixed distance by rail, as well as tests of the best ways of loading cars and coaches.[23] In February and March, 1846, when disorders broke out in the free city of Cracow and Prussian troops were ordered to the Silesian frontier, the War Ministry moved some of them by rail. The Krausenecks and Alsters were giving way to a new generation of men willing to consider the idea that a combination of improved equipment, more track, increased government control, and careful planning might indeed make railroads useful in military operations. The revolutions of 1848 gave them an opportunity to test their theories.

Chapter II

Wars and Rumors of Wars, 1848-1864

From the beginning, railroads added an unexpected dimension to the military problems posed by the revolution. With the first outbreaks largely confined to urban areas, troops could be shuttled from city to city without serious danger of being stopped *en route* by torn-up tracks or destroyed fuel supplies. They could be disembarked at stations held by government forces, eliminating the possibility of having to go into action directly from the trains. Initially, at least, there was little need for cavalry, artillery, and elaborate supply arrangements; infantry task forces could be loaded at one point, unloaded at another with minimal difficulty. The three Prussian battalions rushed to Dresden by rail in May, 1848, in time to serve as the backbone of the counterrevolution, represent only one example of this use of railways to speed the arrival of the mobile fire brigades which crisscrossed Germany in that year of revolt. Nor were the railroads solely tools of the establishment. Writing to his wife in July, 1849, Albrecht von Roon, serving on the staff of the federal expeditionary force in Baden, declared that the rebels' locomotives were among their most potent weapons. Unable to stand against regular troops in the open field, outmaneuvered and outfought at every turn, the revolutionaries persisted in removing themselves from the jaws of disaster—and out of range of pursuit—by rail. "This frustrating war will only end," said Roon, "when the entire railway is in our hands, and to this end the army will advance on

Freiburg"—perhaps the first recorded instance of the railroad directly influencing operations plans.[1]

Even more significant for the long-term relationship of the railways and the military in Prussia was the appointment of Carl von Reyher as Chief of the General Staff in May, 1848. Reyher was interested in utilizing the railways' potential for rapid transport of men and supplies. He found himself, however, with few subordinates having even theoretical knowledge of the problem, and none with wide practical experience. Neither operators nor bureaucrats had devised a workable system of regulating large-scale military traffic. As a rule throughout 1848-49 troop trains remained outside the regular services, moving from station to station in fits and starts as the right of way cleared. The entire process was too slow and cumbersome to be useful against even a normally enterprising foe.

Reyher stressed the importance of keeping up with new developments in railway technology, of assigning military men to study the operation of railroads in peacetime, of closer cooperation between soldiers and technicians.[2] But theory had not been translated into practice when the increasing tension between Prussia and Austria led Frederick William IV to order mobilization on November 6, 1850, and made the continuing weakness of the link between the military and the railroads in Prussia painfully clear to even a casual observer. Men, animals, and supplies piled up at loading centers and shuttled aimlessly from station to station on trains whose destination was a mystery. In the aftermath of the revolution many units of the active army had not yet returned to their peacetime garrisons; detachments of reservists had to be shipped all over Prussia in pursuit of their parent formations. Units in their regular stations often had their mobilization equipment stored at central depots, and bringing the two together brought even more confusion to the already overstrained railway system. Prussia's humiliation was further underscored by Austria's relatively trouble-free transport of seventy-five thousand men to Olmütz by rail in a short time.[3]

The contrast made it plain that something must be done quickly to improve the military efficiency of Prussia's railroads. Prince William, the King's brother, emerged as one of the staunchest supporters of new railway construction. The Ministries of War and Commerce, while remaining as jealous as ever of their respective prerogatives and perquisites, accepted the need for mutual cooperation. Within the General Staff Reyher went so far as to advocate complete military control of railroads in wartime, yet his thinking remained limited. On the whole his memoranda reflected the traditional concept of railroads as primarily a defender's weapon. Reyher wrote of improved mobility making the support of threatened sectors easier, of protecting railways by fortifications, of the overriding importance of linking forts by rail. His attitude is clearly indicated by his warning against adopting the wider Russian gauge for new railway lines in Prussia's eastern provinces. He feared a surprise attack by the strong forces permanently stationed in Russia's Polish and Baltic provinces—and different gauges, Reyher argued, always favor the defense. The German railroaders who struggled to adapt their rolling stock to Russian tracks in 1915 and 1941 would certainly have agreed with him.

The failure of the Prussian railways in 1850 was only partly a failure of doctrine. The existing network had been too thin, the locomotives and cars too few, the administrative organization too haphazard, for large-scale troop movements. But as the General Staff began preparing a theoretical framework for the military utilization of the railroads, their physical structure expanded as well. The dominant figure in the development of Prussian railways in these years was August von der Heydt, Minister of Commerce since December, 1848. For years he had encouraged railway construction; for years he had advocated developing a system of state railroads. In his thirteen years of office he tenaciously pursued both policies. Work on the public-owned Eastern Railway, the *Ostbahn*, was resumed in 1851. At the same time a number of short feeder and connecting lines were built in the Rhineland and Westphalia, including one routed through Halle, Erfurt, and Kassel, which provided a link between the Rhenish provinces and Prussia proper without crossing Hanoverian territory. By 1860 approximately half the 5,700 kilometers of Prussian railroads were state-owned or administered.[4]

Von der Heydt emphasized the railroads contributions to the national interest in small ways as well as large. For example, the *Ostsee Zeitung* reported in January, 1855, that in future all Prussian freight cars were to be given fittings for the transport of men and horses—facilities for benches and rings for reins.[5]

A truly close relationship between the General Staff and the Prussian railways, however, only began in 1858 when Moltke moved into the house at *Behrenstrasse* 66 and assumed the duties of Chief of Staff. From that time, in the words of one biographer,

> hardly a single important railway line was built . . . in Prussia and later in Germany, without Moltke submitting an opinion on the most favorable routing, or the construction of bridges, tunnels, etc. . . . Moreover he endeavored to make clear the general viewpoints influencing his thinking in memoranda to the responsible authorities in order to create understanding for the interests of the military and give them emphasis.[6]

The concepts and perceptions Moltke developed in the early 1840s had been sharpened by study and experience. For Prussia, surrounded by powerful neighbors, lacking natural frontiers, time was all-important. From his first weeks in office, Moltke emphasized his conviction that the best of operations plans could not be executed by the greatest of generals if the mobilization was slow or the initial deployment faulty. It was at the very beginning that the machine must be in the most perfect order. This insistence on the importance of peacetime planning was not new in Prussia; but the opinion that long-range plans were an exercise in futility which could not be harmonized with concrete cases still had many adherents even within the General Staff. This reflected neither intellectual laziness nor simple conservatism. Throughout Prussia's history, the periods of preparation for war had been long enough to enable plans of campaigns to be prepared to fit the given situation. The railroads had brought an end to this grace period. The mobilization of 1850 had demontrated that rapid, large-scale troop movements by rail could not be improvised on the outbreak of war. Yet Reyher, for all his interest in the military potential of the railroads in general, had done nothing to incorporate specific railroads into his theoretical mobilization plans. Though the *Militär-Wochenblatt* had made the Prussian army aware of the French regulations of 1855 for the transport of troops by rail, Reyher continued to base his calculations on foot marches. Wishing to maintain military independence, he was reluctant to initiate a continuing intimate relationship with the Ministry of Commerce, preferring instead to submit individual memoranda on specific problems. Moltke, on the other hand, believed it futile for the General Staff to prepare timetables and loading schedules in a vacuum. The General Staff, the Ministry of War, and the Ministry of Commerce must cooperate as closely as possible, making certain that the railway lines could actually fulfil the demands made on them. He also attempted to convince the War Ministry of the importance of concluding treaties with the small states of north Germany which would provide for mutual use of roads and railroads in wartime.[7] Nothing, however, had been done to implement these recommendations by 1859, when the outbreak of war between France and Austria provided a spur and an example for Moltke's work.

2

A striking feature of Prussia's military development in the mid-nineteenth century was her ability to profit from the experience of her neighbors while being spared the worst consequences of her own blunders. The fiasco of 1850 had clearly demonstrated the wrong way to utilize railroads in a mobilization, but the Convention of Olmütz gave Prussia a chance to digest the lessons in peace. Now in the spring of 1859, trainloads of men and supplies were rolling from every part of France towards the Piedmontese frontier, crushing under their wheels the last traces of doubt that this new means of transportation was eminently suitable for military purposes.[8] Prussia's role in the war which seemed certain to come was as yet undetermined on February 1, when War Minister Eduard von Bonin requested Moltke's opinion on the military measures necessary in case of mobilization—particularly on the strength needed to secure the line of the Rhine. Moltke's reply emphasized the importance of the railways in any contingency plan, and requested Bonin to contact the Ministry of Commerce in order to determine just what could be expected of them under existing conditions.[9] On March 14, he submitted another memorandum declaring that "in the case of war with France . . . the greatest emphasis must be placed on the concentration of the Prussian army on and across the Rhine as soon as possible." This in turn required maximum use of the railroads. The north German railways admittedly represented a marked advance over foot marches, but as Moltke dryly commented, there remained numerous "inconveniences" which were certain to emerge as even more serious in practice than in theory. These inconveniences, he argued, had two underlying causes. First, most lines were still single-tracked. Second, the existing railway network was not sufficiently developed to enable each army corps to have a definite route over which its troops could be transported, without being hindered by other units. At present it would require six weeks to concentrate a quarter-million Prussian and north German troops on the Rhine and the Main. Two weeks could be saved, Moltke argued, by doubling all existing single-track lines and building thirteen new lines of varying length, twelve of which were already projected or under construction. Could the Ministry of Commerce possibly expedite matters?[10]

This ambitious project had no practical effect. Bonin, reluctant to act until the government should decide on a specific plan, reluctant to do anything which might expose Prussia's intentions, refused even to attempt to establish working relations with the Ministry of Commerce. Moltke, learning of this, submitted a stinging memorandum to his chief reminding him of the concrete requirements involved in a successful use of the railroads. The Ministry of Commerce, however, had no intention of sacrificing any more of its hard-won control over Prussia's railroads than was absolutely necessary. Von der Heydt, replying to Moltke's memorandum of March 14, thanked him politely for his useful suggestions, indicated politely certain errors in his reasoning, and expressed the "greatest willingness" to cooperate closely with the General Staff on all questions affecting the military use of the Prussian railway network.[11] A mixed commission to regulate railway transport to the Rhine was finally established on May 2. Handicapped by personal and professional quarrels, it did not complete its work for over three months. By the end of June, however, it had managed to establish three basic transport routes, each controlled by a separate commission of soldiers and officials. At the same time Prussia began negotiating with the north German states, arranging for the use of their railroads and the inclusion of their troop contingents in the overall transport plan.[12]

Six of Prussia's nine corps had been mobilized in mid-June and the first units were scheduled to depart for the Rhine on July 1.

Contracts had been concluded with the railways; locomotives and wagons stood ready on the sidings. But Prince William, who had assumed the regency in October, 1858, and Foreign Minister von Schleinitz, were reluctant to act without the approval of the German Confederation. They cancelled the operation, then changed their minds. When on July 4 the Regent finally ordered five corps to concentrate on the Rhine, much of the rolling stock which had been so carefully assembled was once more scattered to the four corners of Prussia. It would be at least eleven days before troop movements could begin, and Moltke became even more conscious of time as a factor in strategic planning. Above all, he argued, the transport of men and supplies must be uninterrupted; the predetermined timetables must be followed in detail. Faced with the threat of a French offensive from Metz, it was vital to concentrate as rapidly as possible and as far forward as possible—even in view of the fact that it would take at least six weeks to complete the concentration, given the existing state of the Prussian railway network.[13]

Within a few days the entire issue was academic. Austrian distrust of Prussia's intentions in Germany combined with the Austrian defeat at Solferino led to the conclusion of an armistice on July 8—an armistice which for all practical purposes ended the war. The Prince Regent, aware of these developments, held his own troops in their cantonments, and on July 25 ordered demobilization to begin. But if the peace of Villafranca deprived Moltke of the chance to obtain experience "in the grand style" of moving troops by rail, he did the next best thing. He sent officers to France to determine the organization and capabilities of its railway system. Others were assigned to search the numerous official and semiofficial histories and narratives published in France and Austria for guidelines on the role of railways in modern war. The picture which emerged was far from reassuring. France, an aggressive power flushed and arrogant with victory, was now more than ever Prussia's main potential enemy. In the face of this threat from the west, internal conflicts with Austria were unimportant. Strategically as well as tactically, French military doctrine emphasized the offensive, and the French army, with its large cadres of professional soldiers, requiring no long and complex mobilization to reach a war footing, was well-matched to the doctrine. Moltke believed that the most probable

French strategy would involve a surprise attack on south Germany, with the threefold aim of destroying its armies before they had time to concentrate, separating Prussia and Austria, and outflanking the Rhenish provinces. Prussia, with her army based on territorial recruiting, had only two corps stationed in the Rhineland. To reinforce them with units from other regions in peacetime would be to risk a repetition of the confusion of 1850 when mobilization of reserves became necessary. Moltke expected that the railroads would eventually restore the balance, but he realized that given the existing track mileage and the existing capabilities of individual lines, this time had not yet come. If anything, the French railway network was superior to the Prussian—particularly in view of the respective demands likely to be made on each. Moltke, therefore, accepted that any war with France must begin with Prussia on the defensive, holding the line of the Rhine as long as possible while concentrating the bulk of her strength on the Main for an eventual counterattack. And even here, in the heart of Germany, it would require a month for the railroads to transport enough troops to form a defensive line, at least two months for the assembly of sufficient forces to permit offensive operations.[14]

Acting on the basic assumption that Prussia's wars in the immediate future would almost inevitably begin with Prussia on the defensive, Moltke in the early 1860s devoted much attention to problems of fortification and coastal defense. But instead of concentrating on masonry, he emphasized the importance of mobility—mobility secured by an extensive and comprehensive railway network. Conflict between military and commercial interests, he argued, could only arise in frontier zones and along the major rivers. Here, for security reasons, the railroads would have to be constructed with regard to existing fortifications; everywhere else "full freedom of construction is to be allowed." And while Moltke warned that military considerations should never be overlooked, he nevertheless argued that a less suitable line with guaranteed financing was better than none at all—a memory, perhaps, of his days as a railway promoter in the 1840s.[15]

3

If Moltke did everything in his power to increase the military potential of Prussia's transportation network, he also encouraged the development of a common doctrine on the military use of railways throughout the German Confederation. Coordinated plans and timetables, he argued, were indispensable on both military and technical grounds if the German railways were to be of real value. Moltke was not alone in his opinion. For years military writers had stressed both the need to prepare in time of peace for the use of railroads in war and the danger presented by a French railway network so well developed that her generals could concentrate an army of two hundred thousand men in Paris or Châlons and throw them across the Rhine in a day or two.[16] Material considerations, so important in the 1840s, were no longer a major problem. As early as 1854, the German Confederation had almost 12,000 kilometers of railways, and enough rolling stock to transport 170,000 men and 56,000 horses in a day. By 1860, most of the wagons and locomotives of Germany's railroads could be used interchangeably. Individual lines were accustomed to cooperating with each other. The railroads had demonstrated their ability to transport masses of men and equipment. All of the elements for success were present except one. There was still no general plan for converting the railroads from a peace to a war footing. Since 1846 the Confederation's Military Commission had sought to interest the armies of the large and middle-sized states in establishing Confederation control over the railways and influencing their construction with regard to strategic requirements. They had no more success than similar attempts made by officers of the states themselves. As late as 1859 the Bavarian high command proposed to march its troops to the Rhine rather than trust the railroads of neighboring Württemberg. But the events of 1859 inspired still another effort.[17]

On February 7, 1861, a special commission was established to evaluate the suitability of Germany's railway network for military purposes. It consisted of one officer each from Austria, Prussia, Bavaria, and Hanover, but was dominated by its Austrian chairman, Gründorf von Zerbégeny, and by the Prussian Captain von Wartensleben, who had established a justified reputation as one of the few officers in Germany with an understanding of the technical aspects of railroading.

The commission spent several months traveling the railroads of Germany and the neighboring states, talking with owners and officials, determining the capacities of the various lines. Despite the difficulty of distinguishing some of the inspection tours from outright junkets, the officers seem to have done their work well. Their final report emphasized the problems of coordination presented by the wide differences in the construction and administration of Germany's railroads. In the south and east, where commercial and industrial interests were concentrated in the larger towns, where most railways had been financed by government capital, there were fewer junctions and the network as a whole was thinner than in the north and west. There the combination of private investment and the desire of many states to have their own railway system centered on their own capital cities resulted in a combination of short lines and many owners. But nowhere in Germany could the railway officials, lacking experience in military matters and in transporting large masses of troops, be trusted to execute either mobilization or concentration without military supervision. The Commission also echoed Moltke's opinion that only double-tracked lines could fulfil military requirements, describing the fact that three-fourths of the lines were still single-tracked as one of the most serious shortcomings of Germany's railroads. Other specific recommendations were that military movements be made as rapidly as possible in order to free the lines for other purposes, that rolling stock be transferred from one railroad to another only in emergencies, and that military trains follow each other in continuous regular sequence rather than move in "echelons." All civilian traffic, freight or passenger, should be halted during mobilization. Finally, the commission recommended the closest possible cooperation of military and civilian authorities at all levels, with a combined central authority controlling the work of the agencies supervising individual routes.

Ignoring tensions within the German Confederation, the commission had concentrated primarily on coordinating Germany's railway network to meet the threat of a French attack. Their report contained twenty pages of plans for evacuating rolling stock and carrying out systematic demolitions in the face of an advancing enemy. At the same time, the officers prepared detailed plans for the concentration of the *Bundesheer* along the Rhine frontier in case of war with France. This work was, of course, merely a theoretical exercise: even the commission members realized that the moribund Confederation could do little to implement their recommendations. It is significant, however, as the first detailed, comprehensive plan for the military use of German railroads—a plan so theoretically sound that it embodied the basic technical principles used in all projects for a general mobilization against France made before 1870.[18]

The Prussian General Staff continued to do its utmost to improve coordination between soldiers and railwaymen. A Cabinet Order of March 3, 1861, directed that each infantry or *Jäger* battalion garrisoned near a railway station annually detach two noncommissioned officers for training in railway duties. The mobilization plans were also expanded to incorporate a new type of unit, the Field Railway Detachment. Its mission was to repair destroyed or damaged railroads and to supervise the construction of short communications lines when necessary. A comprehensive set of instructions for transporting troops and supplies by rail appeared in May, 1861. These instructions were essentially technical analyses of such specific problems as the best ways of organizing and despatching military trains, of the time required for loading and unloading them, and of determining the respective spheres of authority of civilian and military officials.[19] In a minor key they also illustrate one of the most widely accepted conclusions among historians of modern Germany: the gradual supplanting in the Prussian and German officer corps of men trained in the generous spirit of Scharnhorst and Gneisenau by military specialists.

This interpretation suggests that the broad vision and humanistic ideals of the Era of Reform increasingly gave way before a system of rigid professional training that tended to produce one-dimensional men, realists and technicians whose circumscribed insight contributed greatly to the army's role in the German catastrophe. This changing attitude has been described as a kind of "military positivism" reflecting contemporary trends in philosophy and science. It has been interpreted as a reaction to the bourgeois liberals, whose plans for military reform too often reflected either complete ignorance of the technical problems involved or unwillingness to admit their validity.[20] It was also closely involved with the emergence of technology. Unlike their turn-of-the-century predecessors, Moltke, Roon, and their subordinates were deeply involved with an increasingly technical weaponry. The muskets, cannon, and sabers of the War of Liberation had changed little since the days of Marlborough. Men and animals were no stronger, could move no more rapidly, under Blücher than under Julius Caesar. Yet by midcentury men whose early experience, training, and conditioning had in most cases differed little from that of Scharnhorst or Yorck were grappling with problems posed by rifles which could empty an ammunition wagon in a few minutes, cannon which could hit a target at over a mile, and railroads which could move an army from one end of Germany to the other in a week. And as soldiers began to study the practical military applications of nineteenth-century technology, they learned something:

> All machinery cared about a man was what he knew and what he could do . . . and nobody could fool it on those things. Machinery always obeyed its own rules, and if you broke the rules it didn't matter how important or charming or pure in heart you were, you couldn't get away with it.[21]

Machines made their own laws. The railroads eventually contributed not only to a geometric increase in the size of armies, but to the development of new patterns of warfare as well. Certainly they helped make possible the successful deployment of mass armies along interior lines which remains Moltke's major contribution to the art of strategy. The question of the immutability of the laws of strategy remains moot, but even the staunchest defenders of the concept will usually agree that changing circumstances change the emphasis placed on the various laws. Space and time, two of the key factors in the strategists' equation, meant something far different to Moltke than to Napoleon or Frederick the Great.[22] But the influence of railroads on military doctrine depended on track mileage and layout, on careful organization and precise administration, at least as much as on the speculations of senior staff officers. Theoretical study of the possible influence of railroads on strategy in the pattern of List and Pönitz had not entirely disappeared. It was, however, rapidly losing the limelight to manuals of practical instructions for forming, loading, and controlling military trains. Thus a popular handbook for general staff officers criticized Pönitz's thinking on the subject of railroads on the grounds that he failed to consider adequately the everyday technical problems posed by their use. Trains are derailed, locomotives break down, schedules go awry. The author cited as an example the sixteen days required by an Austrian corps to travel only forty-seven German miles by rails in 1859. They could have covered the same distance afoot in less time, and arrived at their destination ready to fight.[23]

4

Prussian soldiers were further encouraged to master the technical details of railroading by changes in a nonmilitary bureau. Count Heinrich von Itzenplitz succeeded von der Heydt as Minister of Commerce in 1862, but had neither Heydt's force of character nor his technical expertise. Moreover, exemplifying a growing *laissez-faire* trend in Prussian economic circles, he believed that it did not matter who built railways as long as they were built. After fifteen years, private joint-stock companies began to flourish once more as the government, already spending without the consent of the *Landtag*, took itself out of the business of railroad construction. The removal of von der Heydt's strong hand meant that the soldiers were virtually forced to assume primary responsibility for determining methods of using railways in wartime. The outbreak of the American Civil War offered a wide variety of examples of constructing, operating, and maintaining military railroads; the establishment of a permanent railway section in the General Staff has in fact been described as a direct result of the lessons of that war.[24] Increasing tension over the Schleswig-Holstein question, however, rapidly focused the primary attention of Prussia's military planners on their northern frontier.

Moltke's first memorandum on the subject of a possible war with Denmark, written in December 1862, stressed the importance of ending the war as rapidly as possible in order to avoid the threat of foreign intervention. The north German railroads, he declared, could move troops into the duchies faster than the Danish ships, and the concentration would go even more smoothly if the Hamburg Assembly would consent to build a connecting line between Hamburg and Altona. This line could then be used to evacuate the rolling stock of the Holstein railways, keeping it out of Danish hands and making it available to speed the German advance to the Eider.[25] Planning for the contingency of war with Denmark was somewhat restricted, however, by the reluctance of both Roon and King William to fix the size and composition of the Prussian contingent. Moltke evaded this by setting as a General Staff exercise in 1863 the preparation of orders and timetables for the concentration by rail of a Prussian expeditionary force around Hamburg and Lübeck. It was this work which provided the basis for the actual concentration.[26] The origins and course of the Danish War of 1864, while vital for the comprehension of Prussian-Austrian relations and military-political relationships, offered few challenges to the technicians of the Prussian General Staff. Significantly, when Moltke went to Frankfurt in November 1863 as a member of the Confederation commission assigned to work out the details of the initial "Execution," he took with him as his aide Captain von Wartensleben, by this time recognized as the General Staff's leading authority on railway matters—a reflection of the fact that a good part of the four-man commission's task was to determine preliminary routes and schedules for each contingent.

The details of the operation were left to a commission of specialists which met in Leipzig in the first part of December. As the Confederation still had no unified system of military transport, agreements had to be concluded with each government and each private company separately. Moreover, since one of the overriding concerns in planning the operation had been to avoid alarming the rest of Europe, it was considered desirable to interfere with regular traffic as little as possible. Despite the challenges the conference completed its work with a minimum of friction. Its dominant personalities were by this time familiar figures: Wartensleben for the Prussians, Gründorf for the Austrians. These junior officers proved well able to settle the business at hand without alienating their civilian counterparts; Gründorf even convinced the directorate of the Austrian State Railways not to make an extra charge for the use of their specially constructed stock cars.

Given the fact that the German railways had never before cooperated with each other on such a scale, the transport of the "Execution Army" and its reserves went almost as well in practice as on the exercise tables of the various staffs.[27] The first Saxon units left Leipzig on December 15; early on the 18th the whole brigade, almost six thousand men, was in cantonments at Botzenburg. For three months afterward troops, horses, and guns rolled into the theater of war with relatively few delays—a success resulting in large part from the efforts of the redoubtable Wartensleben, who was in charge of directing rail transport to Holstein during December and January.

Things did not always go so smoothly at the unloading points. Neither troops nor railway officials were prepared to cope with a north German winter which often coated ramps and sidings with sheets of ice; nor had the stations around Altona been built to be used by an army. The railway network in Schleswig-Holstein was thin—only two main lines and a few spurs, all single-tracked. Each duchy had its own signal system. There was such a shortage of rolling stock that traffic was restricted to two trains a day until the first armistice in April. The armies, however, did not have to worry about such details. On February 15, with the initial concentration completed, the railway companies assumed the responsibility for unloading military trains and sending them back along the single-track lines, while the military determined the composition of each train and reported its departure. A mixed line commission, stationed in Altona, coordinated the operation, while communications depots were established in Altona, Flensburg, Rendsburg, and Kiel.

Under the unusual conditions in which the war was fought, the system worked well after the inevitable early period of friction and confusion. Casualties were light; ammunition expenditures were low; and a fertile countryside with a relatively friendly population meant that quartermasters were able to purchase forage and provisions locally. Not until the allies entered Jutland did the hostility of the Danish farmers force them to depend on magazines for part of their supplies, and by that time the capacity of the local railroads had been tripled by the expedient of importing wagons and locomotives from Prussia. It was the presence of this rolling stock which inspired Moltke to recommend on October 25, 1864, that the Prussian troops evacuating Danish territory be moved by rail wherever possible. Route marches, he argued, may have been useful at the start of the campaign, but for men going home they were of much less value. The costs of the railway movement would be more than balanced by lower outlays for rations and quarters, and by the earlier discharge of the reservists. The cavalry and artillery, moreover, faced disproportionate wear and tear on horses and equipment should they be required to march back to their garrisons in winter weather.[28] Moltke carried his point. A "Central Commission for the Transport of Large Troop Masses on Railroads" was created on November 5, and when the Prussian troops began evacuating the duchies at the end of the month, most of them rode home. In less than two years they would board trains again, for a different destination and a rendezvous with history.

Die Deutschen Eisenbahnen 1850

_____ Von 1835 bis Ende 1845 eröffnete Eisenbahnen
- - - - - Von 1846 bis Ende 1850 eröffnete Eisenbahnen

Map 1. The German Railway Network, 1850

Source: *100 Jahre deutsche Eisenbahnen: Die deutsche Reichsbahn im Jahre 1835.* Edited by Deutsche Reichsbahn-Gesellschaft (Berlin, 1935), p. 15.

51

Chapter III

Steam, Strategy, and Operations:

The Struggle for Supremacy in Germany

The Schleswig-Holstein campaign and its antecedents had demonstrated that German railways could move masses of troops and supplies, and that soldiers and officials could cooperate to organize the process. Yet the operations in Denmark also contributed, albeit indirectly, to that integration of railroads into strategic and operational planning which had been a major topic of discussion in Germany since the 1840s. Wilhelm Rüstow might continue to grumble that railways could not directly influence the course of a battle, and that no army tied to them could achieve great results. But for the Prussian General Staff the fighting in Denmark had demonstrated that the only way to overcome the firepower of breechloading rifles and rifled cannon was by flank attacks and encircling operations. Yet the range of modern weapons and the size of modern armies meant that flanking movements could no longer be executed tactically. The process must begin earlier; envelopment must be regarded as an operational problem.[1] This doctrine of "strike together, never stand together," was fraught with risk. It implied a division of forces, one part executing the frontal attack, the other the flanking maneuver, with the corresponding risk of being overwhelmed in detail. Even Napoleon had warned against the danger of attempting to concentrate in the face of an enemy; the importance of concentration of force and the advantage of interior lines were basic postulates of nineteenth-century strategists. Clausewitz, the Archduke Karl of Austria, Jomini, von Willisen—their theories agree on these points as on few others. Moltke too recognized and accepted the fact that the strategic advantage still rested with the possessor of interior lines. But dangerous though it might be, dispersion had been made necessary by modern mass armies. Supply problems alone made continuous concentration impossible. Even if wagon trains were kept to a minimum, no more than thirty thousand men—one war-strength corps—could be moved on a single road on a given day. Once concentrated, an army of several corps could not really march; it could only inch itself forward cross-country. To move rapidly it must divide, and this presented an alert enemy with the kind of golden opportunity which Napoleon had feared. Massing troops in a small area, moreover, impelled commanders to seek a decision whether the opportunities were favorable or not. For these reasons, Moltke argued, units should be concentrated only at the decisive moment; to bring even two corps together without a definite reason was an error.[2]

For Moltke as for every strategist, the necessity for concentration of force remained a key postulate in his thinking. His application of this principle, however, differed sharply from that of his predecessors. Concentration of force was to Moltke an equation with three factors: space, time, and mass. It was achieved not when men and units stood shoulder to shoulder on a given spot, but when the distance between units was within the limits allowing their concentric cooperation and mutual support. The art of strategy lay in determining these limits, in "regulating divided marches with regard to concentration at the right time."[3]

Even in the abstract, railroads could play an obvious role in regulating divided marches. And as Prussia's relations with Austria continued to deteriorate, the railroads became increasingly significant in solving concrete strategic problems. Since 1758, Prussian preparations for the contingency of war with Austria had been intimidated by geography. Frederick the Great's seizure of Silesia transformed Bohemia into a giant salient presenting an offensive-minded Austrian army alternative options in the event of war with Prussia. Hapsburg troops could either drive into Silesia or advance directly on Berlin through the Bohemian mountains. For almost fifty years Prussian planners had been attempting to devise an effective counter to this threat.

Typical of their solutions was Carl von Clausewitz' 1827 proposal to concentrate three divisions in Silesia and two on the high road to Berlin to act as defensive anchors, with three corps deployed in lower Lusatia to support either flank as needed. The first major modifications of this plan came during the 1850s. As the Prussian railway network expanded into Saxony and Silesia, during Reyher's tenure as Chief of Staff, he urged the concentration of three corps around the new railheads of upper Silesia and Lusatia: VI Corps at Breslau and Liegnitz, V Corps at Glogau, II Corps at Luckau and Dohne. On the other flank, III Corps would assemble at Torgau and IV Corps at Wittenberg while the Guards remained in reserve around Berlin. This proposal to deploy along a wide front, recalling in many respects the cordon defenses of the eighteenth century, reflected both the common contemporary belief in the lateral mobility conferred by the railways and the hard fact that under existing conditions the number of troops each line could support was relatively limited. It also admitted something that previous plans ignored: successful concentration in the face of a determined Austrian advance would depend almost entirely on the speed with which troops could reach the threatened areas. Dispersion was an acceptable risk if it saved time.[4]

Moltke's first approach to the strategic challenge of the Bohemian salient, a memorandum written in 1860, was dominated by two facts. One was geographic: an Austrian army based in Prague could reach either Schweidnitz in Silesia or Torgau in Prussian Saxony in approximately the same time. The other was technical: the Bohemian railway network could support either maneuver. Moltke was convinced that, whether Austria's aim was the destruction of the Prussian monarchy itself or such a lesser goal as the reconquest of Silesia, its best option would be to march directly on Berlin. The capture of the Prussian capital would be a great moral victory; even more important for the future course of the campaign, the loss of this key railway junction would make it all but impossible for Prussia to draw reinforcements from either west or east. The difficulty lay in blocking this attack. Moltke assumed the Austrians would have the advantage of numbers as well as position. This meant that Silesia would have to make do with its provincial garrison while the bulk of Prussia's manpower concentrated to protect Berlin. Direct defense of the capital he rejected as impractical. The Lusatian railheads were too far foward, too exposed to a determined Austrian advance. Berlin itself, moreover, was unfortified; loss of one battle could mean that the Prussians might be thrown back as far as Stettin in Pomerania before they could regroup. Instead Moltke proposed concentrating behind the Elbe, around Wittenberg and Torgau—even around Dresden, if the Prussian army could occupy Saxony before the Austrians. A static position on the Austrian flank would by itself scarcely hinder their march on Berlin, but Moltke proposed an aggressive defense, a series of flanking attacks from the Elbe bridgeheads which would threaten Austrian communications and, with any success, force them back towards Silesia and their own frontier.[5]

The memorandum is characterized both by its offensive spirit and its willingness to accept strategic and political risks. "It revealed a disinclination to fight away from fixed defensive positions and a preference for one in which the enemy would be checked by the skillful use of space and movement."[6] The increasing importance of space and movement in Moltke's thinking is reflected in still another memorandum on the subject of war with Austria. Prepared in the winter of 1865-66, it reflected Bismarck's hope of securing both French and Russian neutrality. This meant that several corps otherwise needed on the Rhine and the Vistula would become available for operations against Austria and her south German allies. The latter Moltke regarded as a negligible quantity. One corps, reinforced by Landwehr and garrison troops, should be enough to hold them in check. The remaining eight corps could be concentrated against Austria, creating an approximately equal balance of forces. This was still not enough, in Moltke's opinion, to make a Prussian advance from upper Silesia towards Vienna a practical operation. Instead he recommended the concentration of three corps around Dresden and three at Görlitz, with V and VI Corps left in the area of Schweidnitz to cover Silesia. The Austrians would still have the advantage of interior lines; they would still be able either to attack Silesia or to march directly on Berlin. In the latter case, which Moltke considered more probable, the decisive battle would come immediately. In the former, the main Prussian army could either sidestep into Lusatia, join the garrison of Silesia, and continue operations, or it could attack directly into Bohemia, forcing the

Austrians to change front to meet them. In either event, the critical factor would be Prussia's ability to concentrate her strength in time to meet any contingency.[7]

Above all, Moltke believed, Prussia *must* maintain the initiative. A declaration of war should be issued as soon as one of Prussia's neighbors began to arm, and troops should be moved into the theater of war as rapidly as possible. This meant maximum utilization of the railroads. In the memorandum of 1865, for example, Moltke's choice of Dresden and Görlitz as the points of concentration for the main army were governed at least as much by their importance as railway junctions as by any strategic considerations.[8] Another key to success lay in keeping enemies and prospective enemies off balance, in being one step ahead of them. The contributions the railways could make to this process were particularly clear in the case of Saxony, whose Austrian-oriented foreign policy made it as great a threat as in 1756. Here Moltke favored a Frederician solution. It had taken Frederick's army thirty-five days to force Saxony's capitulation—just long enough to give Austria another winter to prepare for war. For Moltke, however, the steam engine guaranteed a different result. Though he was uncertain about the details of Saxony's mobilization schedules, he was certain that they were no faster than Prussia's. Since the Saxons still depended largely on route marches to reach their concentration areas, Moltke was convinced the Prussians could use the railroad to move superior forces to the frontier and overrun most of the kingdom before their adversaries had time to react. Similarly, by the end of 1865, it was increasingly apparent that most of Prussia's neighbors—Hanover, Hesse, the south German states—sympathized with Austria. The VII and VIII *Bundeskorps* together would be over eighty thousand men strong, a formidable striking force. Here, too, steam-powered mobility must be used to counter-balance numbers; offensive action must keep the danger from South Germany *in potentia*.[9]

2

Events during the spring of 1866 transformed the developing relationship between steam and strategy to a kind of symbiosis. By February Moltke seems to have been convinced, distasteful though the prospect was to him, that war with Austria was inevitable. In his opinion Prussia's best course was to strike before Austria could complete her preparations and the other German states decide on a course of action. Bismarck, on the other hand, disliked limiting his alternatives so drastically until the last moment. King William was so reluctant to become involved in a "Brothers' War" that he was hostile both to his Prime Minister's proposed Piedmontese alliance and his Chief of Staff's request for at least partial mobilization.

Moltke's correspondence in the spring of 1866 reflects his increasing frustration at the loss of time which could never be recaptured. "From my point of view," he wrote on April 2, "I must express the conviction that success or failure in this war will depend in large part on the decision for war being made earlier here than in Vienna—now, if possible."[10] The railways were the key to his anxiety. Prussia, Moltke calculated, was able to concentrate its main army on the Saxon-Bohemian frontier in twenty-five days. Austria's circumstances were different. Within the projected theater of operations, Bohemia and Moravia, the railway network was relatively complete. But only one line connected these provinces with Vienna and the rest of Austria, and even this line was single-tracked in places. If the Austrians might have considerable operational flexibility once their concentration was completed, they would nevertheless require at least six weeks to assemble as many as two hundred thousand men in Bohemia. This time, however, could be reduced to a month if Bavaria made the Regensburg-Prague railway available to Austrian troop trains. This fact alone made Bavaria's neutralization, whether by military or political means, a necessity. Victory in war, Moltke argued, was not merely a function of numbers; it depended at least as much on the time needed to bring these numbers into action. But how to convince the King and his civilian advisers?[11]

In the first two weeks of April, as more and more Austrian troops moved into Bohemian cantonments, Moltke watched Prussia's advantage reduced a day at a time. Several of his projected railheads were now exposed to the danger of a surprise attack, but technical considerations did not always permit them to be abandoned. Each passing day fixed Moltke's operational planning more firmly in the structure of the Prussian railway network. Geographically, this was oriented in an east-west direction. Only five lines led south to the Saxon-Bohemian frontier, with their railheads at Zeitz, Halle, Herzberg, Görlitz, and Neisse. In order to regain at least part of the time lost since March, these lines must be utilized to the fullest possible extent. On April 14, 1866, Moltke requested the King's approval of a plan to concentrate seven of Prussia's nine corps along the line Herzberg-Görlitz-Neisse. Strategically this portion offered several advantages. It presented the possibility of falling on the Austrian flank and rear no matter which way they moved. It was a direct invasion route into Austria. It enabled the outflanking of the strong natural positions at Josephstadt and Königgrätz. But Moltke's underlying concern was "the quickest possible concentration of the troops." To ensure it, he was willing to spread them along a 400-kilometer semicircle, accepting all the attendant risks.[12]

For two weeks Moltke worked at convincing the King to approve not only this radically unusual deployment, but also the concentration of Prussia's entire army in the east, leaving the western provinces undefended. Such wide dispersion, he argued, would be dangerous if Austria could concentrate approximately equal forces in Bohemia in the same time. However, as late as twenty-five days after the transport began, two hundred thousand Prussians would face only half that number of Austrians. The initial deployment must provide for the security of Berlin and Breslau, the concentration of the largest possible force in the east, and the maximum use of the railways. And only the projected plan, Moltke declared, could guarantee all three.[13] On April 27, he proposed to modify his original organization even further. Instead of eventually deploying six corps in Lusatia and three in Silesia, he recommended the establishment of two field armies each of four corps, with VIII Corps as an independent detachment. One army would be based in Lusatia, the other in Silesia; thus instead of concentrating, the Prussian army was to spread out—and the unusual extension of the deployment areas allotted to each army multiplied the effect of this process. But despite its dangers, such a concentration had one overriding advantage. It could be completed even more rapidly than the earlier proposals.[14]

With this recommendation Moltke completed the outline of the plan of campaign actually executed in 1866. Far more than was generally realized, it depended on the Prussian railway network. Troops were to be moved as far forward as possible as rapidly as possible on as many railroads as possible, then advanced concentrically against the enemy. Final concentration would take place only for the decisive battle—a true test of Moltke's belief that the art of strategy lay in timing concentrations properly.[15] But for another week the Chief of Staff fumed in his office as telegrams, diplomatic notes, and peace feelers flew back and forth among the capitals of Europe. The terms of the strategic equation had not changed. Prussia had five major railroads leading into the theater of war; Austria had one. Prussia could concentrate its full strength in three weeks; Austria required six. Decisive victory depended on Prussia's ability to utilize this initial superiority, which was declining day by day. The consequences of lost time, Moltke wrote, were "incalculable," but until the King ordered mobilization he could do nothing beyond encouraging the corps to rework their own mobilization tables. Lights burned late at headquarters all over Prussia as staff officers pared hours and days from the time required to prepare their units for the field. Common sense and past experience had taught the wisdom of having newly mobilized troops march for a few days before boarding trains to give them a chance to break in new boots, to become accustomed once more to the weight of a full pack and the heat of a woolen uniform. Horses too found pulling a caisson or a supply wagon a change from the plow, the dray, and the cab. Now, with time dominating all other considerations, men and animals were to be transported to the mobilization centers by rail whenever rolling stock could be made available. Continuing delay might mean that the Prussian army would have to fight even for its concentration areas. Moltke ordered troop trains to be scheduled so as to preserve the tactical integrity of the units involved—and to provide a balanced force of all arms at each railhead as soon as possible to ward off Austrian attacks.[16]

Each day lost meant a corresponding sacrifice of flexibility, a greater dependence on the men and machines responsible for bringing the fighting men into position. Since mid-April, the army's most experienced railway officer, Major Hermann von Wartensleben, had been stationed in Berlin as Chief of the Railway Section of the General Staff, preparing detailed plans for the organization and execution of the move to the Bohemian frontier. Technical responsibility, however, rested with the Central Railway Directory of the Ministry of Commerce, and Wartensleben recommended that a mixed executive commission be formed to coordinate the two bureaus. His detailed suggestions for the deployment, endorsed and elaborated by Moltke, were presented to the War Ministry on May 1. Each of the five axes of advance leading to the theater of operations was to be supervised by a line commission consisting of a general staff officer and a senior official of the railways. This commission would be responsible for controlling the movement of the troop trains assigned to its lines and all subsequent military traffic. Once the concentration was completed, the railways still needed as part of the lines of communication would remain under "military direction acting in accordance with the war plan and war aims." The Central Executive Commission would then operate as part of GHQ. Each field army would also have its own line commission responsible for supply and transport services, demolitions, and repairs. This would provide unity of command while minimizing friction between army commanders and railway directorates. Should disputes arise among the armies themselves, the Executive Commission would resolve the issues, and the presence of civilian officials would prevent the military from making technically impossible demands on the railways.[17]

Wartensleben's suggestions embodied the basic structure used not only in 1866, but in 1870 and 1914 as well. Its first test came immediately. On May 3, King William finally and reluctantly ordered the mobilization of five corps, but still refused to risk provoking war by ordering them to concentrate against Austria. On the next day Moltke reminded the monarch once more that time, not mass, was the crucial problem. Within three days, fifty thousand Austrians could be concentrated around Trautenau, with another thirty thousand threatening Dresden. Intelligence reports spoke of twelve thousand men already at Troppau, with more arriving daily from Galicia. To counter this immediate danger, Moltke wanted to move forward as rapidly as possible, III and IV Corps going to Lusatia, between Cottbus and Torgau, V and VI Corps to Silesia, around Schweidnitz and Neisse, with the Guard temporarily retained at Berlin. But at best it would requce three weeks to complete the concentration—three weeks from the date the first orders were issued. William, whose military virtues were those of a regimental officer, was aware of the problems presented by the railroads without possessing a really deep understanding of the subject. Moltke explained that the necessary preparations for moving a whole corps by rail must be made in the first ten days, while the corps itself, was mobilizing. If this were not done, the transport would be delayed accordingly; therefore mobilization and transport orders must be issued simultaneously.[18]

This warning, combined with Moltke's exaggerated description of the immediate Austrian threat, finally took effect. William accepted—though with some reservations—his Chief of Staff's proposal. It was one of the crucial decisions of his reign. It meant the end of an era—an era when gradual escalation was still possible, when armies could be partly mobilized and held in their garrisons as the last threat short of war. "Ask of me anything but time," Napoleon is reputed to have said, and the railroads had made time too valuable a commodity to risk its waste, even by the day. Moltke's memorandum and the King's reaction to it heralded the beginning of that process of identifying mobilization and deployment which over the next half century came to dominate the thinking of every general staff in Europe, which had gone so far by August 1914 that even the Germans felt unable to reverse the machinery—or stop it. As the troop trains rolled out of the stations in the garrison towns of Brandenburg, of Prussian Saxony, of Posen and Silesia, they were travelling the first mile towards the Marne.

3

It is certain that Moltke had no time for such apocalyptic thoughts during those first days of May. He was deeply involved in the details of transporting and deploying over a hundred thousand men while keeping his senior officers from meddling with the specialists' work. The prickly and erratic Karl von Steinmetz of V Corps resented being told that the railway authorities could not accept direct orders from him without disrupting the overall plan. General von Mutius, the elderly cavalryman commanding VI Corps, had to be reminded that any attempt to use other railroads than those assigned his units meant that "collisions with other transports would take place." Some lines needed more rolling stock. Others had to be cleared of troop trains as rapidly as possible so that supplies and forage could be brought forward—particularly in Lusatia, a poor and sparsely settled area offering limited opportunities to live off the land.[19] At the same time the rest of the Prussian army was mobilizing in fits and starts. King William's continued reluctance to provoke a war meant that nine separate orders were issued between May 3 and May 24 before mobilization was completed. This was exactly what Moltke had sought to avoid. His hopes for a systematic deployment of Prussia's entire armed might were destroyed; he could count no longer on initial numerical superiority. The only solution was to complete the concentration forward, moving the remaining corps from their mobilization areas into the theater of war as rapidly as possible. On May 16 he ordered I Corps, the East Prussian Corps, to concentrate at the Königsberg-Kreuz junction for transportation to Görlitz, where it would act as a link between the two major assembly areas. On the same day, II Pomeranian Corps began its move through Berlin to Herzberg, while the Guard marched towards Cottbus. Finally, Moltke was able to convince the King to approve the transport of VIII Corps and the 14th Division of VII Corps to Halle and Zeitz, in Prussian Saxony, where they would be available either to march on Dresden or to meet a Bavarian attack from the south.

Sketched on a map, the situation was a cautious man's nightmare. Seven and a half corps, almost the whole Prussian army, were extended like beads on a string along an arc four hundred kilometers long. To generals and politicians alike it seemed that Moltke had resorted to the same kind of cordon deployment which had presented such opportunities to the young Napoleon. Theodor von Bernhardi, Prussia's leading civilian expert on military affairs; the Italian plenipotentiary in Berlin, General Govone; Constantin von Voigts-Rhetz, Chief of Staff of the 1st Army; General von Steinmetz—all expressed reservations or objections. King William's Adjutant-General, Leopold von Boyen, son of the great reformer, called the Chief of Staff a superannuated old man. Even among Moltke's own subordinates there was open criticism of his dispositions. Moltke, writing to Steinmetz on June 1, wearily repeated the points he had been making throughout the spring. Austria had six weeks' advantage in mobilization. To counter this it was necessary to use every available railroad to move troops to the frontier as rapidly as possible, and the major railway junctions in Saxony and Lusatia formed a cordon along the border. There was no way either to change this or to deny the Austrians the interior lines given them by the Bohemian salient. But for Moltke, the dispositions made necessary by the railway network were the beginning, not the end, of the army's deployment. Only when the transport was completed "can that be done by marching which could not be done by rail: the strategic deployment."[20] The army would concentrate by advancing concentrically towards the enemy—as soon as the King agreed to issue the orders.

The last point was the crucial one. William was still unwilling to authorize a general advance, and though Bismarck, Roon, and Moltke all realized the dangers of continued delay, Moltke saw them most clearly. The army could not remain scattered among isolated railheads indefinitely; if it could not concentrate forward, it must concentrate laterally. As early as May 29, he ordered the 1st Army to move to the left, toward Görlitz, while the three divisions from the Rhineland, now organized as the Elbe Army, assembled around Torgau. At the same time I Corps, the pivot force, was shifted from Görlitz to Hirschberg in Lower Silesia. Then, just as this complicated and risky maneuver was being completed, 2nd Army Headquarters in Breslau reported that the Austrians were concentrating not in Bohemia, but farther to the east, around Olmütz in Moravia. The army commander, Crown Prince Frederick, and his caustic and competent Chief of Staff, *Generalmajor* Karl von Blumenthal, expected a direct attack on the Silesian capital—an attack which 2nd Army, with only two corps, would have little chance of stopping. Moltke had in fact erred in assuming that the Austrians would concentrate in Bohemia, misled both by faulty intelligence and his own conviction that this was the best strategy. "It is, however, simply not true that the enemy *always* does that which one regards oneself as most reasonable," and Moltke quickly adjusted his dispositions to reality. Second Army was authorized to move farther east, to the Neisse river, and I Corps and the Guard were placed under its command, raising its strength to the four corps Moltke had recommended on April 27.[21]

The result of all this chopping and changing was to establish two main armies of approximately equal strength—a contrast to much of Moltke's earlier planning, which had favored an unequal division of forces with the center of gravity in Lusatia. Moreover, the Prussian dispositions still resembled a string of beads too closely for comfort. The orders of May 29 had reduced the frontage by almost a hundred kilometers, but the southward march of the 2nd Army to cover Breslau had extended it again. The gap between 1st and 2nd Armies was dangerously wide, five or six days' march at best. The three divisions of the Elbe Army were virtually isolated. Many of Moltke's subordinates, even Wartensleben, felt the risks of this disposition outweighed its advantages, and the Chief of Staff's behavior has been analyzed, criticized, and discussed from every conceivable viewpoint. He has been described as defending a course of action he knew to be mistaken in order to "screen the responsibility of his King and his Princes before posterity," while turning all his efforts towards mitigating its evil effects.[22] It has been suggested that he was being true to his own convictions on the dangers of controlling operations too closely from GHQ, bowing to the opinion of the commanders on the spot and hoping to remedy the mistake, should it be a mistake, in the course of the campaign.[23] His decision has been called "the inevitable result of two things: Moltke's lively respect for Benedek's combative nature . . . and the limitations placed on him by geography."[24] In the light of Austria's failure to strike into Silesia, it can be seen that it might well have been preferable to refrain from reinforcing the 2nd Army, but after the weeks and months of uncertainty even a Moltke can be forgiven a temporary lapse, whether of nerve or judgment, especially when the railroads tempted him to change his mind.[25]

Even after the triumph of Königgrätz, Moltke's strategic dispositions were sharply criticized by his contemporaries, and this "remarkable illustration of the conservatism of the military mind" has echoed in texts and articles for over a century.[26] Most of the lines of argument emphasize the dangers inherent in exterior lines of operation. A Napoleon, the critics suggest, would have overwhelmed the Prussians in detail, before they could unite. Instead of accepting this risk, Moltke should either have concentrated in Upper Silesia and thrust towards Olmütz, towards the heart of Austria, or he should have abandoned Silesia, concentrated around Lusatia, and marched directly into Bohemia.[27] One distinguished contemporary military historian even argues that Prussia's concentration was adversely influenced by the railroads. According to Cyril Falls,

> The assembly had actually been clumsier on the Prussian side than it would have been without railways. Lacking their aid and placed in Moltke's situation, Napoleon would have established magazines at and east of Görlitz before moving at all, and would then have concentrated virtually the whole of his force there . . . the Austrians would not have dared to march past it and must have attacked it if they had taken the offensive.[28]

In his excellent study of the campaign of 1866, Gordon Craig describes this criticism as largely based on

> . . . time-honored shibboleths about the dangers of separation when confronting an enemy on interior lines and the sovereign excellence of concentration before battle . . . paying obeisance to principles which were impractical in the new conditions of warfare.[29]

This seems a bit strong; Moltke's dispositions *were* something less than ideal, even by his own admission. Craig, however, rightly scores the use of two of the military historian's favorite phrases—"if only" and "yes, but." Moltke's correspondence between February and June presents all the information required to explain the use he made of Prussia's railway network in preparing for the Seven Weeks' War. It is clear that his preliminary plans had generally favored an unbalanced concentration. It is equally clear that the King's continued refusal to order mobilization had made such a concentration impossible—at least in Moltke's opinion. As for establishing magazines, whether in Lusatia or Silesia, even if King William's consent could have been obtained, such a provocative act might well have resulted in an immediate Austrian declaration of war. For Moltke, it was far more sensible to face the issue squarely and mobilize outright. When the King was finally brought to this viewpoint, however, so much time had been lost that the only solution, inferior as it may have been, was to move every available man to the Bohemian frontier as rapidly as possible. The means at hand must be taken as they were. If this meant spreading the army from railhead to railhead over hundreds of kilometers, there was nothing to do but remedy the situation in the course of the campaign. It was certainly impossible to build new railroad lines overnight to implement the execution of an ideal strategic deployment, and Moltke, like any skilled technician, was never one to let the best become the enemy of the good.

4

The Prussian official history divides the army's movement to Silesia and Bohemia into four periods.[30] The first, continuing throughout May, involved primarily the transport of men, horses, and material to their mobilization centers—an episodic process dictated more by the availability of rolling stock and clear track than by systematic planning. The second period, the concentration of III, IV, V, and VI Corps in Silesia and Lusatia. required little over a week; most of the combat troops reached their destination between May 16 and May 23. The achievement is somewhat diminished on closer examination. The VI Silesian Corps, in its home district, concentrated almost entirely by marching, as did the artillery and trains of III Brandenburg Corps. The real strain on the railroads began between May 23 and June 5, when forty troop trains a day arrived in the theater of war as I, II, VII, and VIII Corps moved into position. As a rule. the lines allotted to each corps could handle eight trains per day without trouble; VIII Corps, using the double-tracked lines from Cologne and Minden to Halle, despatched as many as twelve trains daily— an unheard-of achievement in mass transportation. And the delayed mobilization which caused Moltke such anguish proved to have an unexpected compensation. Knowing what was ahead, the railroads utilized the time to concentrate wagons and locomotives and make administrative arrangements for the movement to Bohemia. With the pride of understatement, the Prussian official history correctly states that the trains arrived at their destination on schedule. To facilitate coordination the Central Executive Commission, headed by Wartensleben of the General Staff and Ministry of Commerce official *Oberbaurath* Weishaupt, who had been the civilian plenipotentiary responsible for planning the troop transports in 1859, assigned overall military control of the transport on each side of the Elbe to an officer of the General Staff. The precautions proved unnecessary; the delays and breakdowns unavoidable in such an operation were few and minor.

By June 5, the major contribution of the railroads to the concentration of the Prussian army was completed—and completed to the credit of everyone involved, from Weishaupt and Wartensleben down to the train crews, the stationmasters, and the transport officers. The fourth period of deployment primarily involved the movements of Landwehr from one garrison to another and the transport of the Guard into Silesia in accordance with Moltke's changed orders. Most of its infantry and cavalry had been kept at Berlin while the artillery and trains marched to Cottbus. When the order to join 2nd Army arrived on July 11, the units on the road swung into the railroad junctions at Guben and Sorau, while those in Berlin and Potsdam boarded waiting trains. Between June 15 and June 21, twelve trains a day arrived in Brieg, the predetermined assembly point; by June 22, the entire Prussian Guard, men, animals, guns, and wagons, was in position and ready to march.[31] It was the kind of operation giving force to the assertion that victory in future wars would require operational plans which considered available methods of transportation as well as time and space.[32]

The Prussians' success in utilizing the railroads to their own advantage is thrown into even sharper relief by the performance of their enemies. *Feldzeugmeister* Benedek, despite his reputation as one of the most aggressive and hard-driving Hapsburg generals, was unable or unwilling to overrule his Chief of Staff. *Generalmajor* Gideon von Krismanic. Krismanic's operations plan stressed the importance of concentrating the Austrian army at a suitable "position" against which the Prussian offensive might shatter itself. His cautious reluctance to move any troops in any direction was strengthened by the technical problems facing him. Once ready for the field, the units assigned to the northern theater of operations faced a serious transportation bottleneck: the *Nordbahn*, connecting these provinces to Vienna. Krismanic and his subordinates rapidly developed an excellent set of orders and regulations governing the use of the railway facilities at their disposal. Despite the handicaps presented by the single-track stretches, an average of twenty-one or twenty-two trains a day came over the *Nordbahn*. It was a performance comparable in every respect with the best efforts of the individual Prussian lines. But it was an improvisation—and it was insufficient to tempt Krismanic to do anything but await the Prussian invasion.[33]

With the exception of Hanover, none of the south German states made remarkable use of their railroads either in mobilizing or deploying their armies. Demolitions, where they occurred at all, were usually amateurish. Even in Saxony, where the Prussian threat was obvious, confusion and lack of preparation reigned supreme. Since the first part of June, the Austrian high command had recommended the evacuation of all rolling stock, public and private. But though the Saxon army began withdrawing towards Bohemia on the night of June 15, most of the railway equipment remained in place to be cut off by the Prussian advance. Only as the Prussian vanguard entered Leipzig on the morning of June 19 were the railroad yards finally evacuated; by the 20th, 142 locomotives and several thousand cars were in Eger, temporarily out of reach of the advancing Prussians. Saxon demolitions, however, were by no means as successful. Their high command seems to have been influenced by the theory, dating from the 1840s, that even superficial damage could render railways unsuitable for several weeks. The work of destruction began only on the night of the 15th. Working in darkness, looking over their shoulders for Prussian cavalry, the Saxon pioneers spent most of the few available hours burning coal, destroying switches and turntables, and dismantling pumps and water towers. Where track was torn up, the rails and ties were neither demolished nor carried away. An attempt to burn the bridge over the Elbe at Rieza resulted in the destruction of only two spans. Within a few days the Prussians had brought the key Saxon lines to almost full capacity once more.

The Austrians planned their demolitions in Bohemia along the same lines as the Saxons. They were somewhat more thorough, twisting rails and burning ties, blowing up bridges and viaducts, and obstructing tunnels. Too often, however, the Austrians seemed reluctant to inflict really massive destruction on their own railway network. The bridge over the Elbe at Lobkowitz, for example, had been mined at the beginning of the campaign, but for a week after July 18, the Austrian garrison of Theresienstadt watched Prussian trains from Turnau cross it on the way to Prague, Pardubitz, and Brünn. Not until July 27 was the mine finally exploded; had it been done earlier, the Prussians would have required at least six weeks to construct even a temporary bridge.[34]

5

If the Seven Weeks' War demonstrated the need for organization and planning to guarantee the best use of the railroads in mobilizing and concentrating an army, it showed even more clearly that these qualities were also required for supplying troops in the field. Moltke's role was still essentially restricted to planning; administration was as yet outside the General Staff's sphere of influence. Roon had been too absorbed in the reorganization of the army to pay much attention to its administrative structure. The Military Economy Department of the War Ministry, also responsible for keeping the army supplied, was slow to shed its peacetime obsession with economy and budget-balancing; moreover, its sphere of influence was too limited to have much effect on the increasingly chaotic supply situation.

Apart from organizational weaknesses, the Prussian army at all levels tended to regard the questions of supply and administration as *Beamtensachen*, unworthy of a soldier's attention. The combination of officers untrained in supply problems and officials unaccustomed to field operations was to prove an expensive luxury. In peacetime each corps had its own intendance service, military officials responsible for purchasing supplies from local contractors and forwarding them to the using units. The system worked well enough to be carried intact into mobilization—and the result was virtual anarchy. With thousands of reservists pouring into the depots, needing rations, uniforms, and equipment, competition among the intendants increased and prices soared. The fact that many of the supply officials were untrained or unfit for field duty further complicated the problem. But the army's real troubles only began when its units left their peacetime stations for the theater of war. No supply trains were included in the General Staff's timetables. Instead each corps was made responsible for bringing forage and rations on its troop trains, and for keeping itself supplied thereafter. Neither Silesia nor Lusatia were particularly fertile areas, and in any case the intendants preferred to deal with familiar contractors in their home districts. Moreover, the War Ministry saw no reason why the ability which the railroads had demonstrated to move troops could not be turned to hauling supplies once the initial concentration was completed. For the first time armies would be freed both from that dependence on magazines and fixed bases which had remained a problem down to the end of the War of Liberation, and from the manifold problems involved in living off the land.

In practice the results were far different. The corps intendants and quartermasters, determined that the men and animals depending on them would be well supplied, purchased and forwarded huge quantities of food and forage in the last weeks of June. The railroads were generally regarded as a kind of magic carpet. Most of the regimental bakers, for example, were retained at the depots in order to make maximum use of the permanent facilities there. As a result inedible loaves of bread arrived in the theater of war from as far away as Cologne. There were no intendants along the lines of communications, no central authority to control shipments and establish priorities. The line commissions could only regulate traffic. They had nothing to do with its content. The War Ministry neither prepared a systematic schedule of supply trains nor designated specific stations as central depots. Moltke, believing Wartensleben too valuable to be left behind in Berlin, took him into the field as his operations officer once mobilization was completed, and the loss of his steady hand did nothing to improve the situation.[35] The railway companies, freed from direct military control, accepted contracts to transport supplies from the various corps intendants, but regarded their duty fulfilled when the goods reached their final destination. The railroads assumed no responsibility for unloading or storage. Local commanders along the lines of communication were often elderly reservists with neither administrative ability nor the manpower to compensate for their lack of talent. Stations and sidings throughout the theater of war were soon jammed with mountains of supplies of every kind. Loaded freight cars stood for days awaiting the services of the few laborers available; empty ones were often left idle on the sidings because no one knew what to do with them.[36]

The effect of this bottleneck was multiplied by the inability of the field armies to maintain contact between the overflowing railheads and the haversacks and nosebags of their forward units. Some Prussian troops fought the battle of Königgrätz on empty stomachs. As late as July 5, Prince Frederick Charles, commanding the 1st Army, desperately reminded his subordinates that great achievements demanded great sacrifices, and that "God who feeds the sparrows will also provide for us."[37] In this case, however, it was Moltke who acted as the *deus ex machina*. With the decisive battle won and the Austrians in full retreat, with his prestige at new heights, the Chief of Staff turned his attention in the first days after Königgratz to regularizing the army's supply system. On July 4 he requested Roon to negotiate with the Prussian Ministry of Commerce regarding the operation of the Lobau-Prague railroad and send Landwehr units forward as rapidly as possible to secure the lines of communication and provide labor services. The 2nd Army was ordered to repair demolitions along the right of way from Pardubitz to Prague and prepare plans for by-passing the fortresses of Josephstadt and Königgrätz with temporary tracks. Finally, the Landwehr and depot troops of I Reserve Corps, concentrating around Dresden, were to advance on Prague as rapidly as possible, repairing the railroad as they went and occupying "this city so important for our supply."[38]

When the Guard Landwehr Division entered Prague it seized a large number of locomotives and wagons which were immediately pressed into service. At the same time the Ministry of Commerce was complaining that all of its efforts to regulate the chaotic supply situation in Prussia were blocked by the hydralike system of separate intendants. As a result, when a *General-Gouvernement* was established in Prague to control the occupied territories, it was given overall responsibility for controlling and regulating the flow of supplies to the troops in the field.[39]

Between the Ministry of Commerce and the *General-Gouvernement*, order began to emerge from chaos. The establishment of field bakeries along the lines of communication ended the absurdity of shipping loaves of bread from Coblenz or Danzig.

Forage and live cattle were purchased locally. Bulk shipments from the corps districts were restricted to such relatively durable items as flour and oatmeal. At some railheads it was necessary to burn large amounts of spoiled or unusable goods in order to clear stations and sidings, but by mid-July supplies were flowing relatively smoothly. The Field Railway Detachments mobilized for the campaign had all the weaknesses of improvised formations without a peacetime cadre; nevertheless they did good work in clearing obstructions and repairing damaged track. Most of the railroads in occupied Austria were kept in operation by local personnel under Prussian control, with strong security guards and the threat of massive reprisals against the local population combining to prevent all but the most minor sabotage.[40] The Prussian army had learned some valuable lessons at limited cost. Four years later their supply system would pass a far more demanding test with credit.

Die Deutschen Eisenbahnen
1870
_____ Von 1835 bis Ende 1865 eröffnete Eisenbahnen
_ _ _ _ _ Von 1866 bis Ende 1870 eröffnete Eisenbahnen

Map 2. The German Railway Network, 1870
Source: *100 Jahre deutsche Eisenbahnen: Die deutsche Reichsbahn im Jahre 1935.* Edited by Deutsche Reichsbahn-Gesellschaft (Berlin, 1935), p. 15.

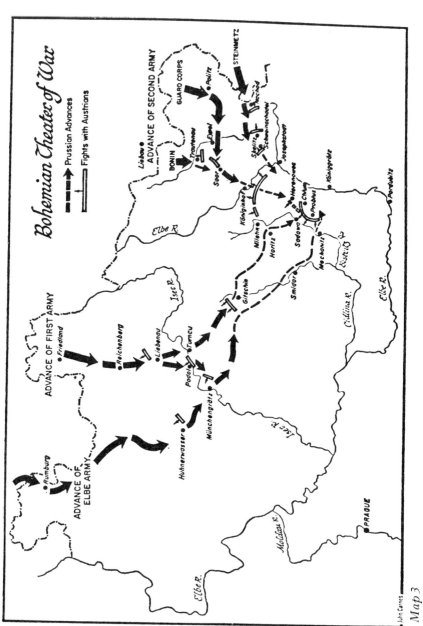

Bohemian Theater of War

Prussian Advances ▰▰▰▶
Fights with Austrians ⊢—⊣

ADVANCE OF SECOND ARMY

GUARD CORPS

STEINMETZ

Politz

Trautenau

Nachod

Soor

Schweinschädel

Josephstadt

Königsberg

Königinhof

Milenne

Königgrätz

Horsenowes

Chum

Pardubitz

Hořitz

Sadowa

Probus

Smidar

Mechanitz

Bistritz

Adlina R.

Elbe R.

Liebau

BONIN

ADVANCE OF FIRST ARMY

Friedland

Reichenberg

Liebenau

Turnau

Podol

Münchengrätz

Hühnerwasser

Rumburg

ADVANCE OF ELBE ARMY

Iser R.

Iser R.

Elbe R.

Molitau R.

PRAGUE

Elbe R.

John Carnes

Map 3

PART II

RIFLES

First impressions of the evolution of infantry weapons and infantry tactics in the armies of Germany between 1815 and 1866 appear to substantiate the often-repeated hypothesis that military men are incapable of coping with technological changes. The smoothbore musket had been obsolescent for years before Prussia finally adopted a modern firearm, the breechloading needle gun. When her neighbors finally exchanged their smoothbores for rifles, the rifles were muzzle-loaders. And even Prussian soldiers appeared to question the wisdom of their radical departure from tradition when they converted thousands of old muskets to rifled muzzle-loaders during the 1850s. More culpable was the apparent failure of the German states to adjust their tactics to the improved range and fire power of their new weapons. Closed formations and shock action were basic to German drill regulations when the Crimean War demonstrated the potential of modern small arms. They remained basic when the German Confederation took the field against Denmark. They survived on the battlefields of Bohemia and Lorraine. The resulting casualty lists stand as *prima facie* evidence of misjudgment at best, stupidity at worst.

Studied in detail, however, this interpretation loses much of its clarity and most of its credibility. The superiority of the needle gun over its muzzle-loading competitors was neither universal nor obvious before the 1860s. Its high firepower and ease of loading were accompanied by relative short range and inaccuracy. The problem of choosing between the two designs was further compounded by a lack of precedents. Before the nineteenth century rifles had been a specialists' weapon used only by a few men and units. No one could do more than speculate on the results of equipping entire armies with these weapons; the lessons of Italy and the Crimea were inconclusive. In any case it was impossible simply to abandon all forms of attack in view of the superiority modern rifles bestowed on the defensive. And if mass formations invited heavy casualties, swarms of skirmishers, each man theoretically acting on his own initiative, posed problems of control which were virtually insurmountable given the existing state of battlefield communications. As the conflict between Prussia and Austria sharpened during the 1860s, armies could no longer postpone decisions on the arming and training of their infantry.

Chapter IV

Genesis of the Needle Gun

Since the general adoption of the flintlock musket in the seventeenth century, technical superiority on the battlefield had lost the importance it possessed between the French invasion of Italy in 1494 and the Thirty Years' War. All armies carried weapons essentially alike. But the needle gun, the breechloading rifle of the Prussian infantry, was a seminal innovation, having more in common with the Maxim gun and the modern assault rifle than the flintlock and percussion muskets it replaced. From the fourteenth century, gunsmiths had sought to develop a firearm combining the accuracy of the rifle with the rapid loading of the smoothbore. Since there seemed to be no way to reduce appreciably the length of time required to force a bullet down the grooves of a rifled barrel, one obvious solution had been the construction of a rifle loading at the breech. Technical difficulties, particularly the problem of designing a gas-tight breech, defeated most designs, and the successful ones were as a rule too fragile or too complicated to be adapted to military use. Ironically, the Dreyse breechloader grew out of an effort to find a solution for an entirely different problem.

Johann Nikolaus von Dreyse was neither an inventor nor a promoter, but a craftsman who spent part of his *Wanderjahre* in Paris, working as a locksmith for a Swiss gunsmith named Samuel Pauly. On the death of his father, Dreyse returned to his native town, took over the family workshop, and began manufacturing caps for the new percussion firearms coming into use among sportsmen. Like those of other manufacturers, Dreyse's early caps were unreliable. Instead of being entirely consumed in the explosion when the musket's hammer struck them, they had a nasty habit of spraying chemicals and metal fragments into the marksman's face. But while his competitors tried to improve the quality of their caps, Dreyse sought to design a cartridge which would be self-igniting, combining the fulminate and the gunpowder in a single entity. In 1812 his old employer, Pauly, had patented a design with the detonating cap at its base; in the 1820s other inventors produced forerunners of the modern rimfire and pinfire cartridges. Despite their efforts the problem of combining reliable detonation with adequate safety remained unsolved. Dreyse proposed to insert a small charge of fulminate at the base of the bullet itself, detonating it by a needle which would first drive through the cartridge paper and powder. Thus the highly volatile fulminate would be protected by powder, lead and paper—the closest possible approximation of a safety cartridge.

One account says that Dreyse first discovered that a needle would detonate percussion caps as well as a hammer while he was seeking a safe and reliable method for extracting the fulminate from percussion caps and salvaging the copper for reuse.[1] In any event the idea seemed worth a trial. The first needle gun was a smooth-bored, converted muzzle-loader, with a needle inserted in the base of the chamber and connected to the cocking mechanism. When the gun was fired, the needle was driven forward and ignited the cartridge. But to develop the weapon, to produce it in profitable quantities, required financial backing, and the most likely sources of this backing in central Europe were the war ministries. Not all of them were indifferent to innovation. Saxe-Weimar began testing percussion muskets in 1824, Hanover in 1825, Prussia in 1826. In some of the smaller states, particularly Württemberg and Saxe-Weimar, the rulers took a direct personal interest in the process. A relatively small contract by military standards—a few hundred or thousand guns—would provide security for Dreyse's struggling firm.

Dreyse's initial attempts to market the needle gun had an aura of low comedy. The Austrian War Ministry dismissed him with the remark that Vienna had quite enough skilled craftsmen.[2]

Prussian authorities were more specific. When Dreyse appeared before them with his right arm bandaged and admitted that a cartridge had exploded while he was ramming it down, they suggested that his design required some improvement.

By 1829 Dreyse had devised a new system. The firing mechanism remained the same, but now the gun was loaded with loose powder in the old style, and the bullet, with the cartridge paper for a wad, was simply dropped onto the needle. A sporting rifle manufactured on this principle caught the eye of a Captain Priem of the 20th Prussian Infantry. Priem in turn brought the new system to the attention of senior officers in the War Ministry and the royal household. As a result Dreyse was asked to convert a number of old flintlocks to needle guns. The weapons, however, were rejected as unsatisfactory. Dreyse had not yet solved the problem of premature firing. If the gun was not cocked before it was loaded, the cap could easily strike the needle and ignite the powder. But the cocked guns had to be handled with care lest they go off while being brought up to the shoulder for firing. Dreyse received 500 thalers, the praise of the testing commission for his ingenuity, and nothing else.

The decision was not final. Both Prince William of Prussia and the Crown Prince—the future King Frederick William IV— had begun using Dreyse's sporting rifles and were convinced that the design had possibilities. In 1832 Frederick William III ordered a more extensive test of sixty improved needle guns in competition with other flintlocks and percussion muskets. By this time Dreyse had returned to his original concept of a cartridge combining cap, powder and ball. He had also developed an improved lock which was easier to remove, facilitating cleaning and replacement of the needle. In October 1833 Dreyse received a contract to produce 1100 of these muzzle-loading smoothbores; by 1835 the fusilier battalions of the 4th and 11th Infantry were receiving the first needle guns to enter Prussian service.[3]

The new musket was still far from perfected. Premature discharges were common, and two even more basic problems remained unsolved: the inaccuracy inherent in a smoothbore and the difficulty in getting the bullet to fit the barrel properly. Nevertheless, for Dreyse the contract represented a triumph enjoyed by few designers in the lean post-Waterloo years. It was tangible proof of his support in high places, and it gave him time and money to develop his gun further. Dreyse's success can in no sense be described as a triumph of inventive genius over the forces of obscurity and reaction. His initial designs had no extraordinary promise as military weapons, nor were they of startling merit ballistically. But Dreyse was able to convince the right people of the worth of his ideas. In Captain Priem he had an enthusiastic advocate with some influence in the War Ministry. The Crown Prince and the Prince of Prussia, who admired Dreyse's sporting rifles, were willing to support him in his efforts to develop a military weapon. There was no guarantee of his success, but at a time when many types of percussion muskets were being tested and manufactured in small numbers, an order for eleven hundred guns seemed a reasonable investment to keep this promising designer contented—and working for the Prussian government.

Even as his workmen began production, Dreyse and the army's testing commission agreed that the muzzle-loading needle gun was at a dead end. Not only was it dangerous to load, but the needle, little stronger than a knitting needle yet exposed to the full force of the explosion, grew brittle and broke rapidly. In a muzzle-loader, even with Dreyse's improved lock, it was difficult to replace quickly. Dreyse's solution was a breech mechanism operating in much the same way as a modern bolt-action weapon —or the bolt of a door. A hollow bolt fitted snugly into the open breech and was locked in place by pushing down the knob or handle. Inside the bolt was a long needle attached to a spiral spring. When the trigger was pressed, the needle shot forward through a small hole in the head of the bolt, and passed through cartridge paper and powder to strike the fulminating cap.[4]

The needle was just as fragile as ever, just as exposed to the explosion. The breech was far from gas-tight. The more rounds a gun fired, the worse the leakage grew; it was not unusual in later years for men carrying old rifles to be unable to put their faces close enough to the breech to take proper aim. Jams caused by overheating were also common; soldiers were sometimes reduced to using stones to hammer open the bolts of their rifles. But the needle gun had one supreme virtue. It worked. Dreyse constructed the first of his breechloaders in 1835. When tested in 1836, not only did it fire twice as fast as any percussion muzzle-loader, but it compared in accuracy with the rifles used by the

Jäger. Dreyse was content with a token order for 150 of these new weapons. Not until 1838 was his design sufficiently refined to be patented; extensive field trials did not begin until 1839. For a year the rifles were tested for accuracy, reliability, and durability under all possible conditions. Dreyse himself gave several impressive demonstrations of their performance. On one occasion he appeared for a rapid-fire test with a hundred rounds of ammunition. The observing committee was convinced that after ten rounds the rifle's breech and barrel would be so hot that the cartridges would explode. But after fifty rounds, fired as rapidly as they could be loaded, the needle gun was functioning as well as ever, and the committee's composure was shattered.[5]

In 1838 Major Priem—the years had brought slow promotion— had boasted to the Crown Prince that with sixty thousand men armed with needle guns and led by a talented general, the King would be able to determine himself the limits of Prussia's frontiers. The final report of the testing commission, while less hyperbolic, was equally enthusiastic, praising the rifle as suitable for the entire infantry, a gift of providence which, if kept secret until a great historical moment, could become a celebrated national weapon.[6] Perhaps influenced by Priem's calculations, on December 4, 1840, Frederick William ordered sixty thousand of the Dreyse needle guns. He accepted the rest of the commission's recommendations as well. The guns were given the cover name of light percussion muskets, and no plans were made to issue them as they were produced. Instead they were to be stored in arsenals, either until there should be enough for the whole army or until a time of national emergency.[7]

2

The introduction of the needle guns meant revolutionary changes for the Prussian arms industry. They were expensive. There was no way existing weapons could be converted to the new system, nor could existing spare parts be utilized. Even more important, the needle gun could not be manufactured in the old way, with the finished product more or less resembling an original model. It was a precision weapon. If it was to function with a minimum of gas leakage and misfires, then every gun and every cartridge had to be identical. The old days of wide tolerances, when a functioning musket could be cobbled together from a French barrel, a Prussian lock, and an Austrian butt, were ended. Both Dreyse himself and Hermann von Boyen, War Minister since 1841, recognized that the necessary standardization could only be achieved by the use of machinery. With a state grant of thirty-five thousand thalers, Dreyse spent the better part of a year converting an old glue factory into one of the first modern arsenals in Germany. It took longer to train his labor force of gunsmiths, apprentices, weavers, and farmers, and to develop techniques of mass production. As late as 1847, Dreyse's output was only around ten thousand rifles annually, and the government complained that at the existing rate of delivery it would be a half-century before the rearmament of the infantry would be complete.[8] By this time, however, the delay was chiefly due not to production considerations, but to the authorities' insistence on preserving secrecy and to a growing debate on the best way to use the needle gun—or the desirability of adopting it at all.

The hindsight presenting the manifold advantages of the breechloader was not available to the men responsible for implementing Frederick William's decision. Advocates of the needle gun claimed that it must be a decisive weapon in the hands of well-trained, well-disciplined troops. The enemy's morale would inevitably suffer when he received a second volley while he was still busy reloading. On the skirmish line a man no longer had to expose himself to ram down a fresh charge; even in open ground he could find cover without sacrificing his own ability to shoot back. The needle gun could be loaded by a small man. It eliminated the chance of ramming down two or three charges on top of each other in case of a misfire. Last but not least, the soldier no longer had to have a certain number of teeth in a certain position to bite the cartridges.

This juxtaposition of arguments reflects the difficulty of evaluating a weapon surrounded by secrecy. Outside of Prussia the needle gun was still so unknown that it was left out of most discussions on the best type of rifles.[9] Where it was mentioned, it was often dismissed as "not well adapted for general military purposes."[10] Even in the Prussian army, misinformation about the needle gun was widespread. A few officers, noncommissioned officers, and armorers from each regiment had seen it test-fired and had been instructed in its care and maintenance. But to date the entire production had gone into the arsenals, and there were many to echo Czar Nicholas I of Russia who, after witnessing a test of the new rifle, was reputed to have described it as more toy than weapon.[11]

Criticism of the needle gun was based on more than technical ignorance and reflex conservatism. Specifically, Dreyse's cartridge was unsatisfactory. Even at 200 paces, about ten percent of the shots fired under test conditions showed an irregular trajectory. The front-to-back combustion and the oval-headed bullet further reduced the needle gun's muzzle velocity and range. With selected cartridges fired by crack marksmen from the best guns obtainable, the needle gun remained ineffective at ranges over 700 paces.

These questions of range and accuracy were particularly important in light of the existing status of the rifle in the Prussian army. Since the days of Frederick the Great, rifles had been the exclusive monopoly of a corps of highly-skilled specialists, the *Jäger*. Initially held in low repute by the rest of the army, they had developed their own esprit, as much pride of craft as military morale. Recruited from hunters, foresters, and gamekeepers, supplemented after 1815 by picked volunteers, the *Jäger* regarded themselves not only as soldiers, but also as members of a guild, initiates of an exotic mystery which could be completely mastered only by those trained from childhood. They preferred quality to quantity both in manpower and firepower. The *Jäger* wanted a rifle able to hit the smallest possible target at the longest possible range. And they could offer a reasonable alternative to the needle gun.

Dreyse was not the only one who addressed himself to the problem of producing a rifle that could be loaded quickly without sacrificing accuracy. In the 1830s several other solutions were developed. The simplest and most practical, designed by the French Colonel Louis Thouvenin, retained the standard percussion lock and inserted a short steel pillar into the bottom of the breech plug. The powder was poured loose into the chamber and settled around this "thorn"; then a small, cone-shaped bullet was rammed onto the thorn, which acted as an anvil. The result was a pre-expanded bullet which when fired caught the grooves and carried as far and as accurately as a patched ball. The Thouvenin rifle could be loaded almost as fast as a smoothbore, the only delay being that involved in ramming the bullet onto the thorn. Its deficiencies—the risk of damaging the bullet in loading, and the problem of keeping black-powder residue from collecting around the thorn and fouling the rifle—were not enough to keep the design from winning great favor, particularly after the weapon's successes in the hands of the French light infantry in Algeria.

Converted to the Thouvenin system, the Prussian *Jägerbüchse M1835* had a maximum range of a thousand paces, was sighted for 700, and was more accurate than the early needle gun. The *Jäger* made no secret of their preference for this design. Their defense of it was so spirited that as late as March 1847 King Frederick William created a special commission to determine whether the *Dornbüchse* was indeed superior to the needle gun. The testing unit was the Guard Reserve Regiment, and the tension was increased by the lively controversy within the regiment on the respective merits of the rifles. Major Graf von der Schulenburg, an admirer of the needle gun, was given the 2nd Company; Major Pallhan was assigned the 3rd Company and his favorite Thouvenins. It was generally considered that Pallhan had an added advantage. His company, recruited from Brandenburg, had a large number of townsmen in the ranks and was generally regarded as a smarter and more efficient unit than the 2nd, composed of Pomeranian peasants. But while the needle gun was outranged by the Thouvenin, it fired two and a half times as rapidly, and proved easier to clean and maintain than the muzzle-loader. Equally important for considerations of marksmanship was the much heavier recoil of the Thouvenin; after a few days sore shoulders and flinching were common in the ranks of the 3rd company. As far as the Guard Reserve Regiment was concerned, the needle gun had won beyond a doubt.[12] The *Jäger*, however, remained unconvinced, particularly when the rifle designed for them, the *Zündnädelbüchse 1849*, turned out to be no improvement ballistically over the original model. Existing percussion rifles converted to the Thouvenin system remained standard issue for *Jäger* battalions until well into the 1850s.

3

The *Jäger* argued that the needle gun was too short-ranged and too inaccurate to be a suitable marksman's weapon. The rest of the army was concerned with another question: fire discipline. The fear of introducing a weapon on the grounds that it uses too much ammunition is easily ridiculed, but in the nineteenth century there was little chance of replenishing the infantry's cartridge boxes during battle. Once out of ammunition, it was argued, the soldier would have to use casualties as a source of supply—and the peculiar construction of the needle gun's cartridge would restrict him to Prussian casualties. Moreover, every regimental officer knew from study, from hearsay, or from his own experience, that once men open fire it is extremely difficult to get them to stop. The image constantly evoked by the opponents of the needle gun was that of a battalion, whether in closed formation or deployed as skirmishers, firing away its ammunition by reflex; the men, deaf to all commands, loading and pulling the trigger until their cartridge boxes emptied, then running away. It had happened often enough in the past to be something more than an imaginary bogey. The projected replacement of muzzle-loader by breechloader appeared to magnify the problem beyond the danger point.

Could ordinary infantrymen be trusted with a weapon whose qualities and characteristics remained such a subject for debate? Even advocates of the needle gun were reluctant to issue it indiscriminately at first. Before rearming the entire infantry it appeared the better part of wisdom to determine the new rifle's performance in the hands of selected men and units. Boyen favored organizing detachments of picked marksmen in each battalion. Other officers favored the rearming of entire battalions or regiments. But to do either would bring drastic alterations in the structure of the Prussian infantry—alterations of questionable utility.

Whatever the qualities of the needle gun, the differences between breechloading rifle and muzzle-loading musket virtually guaranteed the creation of two separate categories of infantry. The men who reorganized the infantry and rewrote its drill regulations after 1806 had developed a tactical doctrine obscuring existing differences between line and light troops.

Half of each regiment, the fusilier battalion and the third rank of the two musketeer battalions, was designated as skirmishers, but every unit was expected to be able to deploy and withdraw under fire, then rally and return to the attack either in skirmish line or column as the situation demanded.[13] If after 1815 instruction in skirmishing and marksmanship was increasingly neglected in favor of close-order drill, the concept of an *Einheitsinfanterie* remained. By 1840 the mission and the training of the fusiliers and the third rank of the musketeers were virtually indistinguishable from that of the rest of the regiment.[14] The reformers' original intention to differentiate these units by giving them the best men had proved impractical—an elite of fifty percent is a contradiction in terms. Thus there was far more likely to be a marked difference in quality between two regiments, Pomeranians and *Rhineländer*, for example, than between musketeers and fusiliers in the same regiment recruited from the same region.[15]

In the years after Waterloo a considerable body of German military opinion favored the creation of a force of light infantry which would be a compromise between the specialists of the *Jäger* and the undifferentiated mass of the line. Rifles, so the argument ran, are murderous weapons in the hands of trained marksmen, but they are complicated. Moreover, their use requires skills which not every man possesses and which cannot always be inculcated by training. On the other hand, all men are not equal in strength and spirit. Mixing them cheek by jowl in the ranks only results in reducing everyone to the lowest common denominator. The best men, the most active and intelligent, should be formed into separate battalions, one or two to a brigade, and given special training in skirmishing, marching, and marksmanship.[16]

Those favoring a separate light infantry often cited the example of France, where the Duc d'Orleans formed the first experimental battalion of *chasseurs à pied* in 1838. The unit proved so successful that nine more battalions were raised in 1840; in 1853 Napoleon III would increase their number to twenty. Armed with rifles, given special training in gymnastics, skirmishing, and marksmanship, the *chasseurs* attracted the attention of Europe's soldiers from the beginning. In Algeria, in the Crimea, in Italy, they and the Zouaves and Turcos formed on the same model more than lived up to their peacetime reputations as elite formations of hard fighters, tireless marchers, and bold adventurers. Their achievement could neither be denied nor explained away; the Prussian army was forced to take note of the French example and justify its reluctance to follow suit.

Assertions that Germans were too slow-thinking and slow-moving to make good light infantrymen were balanced by suggestions that the level of intelligence and adaptability in the ranks was high enough to eliminate the need for special forces of light troops.[17] More demonstrable was the contention that skimming the best men from the line battalions not only damaged the morale of the rest, but presented the danger, especially in a major war, that these elite forces would not be on the spot when needed.[18] Since 1815 the French army had not faced the necessity of committing its entire strength to a war. When campaigns are fought by task forces, by orders of battle drawn up to fit given circumstances, the advantages of a pool of above-average units are obvious. The German states, however, had neither colonies nor imperial commitments. The wars in which they were likely to become involved would probably require general mobilization, and a high average of training and competence would be more valuable than a few elite battalions yoked to a dull and lifeless mass.

4

The Prussian War Ministry maintained this viewpoint until 1848, when the overthrow of the Orleans monarchy and the increasing discontent in Berlin and other German cities suddenly made the concept of an elite fire brigade highly attractive. In March the four fusilier battalions of each army corps were detached from their parent regiments and brigaded under the corps commander.[19] A month later, with revolt still simmering in Berlin, the King ordered all fusilier battalions to be issued needle guns as soon as possible. His decision was confirmed by the storming of the Berlin Arsenal on June 15, which put a number of Prussia's carefully-guarded secret weapons into the hands of the rebels.[20] By the end of 1848 twenty fusilier battalions had received their new guns; nine more were rearmed during 1849.

With troops being dispatched all over Germany to suppress the wave of revolution, there was no time to draw up detailed instructions for the use of the rifle. Officers and noncommissioned officers who had spent time in Dreyse's factory instructed the rest, sometimes converting skeptics by demonstrating themselves what the needle gun could do.[21] The fusiliers' light-infantry heritage had not been entirely lost since 1815; many of their officers were interested in the needle gun as a skirmisher's weapon. Sharpshooters armed with needle guns, it was argued, would be able to shoot almost as accurately as the *Jäger*, but faster and from better cover. Cannon would no longer be able to push to dueling range and spray the infantry's mass formations with canister, as they had done in the Napoleonic Wars. Admittedly the needle gun might waste ammunition, but this danger would be minimized by good fire discipline, enforced by officers who understood that accuracy still remained more important than volume.[22]

There were other ideas of the best way to use the new rifle. Some enthusiasts recommended that an entire corps, preferably the Guard, be armed with breechloaders. But such influential officers as Chief of Staff Carl von Reyher considered such an idea dangerous. Writing to the War Minister on February 19, 1849, Reyher declared that no matter how well the needle gun had performed in tests and on maneuvers, it had yet to prove itself in the field. The rifle seemed well made and easy for the ordinary soldier to repair, but this did not mean that it was sturdy enough to withstand campaign conditions. And only the experience of battle could determine if the needle gun really would waste so much ammunition that it could not be entrusted to ordinary infantry. At present no more than six battalions in each corps should be issued the new rifle, even if enough needle guns were on hand to increase the proportion. In this way it would be tested under the widest possible range of conditions, without the risk of losing the services of a full corps should the weapon prove unsatisfactory. Moreover, Reyher argued, one of the greatest advantages claimed for the needle gun was its versatility. This would be sacrificed by issuing the relatively small existing stocks to the Guard Corps, which would only be put on a war footing in a general mobilization and even then would most likely be held in reserve for decisive battles.

The idea of making the Prussian Guard a tactical as well as a social elite had one other major drawback. The needle guns, Reyher declared, had become so popular with the fusilier battalions which carried them that if they were withdrawn to arm the Guard, or for any other reason, the fusiliers' morale would suffer. Officers and men had been too impressed with the firepower and accuracy of the new guns ever again to have confidence in a muzzle-loading smoothbore.[23]

Combat experience substantiated barracks conviction. Needle guns had been used—unofficially—in skirmishes and street fights virtually since the beginning of the revolution, but their first large-scale tests came in May 1849. In Dresden, the fusiliers of the Alexander Grenadiers and the 24th Infantry used them in the four-day battle which broke the back of the uprising in Saxony. The needle gun might not be able to demolish the barricades which had proved such a formidable obstacle to infantry unsupported by artillery in other cities, but the new rifle's high rate of fire made it possible for detachments of marksmen to pin down or frighten away the defenders while other troops flanked or stormed their position. To the north, in Schleswig-Holstein, Prussian fusiliers and units of the newly raised provincial army used both needle guns and Thouvenin rifles to good advantage against the Danes. The campaign against the rebels in Württemberg and Baden, however, offered an even better demonstration of the needle gun's qualities. If there were no pitched battles, Prussian troops were engaged in enough sharp skirmishes and fire fights spread over a long enough period of time to permit the drawing of reasonably accurate conclusions on what could be expected of the new weapon. On September 22, 1849, Prince William, commanding the expeditionary force in Baden, submitted a long evaluation of the needle gun. In it he declared that even though most of the fusilier battalions had not been armed with the Dreyse rifle long enough to become well acquainted with it, the weapon had on the whole proved satisfactory. Its effect was often more moral than real; particularly on the skirmish line men were prone to become overexcited and fire away their ammunition at long range with no results. But the needle gun's high rate of fire made it a valuable defensive weapon; it outranged the smoothbores which most rebel troops still carried; and battalions armed with the new rifle were firmly convinced of its superiority—and by extension, of their own—over anything the enemy might bring against them.[24]

William's report was not universally convincing. The needle gun had proved itself; the army wanted more of them. Nevertheless such critics as General K. W. von Willisen, a leading military theorist and one of the few Prussian generals with recent battle experience, continued to argue that a rapid-firing rifle was wasted on the ordinary soldier. It was impossible, Willisen declared, to train the entire army to use the needle gun, especially when most of the wartime rank and file would be reservists or Landwehr. Instead he advocated creating thirty-two additional fusilier battalions to supplement those already in existence. Armed with needle guns and given special training in their use, they would be Prussia's answer to the French light infantry.[25]

Willisen's proposal was overruled not by military considerations, but by the Finance Ministry's declaration that the budget could not be stretched to accommodate such a major increase in the size of the army. The Prussian active army included only 126 infantry battalions. Since a third of them—the fusilier battalion of each regiment—were already armed with needle guns, the King accepted Prince William's argument that the best way to increase the proportion of breechloaders was to extend their use in existing units. On June 19, 1851, Frederick William IV ordered future requirements for infantry muskets of every kind to be met by the new production of needle guns.[53] Dreyse's rifle had finally come to stay.

Chapter V

Debate

Initially it appeared that Frederick William's decision might take years, if not decades, to implement. In war Prussia would need over three hundred thousand needle guns for the field army and its reserves. Between 1841 and 1847, only forty-five thousand had been delivered. By 1851, however, production capacity had reached twenty-two thousand a year and this figure rapidly increased as Prussia's arsenals trained men, installed machines, and began converting to the manufacture of the Dreyse rifle. At the same time the state began assuming more direct control over the arms industry. Since the days of Frederick the Great, the Prussian government had obtained most of its muskets and rifles from the factories of Schickler Brothers at Potsdam and Spandau. During the Wars of Liberation a large state arsenal had been established at Neisse, but in 1820 its management was turned over to a civilian contractor. The War Ministry also sanctioned the establishment of new privately-owned factories at Saarn, near Düsseldorf, and Danzig, and purchased much of the output of the arsenals of Suhl, which had been a Saxon city until 1814. In each case the government signed contracts with the manufacturers and attached an inspection committee to the factory to supervise and control the quality of its work. The system was popular, as it was widely believed that a larger number of privately owned factories both stimulated the economy and assured the government lower prices.

The relationship between state and private enterprise had begun to change even before the adoption of the needle gun. The factory at Saarn, never a commercial success, was purchased by the government in 1840 and put under military direction. Schickler Brothers, which by midcentury was a banking house with only tenuous connections to its manufacturing days, willingly sold its installations at Spandau and Potsdam in 1851. Two years later the government also purchased the factory at Danzig. This simply gave official recognition to the fact that these arsenals were now for all practical purposes state institutions. Not only was it necessary to convert and expand facilities as quickly as possible, but the rifle that the factories were to produce had been considered a secret weapon for a decade, and initially at least, the authorities had no intention of selling either the patent or the finished product to any other power. Since the government would have to supply most of the capital for expansion and intended to buy all of the guns, the arguments previously set forth in favor of *laissez-faire* competition lost much of their force. After 1853 only Sömmerda, where the needle gun was first produced, and Suhl, whose rifles remained extremely popular among the *Jäger*, remained in private hands, and their operation and output were closely controlled by a military commission attached to each factory. At the same time the War Ministry began to close down or consolidate its smaller plants. Neisse, which was never tooled up to produce needle guns, became a repair shop in 1851 and closed the next year. Between 1852 and 1855 the Schicklers' old facilities were merged into a single institution at Spandau. As Boyen had predicted a decade earlier, the days of the individual gunsmith and the workshop type of arsenal were over, and the Prussian government had entered the arms business on a massive scale.[1]

The rationalization of small arms production proved successful beyond expectations. By the end of 1851, a total of forty-six infantry battalions had been rearmed. The *Jäger* and *Schützen* of the Guard received needle guns in 1851 and 1852 respectively. A Cabinet Order of July 20, 1854, and a series of supplementary directives prescribed the order for issuing them to the rest of the army—first the line, then the Landwehr. Production, however, was only one element of the challenge posed by the needle gun. If the new rifle had proved itself during the campaign of 1848, just *what* it had proved remained open to debate. Should breechloaders be given to the entire infantry, or to a few chosen units? If the latter, what should be their ratio to other small arms? Should the problem of fire discipline be overcome by training the men in long-range marksmanship like the *Jäger*, or by teaching them to hold their fire until the last possible moment in the Frederician tradition? An anonymous pamphlet written in 1850 and revised in 1852 conceded that units carrying the needle gun were more willing to shoot and more aggressive than those armed with muskets. But the men, often untrained in the proper use of the new guns, tended to open fire at excessive ranges. The needle gun could be loaded safely and easily. But this in turn led to wasting ammunition. In short, the popularity of this weapon was no excuse for giving it to the entire army. No more than one-third of the infantry should be reequipped with breechloaders. And these men should be specially selected, carefully trained, and organized in separate units. The author further argued that men armed with the needle gun could not become really proficient in its use in less than three years—an argument which reappeared in the next decade in justification of the proposed third year of active service for the Prussian army.[2]

This pamphlet, like many of its counterparts, does not demonstrate any particular lack of vision or intelligence. It reflects rather the contradictory nature of the evidence from which war ministries and general staffs were required to draw conclusions. And the problem was complicated by a growing awareness of a new and formidable rival to the needle gun and its breechloading imitators.

During the 1820s a French officer had developed a muzzle-loading rifle using a cylindrical bullet pointed at the nose, hollow at the base. When the gun was fired, the force of the powder gases tended to expand the hollow portion of the bullet, forcing it to take the rifling as well as any patched ball. This idea was subsequently developed and refined by Claude Minié, who in 1849 patented a design for a bullet hollowed conically from the base. A cup-shaped plug of zinc, copper or iron closed the hollow portion of the ball and was driven into it by the force of the explosion, expanding the softer lead and forcing it into the rifling.

The Minié rifle was a weapon with universal appeal. Unlike the needle gun, it looked and handled like infantry weapons had looked and handled for a century and a half. It had a ramrod, a visible lock and hammer, a cartridge that had to be broken open before firing, and all the traditional characteristics of a military weapon. The needle gun, on the other hand, was loaded and cocked the same way a man bolted a door. The manual of arms itself had to be changed to suit it. Given the undoubted virtues of the Minié, it is easy to understand why officers who accepted the fact that the days of the smoothbore were numbered might favor its replacement by a rifle which did a minimal amount of violence to their ideas, conscious or unconscious, of what an infantry weapon should be.[3]

The idea that the Minié was at least as good as the needle gun was not entirely a manifestation of reflex conservatism. A typical Minié was five times as accurate as a smoothbore musket at 300 paces, ten times as accurate at 400 paces. It could hit man-sized targets at 225 meters and targets representing battalion columns or artillery batteries at 750 meters. A good marksman with a good rifle could score consistently at a thousand paces. The needle gun, on the other hand, had been sharply criticized by many experts solely on ballistic grounds. Even with an improved cartridge developed in the 1850s, the needle gun demanded skill in deflection shooting. With selected ammunition fired by crack marksmen equipped with the best guns obtainable, the needle gun was ineffective at over 700 paces. The Minié, with its high muzzle velocity and flat trajectory, seemed to be a weapon better suited to men whose training in marksmanship often remained inadequate.

The Minié had other technical advantages as well. There was no long firing pin to overheat and break, no complicated breech to leak gas, or jam when overheated. The Minié's rate of fire was indisputably slower—one and one-half rounds per minute against five for the needle gun. But this was widely regarded as an advantage, a built-in safeguard against the needless waste of ammunition. The needle gun's cartridge was heavy; the standard issue was only sixty rounds per man—a quarter-hour of rapid fire. The concept that fire superiority was based not merely on the number of hits, but on hits in a given period of time, was difficult to inculcate—and the men who were most interested in improved rifles and improved marksmanship could be as hard to convince as those who regarded any firearm as a kind of glorified pike. Both schools of thought tended to judge a rifle by its accuracy at long range. The concept of it as a rapid-fire weapon in the pattern of the Frederician musket was slower to develop.[4]

In this connection it is interesting to note that the Miniés were commonly described on both sides of the Atlantic as "rifled muskets." Originally there was a solid reason for this appellation —a reason which also contributed much to the Minié's initial popularity in the smaller German states. Existing smoothbore barrels could be rifled, existing muskets converted to Miniés, at relatively low cost. German gunsmiths and designers developed several fine versions of the Minié. The rifle adopted in Baden in 1853 was described by one knowledgeable authority as "a truly ideal gun." Bavaria, Electoral Hesse, Waldeck, and most of the other small German states introduced Miniés between 1854 and 1858, generally adopting a new design as standard and producing it in small quantities while converting their existing stock of smoothbores as rapidly as possible.[5] Nor was this always for want of an alternative. As production of the needle gun increased, the Prussian government began considering its sale to other states of the German Confederation. In Württemberg, however, the breechloader, tested against Miniés, was rejected as short-ranged and unreliable. In 1854 the War Ministry ordered the adoption of Minié rifles for the entire infantry. Cadets in the War College at Ludwigsburg were taught that the needle gun would never prove itself in a war against a first-class opponent. Either the gun would jam or the men using it would fire away their ammunition in a few minutes and reduce themselves to helplessness.[6] And in the mid-1850s even Prussia conceded the worth of the Minié system by converting thousands of its old smoothbores.

2

Had the Crimean War not broken out when it did, the Minié rifle would probably have never made an appearance in Prussia. With their factories tooled up for mass production of needle guns, it is difficult to conceive of the military authorities abandoning their investment and proclaiming to all and sundry that they had been mistaken in their choice of a rifle of the future. But as reports began arriving from the Crimea describing in lurid detail the slaughter inflicted on the heavy Russian columns by the Minié rifles of the British and French; as the French began converting their old muskets into Miniés; as the Russians strained to put as many rifles as possible into the hands of troops in the field; the Prussian War Ministry grew uncomfortably aware of the fact that fewer than half of its infantry battalions had actually been issued needle guns. The rest, line and Landwehr alike, were still armed with percussion muskets little better than those the Russians were carrying. If Prussia was to derive any advantages from the increasing fluidity of European great-power politics, its army had to be at least as efficient as its potential rivals. Diplomacy, no matter how skillful, is essentially a credit operation: sooner or later every state has to face the alternative of paying off in the hard cash of war or declaring bankruptcy. And if the lessons of Jena had dimmed, those of Olmütz were still all too fresh in the minds of Prussia's leaders. If there had not been enough time to remedy all of the army's deficiencies, at least it should not be sent into battle armed with obsolete weapons. The arsenals contained thousands of percussion and flintlock muskets which could be converted to Minié rifles of a sort in a short time.[7] On December 31, 1854, Frederick William wrote to the War Ministry ordering that it begin tests to determine the most suitable means of conversion, simultaneously preparing to carry out these conversions on the largest scale as rapidly as possible. The commission he appointed in January to supervise the process was specifically ordered to concern itself with the methods of carrying out the King's decision rather than with the decision itself, which had been based on the demands of Prussia's political situation.

The committee refused to be hurried. This time there would be no doubts, as there had been with the needle gun. Arguing that the issue was too important to be decided overnight, they convinced the King that each corps should have one company of line infantry and one of Landwehr test the proposed conversions, with the decision to be based on the results obtained. The King agreed on February 22, 1855, and the test continued until the committee met again on April 14. Its deliberations offer an illustration in microcosm of the problem presented by the new technology. Frederick William began by declaring himself satisfied with the results of the tests and reaffirming that the immediate rearming of the infantry was a political necessity. Prince William contradicted his brother, protesting that four weeks of tests had not been enough to determine all the weaknesses of the Miniés. Already there were complaints that the rifling weakened the barrels; that the iron ramrods standard issue in Prussia damaged the grooves; that the new cartridges were so heavy that the soldier could only carry forty-eight of them instead of sixty. Moreover, he argued, Prussia already had over a hundred thousand needle guns—more rifles than any other European power. Why put time and money into giving the army two entirely different weapons with entirely different ammunition? The state would be better advised to devote its resources to increasing the production of needle guns, particularly since the War Minister said that he could double the annual production of 30,000 needle guns and increase the total number on hand to 190,000 by the end of the year.

Other members of the commission, more reluctant than the Prince to challenge their monarch, simply recommended further testing of the Miniés despite chairman Karl von Willisen's argument that over twenty years the French had had no serious problems with the very similar Thouvenin system. But Frederick William's uncertain temper gave way when the *Jäger* General von Werder concluded a discussion of the importance of continuing to issue needle guns by snobbishly suggesting that since the mass of the army could not utilize the advantages of a rifle in any case, they might as well carry smoothbores until enough breechloaders became available. By this time the King was at the end of his tether. He declared that Werder had just attacked the whole concept of infantry rearmament. If the gentlemen wished no more rifles, then he would issue orders to suspend the manufacture of needle guns as well. The subject under discussion was whether or not Miniés should be introduced, and he ordered the committee to vote on this issue. When Prince William and von Werder both voted affirmatively, but made their approval conditional on the continued manufacturing of needle guns, the King flew into a rage. He could not understand, he said, why the needle gun kept entering the discussion. All he wanted was a plain "yes" or "no" on the question of whether a large part of the army should continue to be armed with smoothbore muskets over the next six years, and as far as he was concerned, his brother and Werder had voted against the Miniés.

The final vote was ten to eight in favor of introducing the Miniés. But this ballot by no means demonstrated that almost half of a committee of experts favored smoothbores or muzzle-loaders at the expense of breechloaders. Only two of the eight negative votes were unqualified. One man, General Wrangel, opposed the reduction in the number of rounds each man could carry. Five votes were recorded as negative because the men who cast them insisted that needle guns must continue to be produced and issued. Moreover, four of the ten affirmative votes specifically mentioned that the Minié was a temporary expedient to be replaced as rapidly as possible by needle guns.[8]

Willisen remained unconvinced. He continued to question the value of a rifle which could neither be improvised nor imported in an emergency, and his arguments were reinforced by the speed with which percussion muskets and flintlocks were converted to the Minié system. By November, 1856, over 300,000 had been altered. The rearmament and retraining of the army's musketeer battalions were in full swing. But as early as March of that year Willisen had obtained the King's consent to issue needle guns to the Landwehr units of divisions whose line regiments already had them, instead of carrying out the original plan of arming first the line, then the Landwehr. Since the line and Landwehr were still brigaded together, and since men trained in the line passed into the Landwehr when their active service was completed, this would ensure a uniform armament within each division while enabling reservists to maintain their skill with the needle gun. Frederick William approved this proposal, then agreed to issue needle guns to the rest of the line infantry, then changed his mind again, instructing the War Ministry to assemble a new conference to discuss the whole question of which units should receive breechloaders when.

These decisions may have been reflections of the King's doubts about the needle gun. They may have been manifestations of his growing emotional instability. In either case they were not definitively implemented before Frederick William suffered the first of the strokes which rendered him a helpless invalid. In

1858 Prince William—now the Prince Regent—finally ended the debate by ordering needle guns issued to the remainder of the line infantry, then the Landwehr in the same order as the corresponding line regiments.[9]

4

Minié or needle gun, muzzle-loader or breechloader, rifles did not exist in a vacuum. The Crimean War not only pitted the great powers against each other on the battlefield for the first time in forty years, but also offered the first extensive tests of the potential effect of rifles on infantry tactics. Of the major adversaries, only the British infantry were primarily armed with Miniés. The French line infantry still carried muskets which had been converted to fire expanding Minié balls, giving them greater accuracy. In theory, each Russian corps had a rifle battalion and each regiment a small detachment of sharpshooters, but in fact there were only six thousand rifles in the entire Russian army in 1853. More than any army in Europe, the Russians had emphasized close-order drill and mass tactics, paying no attention to marksmanship and skirmishing. Their light troops were too poorly armed and trained and too few in numbers to be able to screen their closed formations properly. At the Alma and Inkerman the British two-rank line and the French skirmishers and sharpshooters wreaked havoc on the Russian infantry.

Beyond doubt, the Crimea demonstrated the growing importance of firepower on a modern battlefield. It was generally accepted after 1854 that the introduction of long-range rifles would strengthen the defense, prevent artillery from advancing to close ranges, and make cavalry charges in the style of a Seydlitz or a Murat less and less frequent.[10] But the conclusion that tactically the defensive was the stronger form of warfare had been widespread long before the needle gun and the Minié had been more than designers' speculations. The greatest military theorists of the age, Clausewitz and Jomini, agreed in this as on few other points, buttressing their assertions with numerous examples from the eighteenth century and the Napoleonic Wars. Yet while conceding and emphasizing the superiority of the defensive, both men agreed that war could not be won without battle. Clausewitz described war as an act of force to compel the enemy to do our will . . . War, in its literal meaning, is battle, for only battle is the effective principle in the manifold activity which . . . is called war . . . The destruction of the enemy's military force is to be sought principally by great battles and their results . . . the major purpose of great battles must be the destruction of the enemy's military force.[11]

And if Jomini was more cautious, his strategic thinking also regarded "the objective of operations [as] the enemy army, and all geographic objectives were means to that end, without intrinsic value of their own."[12]

How would this decisive action be fought? Clausewitz, drawing on his own experience during the Napoleonic Wars, gave a descriptive account of the "Character of the Modern Battle:"

What do we usually do now in a great battle? We place ourselves quietly in great masses arranged next to one another and behind one another. We deploy only a relatively small portion of the whole, and let it fight it out in a musketry duel which last for hours, and which is interrupted now and again and pushed hither and yon by separate small thrusts from charges at the double and bayonet and cavalry attacks. When this line has gradually exhausted its war-like fire in this manner, and there remains nothing more than ashes, it is withdrawn and replaced by another.

In this manner the battle, with moderate violence, burns slowly away like wet powder, and if the veil of night commands it to stop, because no one can see any longer, and no one chooses to run the risk of blind chance, then an account is taken by each side respectively of the masses remaining, which can still be called effective, that is, which have not yet completely collapsed like extinct volcanoes; account is taken of the ground gained or lost, and of the security of the rear; these results combined with the special impressions as to bravery and cowardice, sagacity and stupidity, which are thought to have been perceived in ourselves and in our opponents, are collected into one single total impression, out of which then springs the resolution to quit the field or to renew the engagement next morning.

But modern battles are not so by accident; they are so be-cause the parties are more or less on the same level as regards military organization and the art of war, and because the violence of war, enkindled by great national interests, has broken through artificial limits and been led into its natural paths. Under these two conditions battles will always preserve this character.[13].

Despite his contention, accepting Clausewitz' description as history did not mean accepting it as prophecy. C. S. Forester has trenchantly compared the British generals of the First World War to savages faced with the problem of removing a screw from a block of wood. Instead of examining the nature of the problem closely, they simply applied more and more direct force in the belief that the screw could be drawn out in the same way as a nail.[14] It would be tempting, but inaccurate, to apply the same analogy to the German tactical theorists of the 1850s. Reduced to its basic terms, the challenge they faced was this: an increasing number of Europe's infantrymen were carrying rifles which could kill at five times the range of the smoothbore musket. Yet no one had devised a way to make men five times braver, five times as willing to die, or even five times quicker on their feet.[15] At the same time, there was little sympathy for what was believed to be the eighteenth-century system of two armies maneuvering from strong defensive position to strong defensive position, each try-ing to force the other into attacking under unfavorable condi-tions. Orthodox military thought rejected the concept of going to ground like a mole and waiting for the enemy to dash himself to pieces against long-range rifles. This was not mere bloody-mindedness. No army could afford to base its training and doc-trine exclusively on defensive tactics. One's own infantry would have to advance on some occasions, if only to complete the enemy's rout. Nor could it be assumed that the enemy would always be the attacker on the battlefield; chance and generalship might well decide otherwise.[16]

Thus the essential question in these years was not *if* the infantry could attack in the face of modern firearms, but *how* it could do so without crippling losses. Since the end of the Na-poleonic Wars, the conviction had become widespread that Clausewitz was right. The combination of skirmish fire and small-scale attacks which had formed the basis of Prussian infantry tactics in 1813 and 1814 might wear down an enemy gradually, but was unable to produce really decisive results. Therefore, rather than becoming involved in a pointless musketry duel, the infantry should keep its fire preparation at a minimum and close with the enemy at the earliest possible moment.[17] The Prussian regulations, for example, as revised in 1847 regarded the fire fight as a preliminary to the decisive attack of closed columns and treated courage as a function of mass. And this reflected neither simple-minded conservatism nor reflex fondness for obsolete formations. Maintaining control over units once committed to battle had posed a problem in 1813 and 1814. As improved small arms turned the prospect of opening battles at long ranges to a certainty, the problem became a crisis. Even assuming the most extreme manifestations of fighting spirit on the part of the individual soldier, should attacking units reach the enemy's positions as an out-of-control mob, they would have little chance of capturing or securing their objective.

Skirmishers too required increased control, particularly in the age of the modern rifle. In Prussia a continuing criticism of the needle gun was its potential for wasting ammunition. To prevent this, Prince William argued, subalterns and noncommissioned officers must be able to control their men in battle just as precisely as on parade, if admittedly in a different fashion. An order of November 15, 1853, ordered all battalions armed with needle guns to cease forming their skirmish lines in traditional fashion, from a single rank with intervals depending on terrain and opposition. In future, skirmishing was to be executed by a varying number of fire teams, small squads under the direct control of a noncommissioned officer directing and regulating their fire and transmitting the orders of the platoon and company commander. The NCO was to be something more than a mere disciplinarian. His new role was that of a junior leader, just as responsible for the actions of the men under him as any commissioned officer—a fact having a salutary effect on promotion policies in many regiments. A supplementary order of October 5, 1854, extended the system to the rest of the army.

This method of *Gruppentiraillement* was hardly designed to develop initiative in privates. Perhaps the man in the ranks could be disciplined to hold his fire, and to cease fire once he had begun.

Perhaps his morale could be made strong enough to send him forward at the officer's whistle, overcoming the temptation to lag behind or lose himself when the bullets started flying. But it was far wiser to have an *Unteroffizier* handy to reinforce the soldier's self-discipline and inner convictions. Nor did these instructions reflect any conviction that closed formations were a thing of the past. Commanders were specifically warned against allowing their skirmishers to deploy in such a way that their parent battalion was uncovered. Prince William repeatedly declared that since a needle gun could do the work of two muskets on the skirmish line, a battalion might very well be able to deploy fewer men. Even firing at long ranges or while advancing was forbidden. The important thing was to come to grips with the enemy quickly.[18]

Advocates of mass tactics could draw support from the events in the Crimea, where instead of meeting the allies' fire superiority by greater deployment, the Russians increased the size of their columns and hoped that there would be enough survivors in each to break through the enemy's front. The ability of these clumsy formations occasionally to get to something approximating close quarters lent credibility to the suggestion that if the Russians had had a larger proportion of trained skirmishers armed with rifles to screen their attacks, their columns would have carried everything before them. As late as 1857 articles in a leading German military journal argued that the mass of the infantry should retain the smoothbore, since the ordinary soldier could do nothing with a long-range rifle except waste ammunition. In any case the fire-fight was only a preliminary to the decisive attack of massed brigades and divisions. To disperse into a mass of small, uncontrollable units for fear of the modern rifle was to invite disorder, confusion, and disaster.[19]

Nor was this viewpoint the exclusive property of anonymous Colonel Blimps. Karl Eduard Pönitz was one of Germany's leading military thinkers. He edited and popularized Clausewitz's works; he was a sharp critic of the Prussian army; he was among the first to recognize the military potential of the railroad. But in a work popular during the early 1850s he could still warn against believing the "peace-time tables" which measured the effectiveness of modern weapons and "proved" that a battalion attacking another battalion armed with modern rifles would be annihilated. Experience, Pönitz declared, clearly demonstrated that if the attacker moves quickly enough, his losses are relatively light.[20] Most of the other articles and manuals published during this period for the guidance of young officers expressed similar opinions. The author of one otherwise perceptive analysis of the importance of issuing modern rifles to the entire infantry concluded it by declaring that since Miniés could force artillery to keep its distance, and could prevent cavalry from charging under normal circumstances, there was no real defense against a bayonet charge covered by a strong screen of skirmishers.[21] The Prussian Prince Frederick Charles conceded that in a battle with both sides armed with modern rifles, mass formations would be decimated in a few minutes. Yet firepower alone was not decisive. It might be able to destroy the enemy if he stood still long enough, but both sides would probably seek a decision by shock action before this happened.[22] In 1838 Jomini had described the battalion column as the best formation for attacking infantry.[23] Twenty years later he admitted that "the bloody affairs of the Alma and Inkerman have attested to the murderous effect of the new firearms," but concluded that improved weapons would not produce any revolutionary changes in tactics. Battles, he declared, would never degenerate into musketry duels with both sides firing at each other at long ranges until one fled or was destroyed: "il faudra toujours que l'une des deux se porte en avant pour attaquer l'autre."[24] The statement is no less true for being obvious. The probable result of such an attack is quite another question—one which could not be answered definitively on the basis of contemporary evidence.

Chapter VI

Decisions

During the 1850s the armies of Germany found themselves in an increasingly tight double bind. It was plain that the range and firepower of modern rifles, whether Miniés or needle guns, would certainly influence future battlefields. The one thing they would not do was force the abandonment of infantry attacks. Generals, colonels, and captains might do their best to go around, but no enemy could be maneuvered to death. Every commander, every set of regulations, had to provide for the moment when it would be necessary to go *through*.

Somehow a solution to the rifle had to be found—a solution enabling infantry to attack without putting an unreasonable strain on the individual soldier's willingness to get himself killed, yet without making him part of a clumsy formation which might develop its own momentum, but would be shot to pieces before it could get close enough to bayonet the enemy or frighten him into running. Even the Crimea, after all, had not offered really decisive proof that well-disciplined, well-armed infantry could *not* come to grips with an enemy, long-range rifles notwithstanding. The tone of German critical opinion was not "it is impossible," but rather, "what else can be expected from the Russians." And in 1859, on the plains of northern Italy, the French army apparently provided Europe with a definitive solution to the problem of men against fire which had occupied military thinkers for a decade. At the outbreak of war, some of the French line regiments were still armed with smooth-bores. The French version of the Minié was inferior in range and accuracy to that carried by the entire Austrian infantry. But on May 12, 1859, Napoleon III issued an order proclaiming that "the new weapons are only dangerous at long range" and declaring that, just as in the past, the bayonet would remain "the terrible arm of the French infantry."[1] Stripped of its rhetoric, the order was a sober recognition of the fact that since the French could not hope to succeed in a fire fight at long range, they must come to close quarters and hope for the best. The decision was by no means a reckless gamble. The French regiments which marched into Italy had strong cadres of long-service professional soldiers; the ratio of officers to men was higher than in any of the German armies. Many were veterans of years of hard campaigning in Africa and the Crimea. Their training, particularly that of the Zouaves, Turcos, and light infantry, had stressed the ability to move quickly and make maximum use of ground. They were better able to cope with the challenge of the rifle than any troops in Europe, and the summer of 1859 gave them ample opportunity to prove it.

From the beginning of the campaign the French maintained military and moral ascendancy over their foes. The furious and successful charges of Forey's division at Montebello, of the Turcos at Robechetto, and the Imperial Guard at the bridges of Magenta, exercised a deep influence on both armies. At Solferino, where Marshal Niel's corps faced the three corps of the First Austrian Army, "when the combat was a fire fight . . . I lost ground. . . . Then I formed a column of attack with one of the battalions of my reserve, and the bayonet gave us more than we had lost with the fusillade."[2] The French high command was so impressed that after Solferino an Imperial Order decreed that even defensive positions ought to be held by a combination of file firing and bayonet charges. The Austrian army might have profited from a similar decision. It lacked recent combat experience against first-class opposition. Its infantry regulations, dating back to 1806, stressed caution in both spirit and letter. This tendency was reinforced when the infantry was issued a muzzle-loading rifle ballistically as good as any in Europe. Training, however, did not keep pace with technology. Units received new rifles, but virtually no instruction in marksmanship or range-taking—a problem exacerbated by the slowness of rearmament. As a result, the Austrians tended to open fire at extreme ranges, wasting ammunition to no purpose. This in turn weakened the men's faith in their weapons and diminished the effect of their fire when the French did close to shorter ranges.[3]

As is common in such cases, what actually happened was far less important than what everyone thought had happened. The general opinion in Austrian military circles was that their infantry had relied too much on the defensive superiority believed to be conferred by modern rifles. Instead of seizing the offensive themselves, or at least counterattacking, they had stood in ranks to be trampled by the French.[4] The Austrian army, demonstrating remarkable powers of adjustment and adaptability, produced in less than three years a new set of regulations embodying and expanding on the lessons they felt they had learned in Lombardy. The regulations of 1862 belittled or ignored fire action, emphasizing instead the bayonet charge delivered by battalion columns advancing at the double. Gymnastic training and wind sprints became an important part of regimental drill schedules. Only a few isolated individuals suggested that it was impossible to outrun bullets. As for breechloading rifles, they were dismissed as being wasteful of ammunition and harmful to the offensive spirit. They were criticized as too complex for an army whose rank and file was largely illiterate and often spoke another language than that of their officers and NCO's. At most their use was advocated only for an elite force of selected specialists.[5]

The Austrian decision was supported by a rash of pamphlets, articles, and essays in the German military press. The weight of battlefield evidence seemed to favor the contention that the French had developed a technique for nullifying the effect of modern rifles. And even more seductive was the argument that morale, dash, and training could overcome fire power. Soldiers were not helpless before machines after all. Officers could still mold their men into a force which would decide battles. Authors lauded French dash and aggressiveness, French determination to charge home with cold steel instead of standing still and firing.[6] In his best-known work, *Ueber die Kampfweise der Franzosen*, Frederick Charles praised the simplicity and directness of the French regulations and the seemingly instinctive knowledge of their soldiers that the best way to avoid being hit was to get as close to the enemy as possible. Above all, he declared, the Italian campaign demonstrated the futility of skirmishing; fire fights only cost time and wasted men.[7]

The Prince and his contemporaries had no doubt that the system which had succeeded for the French would work even better in Germany. The German soldier, they argued, is bigger, stronger, and less excitable than the Frenchman, and therefore can be developed into a more formidable adversary in hand-to-hand combat. Since the German states had short-service armies and no Algerias or Crimeas, junior officers and enlisted men must be given peacetime training in developing judgement and initiative just as they were given close order drill. Skill in these things was not inborn; it could be taught like any other aspect of soldiering. The important thing was to keep the training process from becoming hidebound and formalistic. Training, moral and physical, must be designed to overcome the natural reluctance to close with the enemy: the unit in which every individual soldier regarded his bayonet as irresistible would be irresistible. The heavy losses inevitably suffered in coming to close quarters would be justified by victory—even if the attack were once repelled, no enemy could withstand a second or a third charge delivered in the same way.[8]

Throughout Germany maneuver grounds and officers' messes hummed with proposals for transforming soldiers into warriors. One result in Prussia was mass paper warfare as "every major, yes, every captain, [sought] to invent something special and thereby attract attention to himself."[9] Despite the overactive imaginations, intelligent adaptations to the changed conditions of the battlefield made their appearance in practice as well as on paper. Close combat was still the infantryman's primary task, but the company gained increasing importance as a shock unit, expected to deliver bayonet charges in mass formation when the larger battalion column presented an overly vulnerable target. At the same time skirmish lines were strengthened, deployed earlier, and allowed to open fire at longer ranges.[10] The states below the Main also began incorporating the lessons of 1859 into their military systems. The new instructions and regulations of Bavaria, Württemberg, and Hesse emphasized both bayonet charges delivered by battalion columns and the use of large numbers of skirmishers to weaken the enemy and prepare the way for the charge—possibly a tacit recognition of their lack of a strong artillery. Rifle formations, created in the pattern of the French light infantry by skimming the best men from the line units, flourished. Field exercises and maneuvers became more flexible. Even marksmanship training gained unheard-of importance. Nevertheless, as in Prussia and Austria, fire power remained the handmaiden of moral and physical shock.[11]

2

In light of the events of 1866 and 1870, this reasoning appears either as the product of ignorance and shortsightedness or as the expression of a wistful hope that the new weapons would simply go away and leave everyone at peace. These considerations did play a part in the thinking of some officers, but it is easy to understand how men obsessed for years with finding an answer to the problem of the infantry attack on the modern battlefield may well have regarded the events of 1859 as heaven-sent, definitive proof that rifles were not really as dangerous as their advocates proclaimed. It was, of course, possible to argue that had the Austrians known how to use their rifles properly the French would have met the fate of the Russians at the Alma and Inkerman. As early as 1855, for example. Colonel von Glisczinski, Chief of Staff of the Prussian Guard, argued that the new firearms had given war an entirely different character. Far from advancing rapidly and boldly, infantry would no longer be able to attack without the trench and the gabion. The hero of the future, the man on whom victory depended, would be the field engineer. Both before and after 1859, he contended that too many officers unthinkingly accepted the argument that fire tactics wasted time and men to no positive result. This fixed assumption, restricting fresh approaches, became a self-fulfilling prophecy regardless of its intrinsic merits or shortcomings.[12]

Glisczinski's recommendations found few auditors. Writing in 1861, a Bavarian major stressed the fire power of skirmish lines instead of their shock potential and suggested that future infantrymen must learn techniques of field fortification to protect themselves from rifle and artillery fire. But his was only one of dozens of pamphlets, books and articles.[13] Even those men who concluded that the Italian campaign had not reversed the course of history, that the French had not found a way to make their men bullet-proof, were seldom able to deduce what this meant to the infantry attack. Lieutenant-Colonel Wilhelm von Plönnies, Electoral Hesse's foremost authority on small arms and infantry tactics, declared that the infantry could affect an enemy only through fire action. Caesar Rüstow, author of a major work on small arms, was also convinced that rifle fire could lead to greater results than the most dashing bayonet attack. But Rüstow argued that since the Italian campaign had proved that rifles were ineffective at long range, fire fights should be conducted in Frederician style, point-blank. He proclaimed the controlled volley "the crown of fire" and stated that mass formations were by no means obsolete, since they were the only way for a commander to influence the course of a battle—the effect of smaller units was wasted. As for the use of cover, there was no reason why a battalion could not lie down to fire as well as an individual or a squad. Plönnies too declared that the battalion was still the basic tactical unit; commanders should guard against deploying it too early and risking loss of control. Otherwise, whether armed with rifles or muskets, most men would still fire without aiming and hope to frighten their target to death by the noise.[14]

It was, of course, possible to offer an operational solution to the tactical problems posed by modern rifles. As early as 1855, Frederick Charles had suggested that faced with a position too strong to be attacked frontally and whose flanks are secure, an aggressive general would make war with his men's legs by marching around it, thereby forcing the enemy to retreat.[15] In a memorandum of 1858 the new Chief of the Prussian General Staff, Helmuth von Moltke, argued that the goal of future commanders must be a defensive battle ending in a counterattack.[16] After the peace of Villafranca he despatched officers to Italy and France to prepare detailed reports on the returning armies and the nature of the battlefields, and obtained a permanent military attaché for the Paris Embassy. Basing his thinking on the resulting flood of information, Moltke began to form specific conclusions about the reasons for the Austrian defeat—conclusions first expressed in the history of the war which he composed in 1861. Not French bayonet charges, but Austrian passivity, their inability to use either the terrain or their rifles properly, their failures of generalship and leadership, had brought about Magenta and Solferino. Bayonets had not crossed in 1859 any more than they had in the eighteenth century or in the days of Napoleon. What the French had done in fact was advance close enough to be able to use their own inferior weapons effectively; they had fired as many rounds as the Austrians in the course of the war.[17]

This conclusion, however perceptive, did little to solve the problem of infantry attacks in the face of long-range rifles. Increasingly Moltke accepted Frederick Charles's reasoning. He suggested that the best way of meeting the problem of modern weapons was to force the enemy to assume the tactical offensive by a combination of superior strategy and hard marching. Offensive operations must depend increasingly on envelopments and flanking maneuvers; and as the range and effect of the new firearms would make such maneuvers impossible in the face of the enemy, campaign and battle would become more and more closely related, one leading into the other.

The Chief of Staff's thinking was also affected by the fact that France and Austria were Prussia's likely adversaries in the immediate future. The willingness of orthodox officers in both nations to send their infantry forward under most conditions could easily be turned to advantage. Particularly against France, Moltke argued, Prussia's strategy should be offensive, her tactics defensive. The increasing range and precision of modern firearms gave the defender an overwhelming advantage, particularly if he could anchor his position in villages, woods, or similar terrain features. Once troops had time to settle into a position, prepare cover for skirmishers, and mark the ranges, attacking *tirailleurs* firing at unknown ranges, exposed to enemy fire, could not expect to prepare the way for a mass attack as they had done in 1813-15. Building up the skirmish line with the hope of gaining fire superiority would only result in increased casualties for no result; columns advancing with the bayonet would have to face the enemy's unweakened skirmishers as well as the closed formations of his reserve. Nor could artillery fire alone prepare a decisive attack. Unable to decide the action either by a long-range artillery duel or a static fire fight between skirmish lines, the enemy would almost certainly be forced either to charge or to retreat. And nothing in French or Austrian doctrine suggested the possibility of withdrawal under such conditions.

The needle gun, Moltke suggested, would be the key to repelling such attacks. It was accurate up to 600 paces; it could be fired three times as rapidly as its muzzle-loading competitors. And these advantages could best be utilized in stationary combat. Prussian infantry must remain calmly in position, wait until the last possible minute to smash enemy assaults with superior firepower, then charge the survivors with bayonet and gun butt. This did not mean that no advance should ever be made against a sheltered enemy, but no officer should storm forward when standing still was of visible advantage. It must never be forgotten, Moltke declared, that the greatest bravery will shatter against an immovable obstacle. A good horseman did not drive even the boldest steed against a barrier it cannot hurdle, whether that barrier was a six-foot water-filled ditch or an open front which gave the firearm a chance to work its full effect.[18]

Prussian tactics were by no means as defensive-minded as Moltke's writings might indicate. This was clearly shown by the new maneuver regulations issued in June, 1861. They were intended not only to adjust the conduct of maneuvers to improved weapons, but also to provide a coherent system of field service regulations for the entire army. Future infantry combat, the regulations suggested, would ideally involve engaging the enemy in a fire fight, maneuvering him into the open, absorbing and exhausting his reserves, then destroying him. They stressed the use of flexible company-strength columns, able to maneuver rapidly, to probe for flanks and weak spots, and to take maximum advantage of every bit of cover both in defense and attack. Company columns were, in fact, recommended as the normal combat formation. Yet this tactical flexibility, as yet unknown in the French, Austrian, or Russian armies, was accompanied by a continued reluctance to accept the supremacy of fire on the modern battlefield. Closed formations might be dangerous, but official Prussian opinion still considered them necessary. Battalion columns were encouraged as fostering concentration and rapid movement. The needle gun's fire power was utilized to reduce the strength of skirmish lines. The section of the instructions dealing with company columns sternly warned against letting them dissolve into unmanageable swarms of skirmishers.[19] Moltke himself recommended that skirmish lines be used to deliver bayonet charges. Properly executed, not only would they neutralize the enemy's skirmishers, but, by drawing in his reserves, they would render him more vulnerable to the attack of the closed formations *in which the real power of decision rested.*[20]

Initially the Prussian army remained even more firmly committed to existing tactical forms than its regulations indicated. During the maneuvers of 1861, senior officers of both sides deployed their men in battalion columns at close ranges, attacked even strong positions frontally without any preparation, disregarded terrain features whenever it suited them. Foreign observers, French and British, made no secret of their criticism, holding the Prussian tactics up to scorn in regimental messes and newspaper columns alike. Nor was obvious royal displeasure enough to remedy the situation. In 1861 the Crown Prince sharply criticized the artificial formations and the clumsy tactics of the Prussian Guard. Two years later, maneuvering against III Corps, the same officers made the same mistakes, embarrassing even the observers. When the French General Forey suggested that the Prussian army was compromising the military profession, he was hardly motivated by jealousy.[21]

3

The image of the Prussian army as something less than a first-class opponent was seemingly confirmed on the outbreak of war with Denmark. In December, 1863, William had appointed Frederick Charles commander of the Prussian contingent. In three years the Prince had made his III Corps the best in the army. Now he was ordered to show Europe the true worth of the Prussian military system. The "suggestions" he issued to his officers on December 15, 1863, recommended the column as the decisive formation, the bayonet charge as the decisive maneuver, and close combat as the decisive way to win great victories. The

relationship of rhetoric to reality in this document is best indicated by its suggestion that in a hand-to-hand fight only the foremost adversaries should be bayonetted. "The others are to be
taken prisoner by shouting a request to them to throw down their
arms and surrender. This . . . is more practical than killing,
since in the time it takes to kill one, five prisoners can be tak-
en."[22] Anything less like the aftermath of a bayonet charge can
scarcely be imagined. To the surprise and chagrin of many of
his fellow officers, however, Frederick Charles ignored his own
suggestions. Instead of translating into action the offensive
spirit embodied in his essays and articles, he showed himself
to be a cautious, methodical officer unwilling to risk either the
lives or the morale of his men. His attempt to avoid storming
the Danish redoubts at Missunde was not regarded enthusias-
tically by the rest of the Prussian army. The Union infantry
which had bled in front of Marye's Heights at Fredericksburg,
the Confederates blown away by the guns of Gettysburg, could
have imparted some useful information on the problems of
attacking even improvised field fortifications. Whether their
words would have been heeded was at best questionable—
particularly in view of the open rivalry existing between the
Prussian and Austrian halves of the expeditionary force.

Since the allies crossed the frontier, their officers had been
comparing tactics, doctrine, weapons, organization, and life
styles. But while the Prussians ingloriously maneuvered around
Missunde, the Hapsburg double eagle was being carried to
triumph against the Danish positions to the west. Eager to test
their new infantry drill regulations against live opposition,
the Austrians seized every opportunity to attack with the
bayonet, and in the early days of the campaign their battalion
columns won the kind of successes predicted only by their firmest advocates. On February 3, the Austrian Brigade Gondrecourt
carried the village of Ober-Selk and the heights beyond against
superior Danish forces—a victory which contributed no little
to the Danish commander's decision to abandon his forward
defenses and retreat on Düppel. Three days later, at Oeversee,
three battalions of Brigade Nostitz, the elite Black and Yellow
Brigade, made headlines by storming three successive positions
with the bayonet. To the Austrians and to many neutral observers as well, the charge seemed definitely established as the

only corrective to the modern rifle. Prussian officers at GHQ grumbled that the Danish troops were by no means the equal of the Austrians either in numbers or quality, and that the weak Danish artillery had allowed the charging columns to get to close quarters almost unscathed. Troops attempting such head-on tactics against a real enemy would remain on the field permanently—as corpses.[23] Casualties in the assault units had in fact been uncomfortably high, particularly among senior officers. The Austrians, however, could point to the equally high Danish losses and, more significantly, to the moral ascendancy which their bayonets had won. In the light of subsequent events it is easy to regard the Prussian critics as men of perceptive vision, but at the same time their condemnation of Austrian methods bore the unmistakable taste of sour grapes.

When the Danish army shut itself up in the redoubts of Düppel, the Prussian infantry lost its chance to show what it could do in a major battle. From February 22 to April 18, while the Austrians overran the rest of Jutland, Frederick Charles's men waited for the heavy guns to overcome stubborn Danish resistance. The assault itself brought glory, medals, and casualties to the units involved without teaching any new lessons. Nor did the amphibious assault across the Alsen Sound on the night of June 29 present a serious challenge to Prussian skill and discipline. It did demonstrate the value of rapid-firing breechloaders in defensive fighting. The Prussian troops, disorganized by the confusion of the crossing, managed to turn back every Danish attempt to drive them into the sound. Attacking columns melted away under the fire of the needle gun; demoralization and casualties made the Danes easy victims of Prussian counterattacks.

The Prussian infantry's new firepower also proved itself on the Jutland peninsula. On July 3, a company of the 50th Prussian Infantry, 124 men strong, bivouacked around the village of Lundby, was surprised by a Danish company which immediately launched a bayonet charge. The Prussian commander kept his men in hand until the enemy column was within 250 paces of his position. Three separate volleys, the last fired at point-blank range, halted the Danes in their tracks and drove them to cover. When they attempted to use their rifles, they exposed themselves and their positions while reloading. Prussian sharpshooters and platoon volleys inflicted such heavy casualties that within minutes the survivors began to abandon the firing line. Twenty minutes after the first Danish attack the Prussians had no more targets. Of the 180 men of the 5th Company of the 1st Danish Regiment, twenty-two had been killed and sixty-six wounded; some of the bodies had been hit seven or eight times. Three Prussians were wounded.

It was a meaningless outpost fight at the end of an ignoble war. There was no glory, no material for an epic poem, nothing but twenty minutes of target practice.[24] The outcome was hardly surprising. Even the Austrians realized the need for better odds than three to two if a bayonet charge were to succeed against an unshaken enemy. Moreover, after six months of defeat the Danes could hardly be described as first-class troops. More significant for those studying the lessons of the war were the ease of the Prussian victory and the fantastic imbalance in the casualty lists. Even the firmest believers in battalion columns and bayonet charges could not afford to overlook the fate of the Danes at Lundby. But neither could they overlook the tactical deficiencies the Prussian infantry had displayed during the storm of Düppel and the fighting on Alsen. In particular, the Prussians appeared to sacrifice control for dispersion. Even their company columns quickly got out of hand. The Austrian official history commented superciliously that "the Prussian . . . tactics could have been very dangerous against an enemy who knew how to keep his forces concentrated."[25] A Swiss observer, Colonel Emil Rothpletz reported that the company column had lost favor among Prussian officers, who increasingly favored the use of whole battalions for offensive operations whenever the terrain permitted.[26]

4

The campaign in Denmark might have left the Prussians more concerned with tactics than with weapons. Their rifle nevertheless attracted more and more attention elsewhere in Europe. Colonel Rothpletz described the needle gun as a durable, reliable weapon with few mechanical defects not directly caused by individual errors. Admittedly the rifle was heavier, its recoil stronger, than was theoretically desirable. It was less accurate than the Minié rifles of the Swiss Confederation. On the other hand it was simpler and easier to load. The soldier had no need to expose himself to ram down the cartridge. Even the most frightened or ignorant private could not load one round on top of another, or load the cartridge backwards, or fire off his ramrod. Fire discipline posed a difficult challenge in a unit armed with breechloaders, but if officers and noncommissioned officers could not control their men, then they had no right to their rank. As for ammunition supply, Rothpletz declared that if he could win battles with the needle gun, it was of no concern to him how much the arsenals and the supply officers complained or how hard they had to work.[27]

Rothpletz was not alone in his opinion. Since 1861 the Military Musketry School in Spandau had provided a central institution for training officers and noncommissioned officers in the use of the needle gun. Its six-month courses included men from every regiment in the Prussian army, and did much to make all ranks aware of current developments in weapons and tactics. When the French General Bourbaki attended the Prussian maneuvers in 1864, one of his first requests was to be allowed to inspect the Musketry School. Captain Freiherr von Löe, Prussia's military attaché in Paris, protested. The French, he argued, had so far largely ignored fire tactics; knowledge of what was happening in Spandau might induce them to adopt a breechloader of their own. King William, in a gesture which can be interpreted as either shrewd or stupid, ordered that Bourbaki be shown everything. The French, he proudly told von Löe, can copy our rifle, our organization, and our regulations; they cannot copy the quality of our leaders or the training of our men. Bourbaki was suitably impressed. His reports informed Napoleon III and the War Ministry that the needle gun was an outstanding weapon and the Prussian infantry's musketry was the best in the world, deadly up to 400 meters. Coming from one of the Second Empire's most respected field commanders, this exaggerated claim might not have been enough by itself to keep France neutral in 1866. It certainly helped, however, to spark the development of the rifle and the tactical doctrine which were to cost so many German lives in the summer of 1870.[28]

The lessons of the Danish campaign gave added impetus to

the military reforms which most of the small and middle-sized states had been introducing or considering since 1859. New rifles, new organizations, new tactical forms, appeared everywhere in Germany. But it was the needle gun which made the deepest impression on the Confederation's military experts. Wilhelm von Plönnies, the Hessian major who had done so much to introduce the Minié rifle to south Germany, was convinced that in the future only a small-caliber breechloader would deserve the name of a military firearm.[29] Experts like Plönnies, and the Württemberg General von Hardegg believed that well-disciplined troops would be unlikely to waste ammunition, and that the breechloader's firepower and ease of handling outweighed the Minie's admitted superiority in range and accuracy.[30] The challenge, as usual, lay in convincing the war ministries and governments to take any action at all—and this time inertia was reinforced by considerations of high state policy.

Events in 1859 had made plain the need for greater cooperation among the armies of the German Confederation. Many contingents copied more or less closely the patterns and examples of their more powerful neighbors. Hanover continued to go its own way, adopting a Minié rifle which could use the ammunition of no other contingent. The battalions and brigades of other north German and Thuringian states, however, were usually organized and armed along Prussian lines, trained and even sometimes commanded by Prussian officers. Saxony, after an abortive effort to improve the organization of IX *Bundeskorps*, accepted the position of an Austrian auxiliary. But as the conflict between Prussia and Austria sharpened, military innovation implied political commitment as well. Adopting the weapons and tactics of a state might not be a firm statement of alliance, but it did mean a certain loss of flexibility—the exact degree of loss varying with one's dependence on Prussian or Austrian arsenals. This was a problem of particular concern to the states below the Main. Before the Danish campaign, adopting a common caliber for the new Minié rifles just going into production had seemed an excellent compromise between the claims of national sovereignty and the demands of military efficiency. The Bavarian Podewils, the Austrian Lorenz, the Wild rifles carried by Baden, Hesse, and Württemberg, might differ in details of construction, but at least their ammunition was interchangeable. It had taken forty years to get even the contingents forming VIII *Bundeskorps* to accept this limitation on their sovereign rights. Now it was proposed to start from the beginning with a weapon which would require completely new machinery for its manufacture, which would separate south Germany from Austria once more, and which might well serve as merely an entering wedge for a Prussia altogether too ambitious to suit her south German neighbors. Baden had adopted Prussian regulations and training methods after 1848, but she was as far from direct contact with Prussia as any of the small states. Moreover, her exposed position along the Rhine led her to regard the threat from Paris as far more immediate than that from Berlin. Bavaria had only completed rearming with Podewils Miniés in 1862—a costly process compounded by the War Ministry's decision to supplement inadequate domestic production facilities by placing large orders in Liége. Hesse too had no money to spare for innovations. Instead the students at the War School were required to discuss "the ten disadvantages of the needle gun" as part of their final examination—a transparent and ineffectual attempt to reduce the respect and fear many junior officers felt for the Prussian rifle.[31]

The controversy over the needle gun was reflected most clearly by events in Württemberg. By the spring of 1866, army and government agreed that the advantages of arming its infantry with breechloaders outweighed even the sacrificing of the hard-won commonality of VIII *Bundeskorps*. But the experimental weapons produced by local artisans and officers had proved unreliable, shorter-ranged and less accurate than the Miniés they were proposed to replace. The new world offered a possible alternative source of breechloading rifles, including designs proved and tested in combat during the American Civil War. The results of Swiss researches made available to the Württemberg army indicated that at least three of the U.S. rifles were ballistically superior to the needle gun. No one in Württemberg, however, had actually observed Sharps or Spencer rifles being used by troops. Purchasing from American firms also meant that even if the order could be promptly filled from available stocks, the rifles would still have to be shipped across an ocean. This entailed both an initial loss of time and an increased risk of

119

having imports cut off in case of war. Problems of maintenance and ammunition supply which had influenced earlier opposition to purchasing needle guns would be multiplied by introducing a non-European weapon. And while these difficulties might be overcome by establishing production and maintenance facilities in the using state, the costs and the time involved made this solution unacceptable as Germany moved towards war. If the needle gun, on the other hand, no longer represented the peak of small arms technology, it had been a subject of discussion for years. It had been extensively tested in Württemberg arsenals. Its strong points and shortcomings were reasonably familiar. Unlike its transatlantic competitors it was immediately available in quantity. If Württemberg was not able to reach a final decision on rearmament before the outbreak of hostilities, the authorities nevertheless tended to favor adopting the needle gun as standard equipment for the infantry.[32]

Chapter VII

Test

In 1866 the Austrian army was widely regarded as second only to that of France in general efficiency. Its rapid adjustment to the lessons of 1859 appeared to contrast favorably with the Prussian deficiencies and weaknesses broadcast throughout Europe both by proponents and opponents of military reforms, and displayed obviously in the maneuvers of 1860 and 1861. The Prussian victories in Denmark, won when the war had been relegated to the back pages of the European press, had not attracted the attention given to the dashing Austrian attacks at the beginning of the campaign. Opinion makers and experts alike, in short, tended to agree that Prussia was inferior to her adversary:

> in organization of detail, in adaptation for, and experience in, warfare . . . , in spite of the needle gun, the odds are against the Prussians, and if they refuse to be beaten in the first great battle by the superior leadership, organization, tactical formation, and *morale* of the Austrians, and last, not least, by their own commanders, then they must certainly be of a different mettle from that of which a peace army of 50 years' standing may be expected to be.[1]

Nor had the Austrians rested on their Danish laurels. Events in Schleswig-Holstein had changed a good many minds about the military potential of breechloading rifles. Some of the cob-webbed experts at the War Ministry were difficult to convince. Francis Joseph's faith in the bayonet initially led him to oppose any innovation which might lessen its effect. By the winter of 1865/66, however, an increasing number of key senior officers and military bureaucrats were arguing that the muzzle-loader's days as a first-line weapon were numbered. The army must adopt some form of breechloading rifle.[2] Implementing this conviction did not depend on choosing from among the designs under study in the Vienna arsenals. Test models do not fight. If the War Ministry had resisted the introduction of breechloaders for years, the new locus of opposition was the ·Ministry of Finance. Keeping pace with military technology is expensive. In the preceding decade, not only had the Austrian infantry been completely rearmed with new Minié rifles, but almost all of the artillery's smoothbore cannon had been replaced with muzzle-loading rifles—a double strain on the state's budget which made civilian ministers and civilian deputies less than eager to grant another of the seemingly endless demands for new weapons. The proposed innovation would cost at least two million gulden. Those like Count Mensdorff, Foreign Minister between 1864 and 1866, who advocated finding the money somehow, were unable to prevent the issue from being submerged under the pressure of the urgent foreign and domestic crises which plagued Austria in this period. By 1866, when Francis Joseph finally approved the production of breechloading rifles, the War Ministry had only enough cash on hand to pay for 1849 of them.[3]

The technical side of rearmament was in fact of secondary importance. Had the final decision been made and the money been available as far back as 1863, it is questionable whether a design could have been adopted, produced in quantity, and issued to men trained in its use in time to influence operations in 1866. More significant was the failure of the men who recognized the importance of firepower to exercise any real influence on Austrian tactical doctrines. The needle gun's superiority over the *Lorenz-Gewehr* was not universal. The Prussian rifle could fire faster. It could be more easily loaded from a prone position. But its normal effective range was only around six hundred paces. The Austrian rifle, on the other hand, had a range of nine hundred paces. Austrian artillery, moreover, was superior to the Prussian in training and equipment. To counter the short-ranged, rapid-firing needle gun, individual writers suggested that the Austrians use their artillery to force the Prussians into attacking, then destroy their skirmishers and company columns with accurate rifle fire at long range.[4] But the overwhelming weight of opinion at regimental levels in the Austrian army continued to regard the rifle as a glorified pike, and to see victory as depending on shock tactics. Any officer who spoke against them to the Emperor did so at the risk of his career. Generals and regulations alike instructed platoon and company commanders to take every opportunity to indoctrinate their men in the invincibility of the bayonet charge delivered by battalion columns. These columns, it should be remembered, were not as cumbersome as their name might suggest. They were really shallow rectangles, six companies massed two by two, two or three paces apart—a formation sixty men broad and twelve deep. Even Austrian advocates of the breechloader argued that such a column so armed would be more effective because it needed to deploy fewer men as skirmishers; it could provide its own fire support as it charged.[5] Handbooks, tactical studies, and articles suggested that the best defensive maneuver was the attack, that the results which the needle gun may have achieved on the target range were not applicable to the battlefield.[6]

In evaluating this apparent conservatism it must be understood that the Austrian infantry had just spent five years adjusting its doctrine, training, and indoctrination to the conclusions drawn by the High Command after 1859. To change again, virtually overnight, would demand a degree of technical and intellectual flexibility found in few human institutions. On the whole, moreover, officers and men were confident in their tactics, confident that courage and dash meant more than firepower. Perhaps it was to preserve this confidence that on May 19, 1866, Field-Marshal Benedek, commanding the *Nordarmee*, issued a directive reaffirming the principles of shock action. Fire fights must take second place to massive blows delivered by closed formations. Benedek went so far as to suggest that frontal attacks would succeed in most cases because the Prussians, believing such a maneuver virtually impossible, would be too surprised to react quickly. The best way of countering the needle gun, Benedek declared, was never to offer it a stationary target, but to close rapidly to within two or three hundred paces of the enemy and throw him out of his own positions with the bayonet.[7]

The Austrians were not indulging in sheer self-deception. The contention that closed formations held together at all costs could carry an objective with losses which, if higher than those of the same force deployed as skirmishers, would still be an acceptable price to pay for keeping the troops in hand, was based solidly on battle experience. Across the Atlantic, two improvised armies were coping with modern firepower by giving the junior officers and enlisted men the opportunity to study the terrain before attacking, by making maneuver plans simple enough to be executed under most conditions, and above all, by using the skill with spade and axe which was widespread on both sides. But most of the books and articles which would disseminate this information in Germany were yet to be written; the authors were still drawing conclusions from their sojourns in the new world.[8] Nor were American methods panaceas. If the argument that mass formations were obsolete was proved correct from Gravelotte to Passchendaele, the answer that ordinary men, the stuff of which a modern conscript army was made, could only be controlled and maneuvered *en masse* was defensible as well. Open-order tactics might be desirable in theory, but many veterans of the fighting in Schleswig-Holstein argued that only men in their third year of service could be trusted on the skirmish lines. Younger soldiers too often either failed to fire at all or simply blazed away in the general direction of the enemy without doing any damage.[9] Both Prussians and Austrians had used columns successfully in the recent war. To abandon them was to abandon command and control as well, to make the battlefield merely a conflict between armed mobs incapable of adjusting to changing situations, able neither to pursue a defeated enemy nor to rally after their own defeat, to consolidate a victory nor execute a withdrawal.

Events in 1870 indicated the merits of this contention. If even company columns were destroyed by French rifle fire, the loose swarms of skirmishers which took their place also proved unable to produce decisive results without heavy casualties. After 1864 Prussian commanders increasingly emphasized firm discipline and well-executed company drill. They trained enlisted men to accept the leadership of strange officers and NCO's and, if necessary, to push forward independently to the objective. But closed formations retained an important place in the doctrines of Prussia as well as Austria. The crucial difference between the two armies lay in their views on the tactical defensive. Even before Lundby Prussian instructions and training manuals increasingly emphasized the needle gun's potential as a defensive weapon and the difficulty of making frontal attacks against modern rifles. Moltke declared that in the age of the breechloader, no combination of bravery and superior numbers could carry to success a frontal attack over open ground. The strategic offensive, he argued, must in future be linked to the tactical defensive by executing flanking movements or choosing defensive positions "of so offensive a nature strategically that the enemy will be forced to attack . . .," and only then launching a counterattack.[10] Frederick Charles, who commanded the Prussian First Army in 1866, suggested that his men lie down under fire, as the British army did. Officers should dismount on the battlefield instead of making targets of themselves and the men around them. Let the Austrians charge, he urged, and meet them with five or six well-aimed volleys before resorting to the bayonet.[11]

2

The respective recommendations of Benedek and Frederick Charles faced their first test on June 26, at Podol on the Iser River. It was 8:30 P.M. when the First Army's vanguard struck the Austrian outposts guarding the village. The Prussians cleared the town, then lost it to the charge of an Austrian brigade. When the Prussians brought up reinforcements and counterattacked in turn, the Austrians charged the advancing company columns with the bayonet in approved textbook fashion. In equally approved fashion the Prussians halted, deployed their forward sections, and opened rapid fire. The Poles, Bohemians, and Magyars of Brigade Poschacher had never experienced or imagined anything like the hail of lead the needle guns poured into their ranks. A single company of the Prussian 71st Infantry fired 5,700 rounds in thirty-three minutes, an average of twenty-two per man.[12] If it was too dark to aim properly, it was also difficult to miss at ranges as close as thirty paces. Only occasionally did bayonets cross in the streets of Podol. The Prussians shot their way forward, inflicting such heavy casualties that the Austrian corps commander finally abandoned both the village and the bridgehead and ordered a general retreat across the Iser.[13]

Each side put approximately three thousand men into action. But while Podol cost the victors one hundred thirty casualties, the Austrian official history gives their losses at 1,048 killed, wounded, and missing. The striking discrepancy between the casualty lists was not lost on the junior officers and enlisted men of both armies. Even when the Austrians attempted to use their rifles during the street fighting, they soon discovered the difference between executing the complicated loading drill of the Minié on the parade ground and trying to repeat the motions at night, with the sick feeling of being helpless targets as they bit their cartridges and wielded their ramrods. It is little wonder that the Prussians shouted to each other "shoot low; the Austrians all shoot too high"—or that the Austrians complained that "the Prussians don't fight like honest men."[14]

To the east, in the foothills of the *Riesengebirge*, the Prussian Second Army was teaching the Austrians a similar lesson in infantry tactics. On June 27, the Prussian V Corps emerged from the mountains onto the plateau of Nachod, taking position only hours ahead of the Austrian VI Corps.[15] When the Austrians reached the field, they promptly launched a series of bayonet charges which achieved some local successes, but made no permanent headway against the steady and rapid fire of the Prussian rifles. By 12:30 the contest of "muzzle-loader against quick loader, target against marksman"[16] was over. Disheartened by their heavy casualties, demoralized by the fire poured into their ranks by Prussian skirmishers invisible in the powder smoke, the Hapsburg battalions began to melt away. At 1PM the Austrian commander ordered a general retreat. If there had been nothing to choose between the combatants in terms of courage, the casualty lists told a different story. Two hundred seventy-five Prussians were dead and 900 wounded while VI Corps had lost 2,200 dead, over 2,500 wounded, and almost a thousand prisoners—over twenty percent of its strength. Prussian firepower had been a devastating surprise. A wounded officer told his captors that the first time his company stood upright to reload, half of them were shot down, and the survivors preferred to continue the fight with empty rifles. The large number of unwounded prisoners included many who surrendered rather than risk further movement in range of the needle gun. As the defeated Austrians bivouacked for the night, the first shock of combat was replaced in too many men by depression and fear.[17]

Now did victory prove an antidote for the malaise caused by the breechloader. On the day of Nachod, the Austrian X Corps under General Gablenz won a hard-fought action against I Prussian Corps at Trautenau. In an afternoon of stubborn fighting, Gablenz's battalion columns, skillfully handled and bravely led, forced the Prussians out of two successive positions and back into the Bohemian mountains. But this apparently brilliant triumph of the bayonet found few to cheer it. Thirteen hundred Prussians had been killed, wounded, or captured. Gablenz's four brigades lost over 4,400 men, plus 373 unwounded prisoners. Seldom in the modern history of warfare had the victor lost over three times as many men as the vanquished, and most of these casualties had been inflicted by the needle gun. From headquarters to company campfire it was clear that two or three more victories like Trautenau would reduce X Corps to the size of a burial detail. On June 28, VIII Corps under the Archduke Leopold learned the same lesson at Skalitz. Instead of obeying orders to retire before the Prussian advance, the Archduke sent his men forward. The Prussians occupied the woods and the railway embankment to the east of the village, and allowed two Austrian brigades to dash themselves to pieces making one headlong charge after another against their invisible enemy. When the Archduke's corps rallied that evening, over 5,500 of its men were missing. The brigades which bore the brunt of the action had lost over a third of their effectives, and the morale of the whole corps was broken. For the remainder of the campaign it was to prove untrustworthy in action.

The Austrian defeats in the first week of the campaign must be attributed to failures of command and strategy as well as to the impact of the needle gun on their bayonet charges. But it was the moral and physical effect of Prussian firepower which had the greatest influence on both sides. Benedek, shocked by

127

casualties as high as fifty percent in some regiments at Nachod, had issued an order on June 28 forbidding bayonet charges without artillery preparation.[18] It came too late, however, to influence Trautenau and Skalitz. The Austrians continued to do the Prussians' work for them by presenting better targets than the rifle ranges of a garrison town:

> The Austrian soldiers fired only a few volleys before they charged, then with fixed bayonets they followed their officers to within 200, 100, even 50 paces of the enemy; they saw every sixth, every fifth, in some cases even every fourth or third of their comrades fall. Under such frightful casualties the Austrians first hesitated . . . followed the shouts of their advancing officers for a moment, then . . . certain death before their eyes, they fled . . . The Austrians undertook the assault with heightened vitality, with hammering pulses; then . . . suddenly the rapid fire of the new weapon strikes them in a way never anticipated: the moral effect of this recoil is frightful. Rapid fire follows the fugitives, and not a few of them, overwhelmed by the rapidly-changing sensations, throw themselves to earth to escape the bullets, physically and emotionally so exhausted that they are easily made prisoner by the pursuing enemy.[19]

The Prussians for their part had seen their rifles alone turn back the vaunted Austrian columns with ease. They had taken prisoners shocked into incoherence by the needle gun's hail of bullets. The tales of victory lost nothing in the telling as they spread from regiment to regiment. Morale soared. And when Prussian infantry attacked or counterattacked, they found that the Austrians were committed to shock action in defensive as well as offensive operations. Their rifle fire was too high and too slow to stop a determined attack; their skirmishers were unable to keep Prussian riflemen at a distance from the closed formations. Each Hapsburg brigade had a *Jäger* battalion, elite troops which displayed reckless courage and an almost fanatical disregard for casualties, but whose doctrine and training denied their name. Instead of developing open-order tactics and skill in marksmanship, the *Jäger* had concentrated since 1859 on bayonet charges executed even more rapidly and in even closer order than those of the line regiments.

The usual result of these tactics was that the Prussians simply closed around the Austrians' front and flanks, shot the columns to pieces, and followed the survivors into the position they were supposed to be defending. Thus on June 28 the 1st Prussian Guard Division delivered a number of spirited and successful attacks against two Austrian brigades around the village of Neu-Rognitz while losing only half as many men as its opponents. But Austrian tactical and technological shortcomings did not make their situation hopeless. When the Prussian 1st Army struck the positions of the Saxon Corps and I Austrian Corps north and west of the town of Gitschin on the morning of June 29, the course of events was far different from Nachod and Skalitz. Crown Prince Albert of Saxony, commanding the allied force, was an outstanding soldier whose men were under orders to hold ground rather than capture it. They had been deployed on high ground; their own artillery was in position to cover them; they were supported by ample reserves. This time it was the Prussians who struggled in the swampy meadows and broken terrain around Gitschin. It was Prussian company columns which lost direction; Prussian skirmish lines which were overrun by well-timed bayonet charges; Prussian troops who felt the sting of Minié balls at a thousand paces. But the potential impact of this skillfully conducted action on future operations was lost at 7:30 PM when a courier reached Prince Albert with a despatch from Benedek ordering him to retreat immediately. The allied troops suffered heavy losses disengaging, and heavier ones when the Austrians panicked and fled before the Prussian rifles. When I Austrian Corps finally rallied, almost 5,000 of its men were missing—3,000 dead and wounded, 1,900 unwounded prisoners. By contrast the Saxons, who had retired in comparatively good order, suffered only 600 casualties.

If the defeat at Gitschin contributed more than any other single factor to the collapse of Austrian morale, it also clearly demonstrated the superiority modern weapons properly used conferred on the defense. Until the arrival of Benedek's order, the Saxons and Austrians, despite their muzzle-loading rifles and shock tactics, had thwarted all Prussian efforts to break or flank their lines. The allies had inflicted for the only time in the campaign at least as many casualties as they sustained. But these facts were eclipsed at Austrian headquarters by the overwhelming evidence of defeat. In four days the *Nordarmee* had lost over thirty thousand men. Some of its finest combat units had been reduced to skeletons. Benedek despairingly wrote to his wife that "it would really be better if a bullet found me" and wired Francis Joseph urging him to make peace at all costs. The Emperor's refusal, ending with the question "has a battle been fought yet?" may have stiffened Benedek's spine. He may have feared to risk a running fight with the Prussians. His own mercurial temperament might have convinced him that victory was possible. Perhaps in the aftermath of Gitschin he or someone on his staff had been converted to the concept of the tactical defensive. In any case, Benedek decided to make a final stand behind the Bistritz River, on the hill chain of Lipa-Chlum eight miles northwest of Königgrätz.[20]

3

As the Austrian troops fell back towards Benedek's chosen battlefield, his engineer and artillery officers began constructing battery positions and field fortifications in an effort to give his troops some protection from the rifles which had wreaked such havoc on them in the open. Benedek was convinced the Prussian 2nd Army was too far away to support Frederick Charles, who would be forced to exhaust his strength against fixed positions as the Austrians had done on the frontier.[21] His optimism was not shared in the ranks. If many regiments sang as they took up their positions on the morning of July 3, the prevailing mood was nevertheless one of resignation. A veteran of the *Nordarmee* wrote a year later that the preceding week had convinced the troops that "the mass attacks with the bayonet which had been considered the last word in military wisdom were infamous against the rapid fire of the needle gun." But despite Benedek's order of June 28, the army could hardly adjust to new methods of warfare in a week. The course of the day clearly showed that under pressure, Austrian soldiers fought as they had been trained to fight in peacetime, even if they died doing it.[22]

The opening hours of the battle, however, seemed to justify Benedek's decision to stand and fight. On the Austrian left wing, the Saxon Corps demonstrated that its performance at Gitschin was no accident by easily containing the attacks of the Prussian

Elbe Army. Saxon rifles and Saxon artillery kept the needle guns of Prussian skirmishers at a respectful distance and beat back a series of disorganized attacks on the village of Nieder-Prim. Around noon, Prince Albert even launched a series of counterattacks, bayonet charges which drove the Prussians back nearly to the Bistritz River. In the center of the line, the three Prussian divisions which crossed the Bistritz around 8:30 were almost immediately pinned down by Austrian sharpshooters and Austrian artillery. Breechloading rifles were of little use against two hundred cannon amply supplied with ammunition and protected by open ground to their front. Attempts to charge the Austrian positions only increased casualties. By 11 AM, Prussians were straggling back toward the Bistritz in twos and threes. By noon, whole battalions were melting away, and a general panic was becoming a real possibility.

But the battle of Königgrätz was not decided along the Bistritz. The stage for an Austrian disaster was set slightly to the north, when the Prussian 7th Division occupied the wood of Maslowed, the *Swiepwald,* and pressed forward into the village of Cistowes. The Austrians immediately counterattacked. A bayonet charge rapidly cleared Cistowes of its disorganized conquerors, but in the *Swiepwald* events took a different turn. *Generalmajor* von Brandenstein deployed his whole brigade, seven battalions, against the Prussian position. Half his troops never reached the wood. Those who did were caught up in a smoke-shrouded inferno with no flanks or rear, where an officer's authority extended only to the men on either side of him. It was a battle of ramrod versus bolt, with the piled-up Austrian corpses in the clearings as ghastly evidence of the effect of rapid fire at close range. Brandenstein was mortally wounded; his brigade, destroyed as a fighting force, was forced out of the *Swiepwald* thirty minutes after it first entered it.

In the words of the Austrian official history, the wisest course would have been to accept the local defeat. The *Swiepwald* was commanded by Austrian artillery around Chlum and Maslowed; the 7th Division would have found it no easier to advance than had the Prussians along the Bistritz.[23] But Count Festetics, commanding IV Corps, to which Brigade Brandenstein belonged, was determined to restore his original line and avenge his casualties. When he was wounded his successor,

131

Lieutenant Field Marshal Anton von Mollinary, continued and extended the operation. Mollinary was convinced that he had a chance to rout the Prussians in the *Swiepwald*, envelop the line of the Bistritz from the left, and crush the First Army before the Second could intervene. He was so confident that he not only defied Benedek's direct order to avoid further offensive movements; he also requested support from II Corps. Benedek had posted this corps on the heights of Chlum to screen his right flank against the Prussian Second Army.[24] Like IV Corps, it had not been heavily engaged before July 3. Whether officers who had seen regiments lose half their men to the needle gun in a few minutes would have been quite as anxious to throw their men into the *Swiepwald* is questionable. What is certain is that first Brigade Fleischhacker, then Brigade Poeckh, of IV Corps charged the woods as if Nachod and Skalitz had been merely names on a map, cheering and shouting, played into action by their buglers.

By this time Prussian organization had dissolved into a jumble of small units commanded by anyone who could set an example, and the appearance of these fresh Austrian masses strained the exhausted men to the point of collapse—but not beyond it. When the forward battalions of Brigade Fleischhacker attempted to push forward into the *Swiepwald*, they were cut to pieces by the needle guns of the desperate Prussians "forced into this . . . part of the woods . . . partly through the loss of Cistowes, partly through the . . . attack of Brigade Poeckh."[25] The latter brigade, suffering heavy casualties, drove almost to the far edge of the *Swiepwald*, pushing the disorganized defenders aside by sheer mass as the prow of a ship parts the ocean. But like water, the Prussians flowed around the Austrians, firing into the unprotected flanks of the columns struggling through the underbrush. The first wave of Brigade Poeckh had just paused for breath when "on a tree-covered height on the right flank, masses of Prussians . . . opened a murderous fire on the extremely vulnerable brigade."[26] Poeckh and all but one of his staff officers were shot, and less than half of the 4,000 men of the first wave managed to escape through the Prussian rifle fire. One battalion could muster only forty-two files that evening.

As the first Austrian fugitives streamed out of the woods, two fresh brigades entered it. Mollinary still believed he had a chance to crush Frederick Charles's left flank in the *Swiepwald*. Responding to his request, Count Thun, commanding II Corps, loaned him Brigades Württemberg and Saffaran. Mollinary promptly sent them forward around 11 AM to complete the work IV Corps had begun. Writing three decades later, a Prussian colonel described the frontal attacks of the Austrian battalion columns as theatrical productions. The men on the spot at front row center were not so casual. Losses had been heavy, particularly among the officers. Ammunition was running low. Division Commander Eduard von Fransecky's requests for reinforcements had been disregarded. Only two battalions held the sector of the *Swiepwald* against which Brigades Württemberg and Saffaran now advanced. Exhausted by a two-hour fire fight, they could not stop ten Austrian battalions by themselves. At close range the needle guns decimated the onrushing columns. One *Jäger* battalion lost half its strength in a few minutes. But it was not enough. By noon the Austrians had once again reached the far edge of the *Swiepwald,* and Prussian commanders were desperately encouraging their men to meet the·next attack —an attack which, it seemed certain, would be the final one.

It did not come because there were no troops left to make it. Even the Prussian official history, written in 1867, had no clear understanding of the havoc wrought by the rifles of the *Swiepwald's* defenders. Of the fifty-nine battalions which had formed the Austrian right flank, forty-nine had been drawn into the fighting around the *Swiepwald*. Only thirteen remained intact. Eight more had been rallied and reorganized. The other twenty-eight were either tangled somewhere in the woods or had been destroyed by the needle guns of Fransecky's division.[27] In later years Prussian historians tended to attribute this victory to training and leadership rather than superior armament. Certainly the excellent fire discipline of the men, their generally high morale, their willingness to fight under strange officers, and the tactical skill displayed by these officers were all vital factors in the ability of the Magdeburgers to hold the *Swiepwald* for so long against superior numbers. The Austrians also contributed to their own defeat by failing to attack with more than two brigades at a time. But underlying all other factors was the needle gun. It was superior firepower that made the improvised Prussian detachments so dangerous to the Austrian columns, that gave small numbers of men strangers to each other and to their officers the confidence to stand their ground against a charging battalion, then close in and harrass it once it passed. Such hand-to-hand fighting as there was occurred only when the Prussians had no time to reload.

The final attack on the *Swiepwald* marked the high tide of Austrian fortunes. Benedek had originally intended to move VI Corps from reserve to fill the gap on his right caused by Mollinary's insubordination. Then he hesitated. As a result, when he received a message at 11:30 informing him that the Prussian Second Army was not only closer than he had believed, but could be expected on the field hourly, Benedek found himself with a flank of seven kilometers defended by only nine battalions. It was too late to move VI Corps. Mollinary and Thun, when ordered to evacuate the *Swiepwald* and return to their original positions, protested vigorously against abandoning the terrain which had cost such heavy casualties. When they finally decided to obey, detaching their forward units proved as costly in time, lives, and morale as it had at Gitschin. Tired and dispirited, the Austrians were hardly in condition to withstand this new threat from the north.

Crown Prince Frederick's units had been delayed by weather, terrain, and incompetence. Nevertheless the 1st Guard Division captured the heights of Horenowes from elements of II Austrian Corps by 1 PM. Ninety minutes later, *Generalleutnant* Hiller von Gärtringen sent his division against the pivot point of the Austrian line, the heights of Chlum. Deployed in half-battalions and company columns, the guardsmen went forward through standing grain and broken ground that combined with the smoke-thickened mist shrouding that part of the field to conceal the scope of their movement from the Austrian infantry. The Austrians' attention was so firmly focused westward, on the *Swiepwald*, that their positions do not seem to have been screened by even an outpost line. The troops in the redoubts around Chlum, Brigade Appiano of III Corps and Brigade Archduke Joseph of IV Corps, had seen little action themselves, but had had ample opportunity to observe the effect of the needle gun on their comrades. Suddenly, emerging from the fog like ghosts, the Prussians were on them, pouring volley after volley into their ranks. The Archduke's men broke and fled, carrying their supports with them, abandoning entrenchments and guns alike. The two battalions of Appiano's 46th Regiment garrisoning Chlum were surrounded and destroyed by close-range rapid fire. It was the kind of confused melee ideally suited to Prussian tactics and Prussian armament, where detachments two or three hundred strong led by officers quick to grasp the initiative could exercise an influence out of all proportion to their numbers by superior firepower and fire discipline. Austrian battery positions were rendered untenable in minutes by the rifles of Prussian skirmishers. Austrian cavalry charges were turned back by units which did not take the trouble to form square before opening fire. Three companies seized the village of Rosberitz and inflicted heavy casualties on disorganized crowds of Austrians which streamed past the village "as silent and inactive as a moving target."[28] Hundreds of them surrendered. By 3 PM the Prussians were victorious all along the line.

Field-Marshal Benedek remained unconvinced. Riding forward under fire, he personally led a futile bayonet charge against the village of Chlum. Local counterattacks on other detachments of guardsmen proved equally unsuccessful. The Austrians advanced in close order; the Prussians mowed them down with rapid fire at close range. It was plain that isolated brigades and battalions could accomplish nothing against the needle gun, even when its wielders were disorganized by victory. But after his brief reversion to the role of field officer, Benedek ordered VI Corps to throw the Prussians out of Chlum and Rosberitz. Its commander had learned something since Nachod. Ignoring Benedek's appeals for haste, he delayed his attack almost an hour while 120 guns bombarded the villages and the heights behind them. Once committed, the Austrian infantry managed to capture Rosberitz in a quick rush. Beyond the village, however, their charging columns were again shattered by Prussian fire. Numbers and bravery gained ground a yard at a time, but just as in the *Swiepwald* the Austrians were never able to break the Prussian line. Disorganized and exhausted, replenishing their ammunition from the pouches of the dead and wounded, the infantrymen of the Guard maintained their positions until the arrival of I Prussian Corps shortly after 4:30 made further Austrian attacks in the Chlum sector pointless.

The Austrian left wing had collapsed ninety minutes earlier. The success of his local counterattacks led Prince Albert to plan a more elaborate maneuver. While two Austrian brigades from VIII Corps advanced to protect his exposed left flank and occupy Stezirek Wood, two Saxon brigades would press home an attack on the center of the Prussian position. The Saxons carried out their assignment as well as any troops that day. But the Austrian Brigade Schulz, pushing through Stezirek Wood with skirmishers only a few paces in front of its battalion columns, ran headlong into a Prussian regiment. This brigade had been only lightly engaged at Skalitz, but the stories told by their comrades had not been forgotten. Now, facing the needle gun at point blank range, the leading Austrian regiment broke and ran, carrying the rest of the brigade with it. The Prussian colonel deployed all three of his battalions in line, and their rapid fire gave the Austrians fresh momentum. Fleeing for their lives, half of them fell back on the village of Ober-Prim. The other half rushed blindly into the left flank of the Saxon 2nd Brigade and threw it into confusion, a helpless target for every rifle the Prussians could bring to bear.

Even this disaster demonstrated the worth of firepower: a single Saxon battalion, deployed in line, let the swarm of fugitives through, then closed ranks and held off the pursuing Prussians with well-timed volleys. But isolated gallantry could not stop the Elbe Army from closing in on the front and flank of the allied position. The Austrian brigade around Ober-Prim had been cut to pieces at Skalitz and, except for a single battalion in Ober-Prim itself, offered only a token resistance. However, the Saxon defenders of Problus and Nieder-Prim made the Prussians pay a stiff price for their victory. Even company columns proved too vulnerable a formation to risk against the rifles of Prince Albert's men. The final attack on Problus was made by a disorganized swarm of skirmishers, and when the Austro-Saxons finally disengaged around 3:30, the forward Prussian units were too tired, hungry, and disorganized to pursue them effectively.

With both flanks broken, with their line of retreat threatened, the corps which had held the Prussians in check along the Bistritz all day now fell back along the Königgrätz road towards Rosnitz. Frederick Charles's men followed, his vanguards occupying the heights from which the Austrian guns had tormented them since dawn. The Guard and I Corps closed in on the Austrian line of retreat from the north, and a desperate Benedek played his last cards. While two cavalry divisions rode against Frederick Charles's forward units, three brigades of I Corps, the only Austrian infantry as yet unengaged, charged the Prussian lines at Chlum, no longer with the hope of victory, but simply to hold open the road to the south. Both efforts succeeded. The Austrian cavalry, though it suffered heavy losses every time it rode into range of the needle guns, delayed the advance of 1st Army for an hour. As for I Corps, the Prussians allowed its columns to close to 300 paces, then opened fire. Twenty minutes later, six thousand Austrians were dead or wounded—almost a third of the men who had begun the attack. Twenty-eight hundred more surrendered, many of them in a state of shock. Before I Corps could extricate itself from the Prussians who were closing on it from three sides, its losses rose to over 10,000—half of its strength, and a quarter of the casualties suffered by the Austrians on July 3.

An energetic pursuit might well have destroyed Benedek's army. Only the final desperate charges of I Corps and the cavalry, together with the bravery of the Austrian reserve artillery, which kept the Prussians under fire until nightfall, effectively concealed the fact that the allied infantry was effectively *hors de combat*. Over 41,000 Austrians were dead, wounded, or missing. Twenty thousand had surrendered unwounded. Italian regiments had collapsed under the Prussian rifles. Hungarian, Polish, and Bohemian units were showing signs of wavering. The Saxon corps, whose sensible tactics and steady courage brought it out of action with only 1,500 casualties, was fighting for homes already under Prussian occupation. As the defeated army crossed the Elbe the discipline that had kept it together on the field of Königgrätz dissolved. Regiments degenerated into mobs of stragglers. For all practical purposes the *Nordarmee* was finished as an effective fighting force. Benedek fell back on Olmütz ostensibly to reorganized and reequip his army, but rather than risk another pitched battle, when the advancing Prussians cut his communications with Vienna he retreated across the Carpathians and reached the capital via Pressburg. Though the preliminary treaty was not signed until July 26, the struggle for mastery in Germany had ended July 3, in the *Swiepwald* and on the heights of Chlum.

4

The increasingly close association of the south German states with Austria after 1864 resulted in a corresponding tendency for their armies to adopt Austrian shock tactics. If the south German Miniés were slower to reload, in defensive positions their greater range and accuracy might well have outweighed the other advantages of the needle gun.[29] On several occasions in 1866, the Podewils rifles of the Bavarians inflicted relatively heavy losses on Prussian company columns in the broken Franconian terrain. At Hammelburg on July 10, for example, two Bavarian battalions, their flanks protected by high ground, stopped the advance of a Prussian division for several hours. In the hands of good marksmen, the Podewils rifle showed itself fully equal to the needle gun during the fire fight. South German staffs, however, tended to ignore the potential advantages of the tactical defensive followed by a counterattack. This oversight was compounded by the shortcomings of their infantry. If decentralization and open-order tactics offered too many opportunities for laggards to hang back or lose themselves, pushing home the attack of a battalion column against determined defenders required qualities not always found south of the Main in the years before 1866. Admiring the dash and initiative which the French had shown in Italy, most of the south German armies attempted to instill it into their own men by incorporating "a certain light, not to say careless" tone in both regulations and practice.[30] However, these concepts of initiative and flexibility too often served as cloaks for lax discipline and inadequate training.[31] And while the French army had the stimulus of constant campaigning in distant theaters of war, the south German contingents were restricted not only to their own borders, but as agriculture and industry expanded, to ever-shrinking maneuver areas as well. In Hesse-Darmstadt, for example, the field exercises had been carried out in the same area for so many years that a peasant would occasionally inform a new subaltern that he had stationed his outpost incorrectly: ". . . it belongs here by the cherry tree, where it has always been."[32]

Like the Danes in 1864, the Hessians, the Bavarians, the Württembergers were only able to comprehend the true meaning of a rifle which could fire five times faster than anything in

Europe when they had once faced it in battle. From their perspective the Prussians simply enjoyed target practice at the expense of half-trained reservists fumbling through the complicated loading drill of the Minié. Even at their best and bravest the south Germans could make no headway against breechloading firepower. On July 13, for example, fusiliers of the Prussian 15th and 55th Infantry held the village of Frohnhofen in Bavaria and the railway embankment beyond it for almost four hours against the battalion columns of the Hessian Division of VIII *Bundeskorps*. The Hessians came on time and again, bands playing, against the Prussian rifles. Nor did their tactics reflect a simple faith in shock action. They made good use of what cover the terrain afforded. All of their attacks were screened by skirmishers. But the courage and self-sacrifice of the Hessians served only to swell their own casualty lists. The six battalions engaged at Frohnhofen lost 32 officers and 745 men killed, wounded, and missing. They killed three Prussians and wounded sixty-five—a repetition of Lundby on a large scale which did nothing to encourage other south German troops to press home their own attacks against Prussian positions. It did however, inspire major postwar reappraisals of doctrine and tactics in the states below the Main.

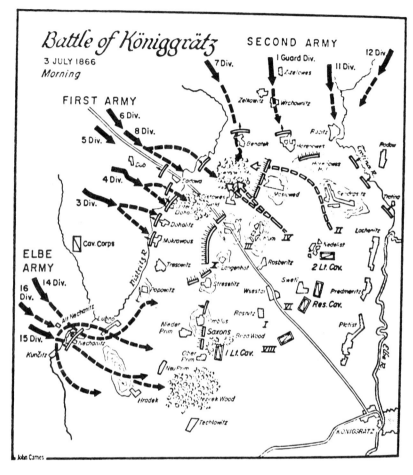

Map 4

PART III

CANNON

In the armies of Germany after 1815 artillery tended to be regarded as an expensive branch of service officered by desiccated pedants. It was a consistent victim of economy drives; even when war ministries agreed to purchase new material they refused to authorize enough horses to move it. At this stage of Germany's economic development industrialists hardly acted as a force for change. Cannon were manufactured by the state, and states were reluctant to risk depending on private entrepreneurs. Even Alfred Krupp, whose name has become almost synonymous with the growth of the German military-industrial complex, was primarily a salesman attempting to peddle his steel for any purpose whatever. He sought government contracts merely in the hope that they would be larger and more stable than those offered by private firms, and exercised no significant influence on decision-making.

Despite these temptations to stagnation artillerymen, especially in Prussia, were surprisingly successful at avoiding complete absorption in parade-ground drill and technical minutiae. They addressed themselves to questions of new gun metals, of the relationship between fire-power and mobility in artillery equipment, of improving the artillery's efficiency as a battlefield instrument. Particularly in technical matters their achievements were greater than is generally conceded. Early criticisms of cast steel as a gun metal involved its cost-effectiveness and its reliability; they were not manifestations of inflexible conservatism. Similarly the long debate on the introduction of rifled cannon did not involve a choice between riding the wave of the future and remaining committed to the material of the Napoleonic Era. It was rather a fundamental disagreement over the desirability of long-ranged precision weapons whose individual rounds were not particularly effective as opposed to an equally-modern design of smoothbore cannon whose shorter range was arguably compensated for by greater blast effect. Even breechloading was not an obviously desirable innovation. Until the development of recoil mechanisms, rate of fire depended more on the time required to bring a piece back into battery than on the end from which it was loaded.

In their concern for drawing proper conclusions from ambiguous evidence, Prussian gunners tended to concentrate on weapons rather than on how to use them, an error not repeated by their Austrian rivals. But the tactical and operational weaknesses which handicapped the Prussian artillery in 1866 cannot be described as structural faults. By 1870 they had been generally alleviated, and Prussian guns played a decisive role in toppling the Second French Empire.

Chapter VIII

Matrix

If the artillery had been the stepchild of the Prussian army before 1806, in the period after 1815 its status approximated that of an illegitimate half-brother—semirespectable, but uncertain. And like many another military bastard, the artillery tried harder. Gerhard von Scharnhorst had made his reputation as a gunner, and during the Era of Reform he paid particular attention to his old branch of service. He personally supervised its integration into the mixed brigades of the new Prussian army, the preparation of its comprehensive drill regulations, the training of its officers. His three-volume *Handbuch der Artillerie,* a seminal work in its field, remained a source of principles and inspiration to the Prussian gunners for a half-century. He was responsible for the appointment of the King's brother, Prince August of Prussia, as Inspector-General of an arm whose bourgeois officers and civilian drivers had traditionally been objects of ridicule to the nobles of the infantry and cavalry. And he established the *Artillerie-Prüfungs-Kommission,* with responsibility for keeping the Prussian army abreast of foreign and domestic developments in weapons technology.

Scharnhorst originally viewed this body as a kind of technical general staff, with the members serving regular tours of duty with troops in an effort to keep them from becoming deskbound. Prince August's decision in 1824 to assign officers permanently to the commission ended this experiment, and in 1830 the functions of the APK were restricted exclusively to research. If these reorganizations encouraged preoccupation with details and a corresponding tendency to disregard practical problems, service on the commission nevertheless continued to offer an opportunity for officers to present their opinions on a wide variety of technical problems. Prince August not only allowed free expression of opinion; he ordered it. An officer reluctant to express his own views or overly concerned with conforming to those of his superiors ran the risk of being returned to troop duty with an unsatisfactory report. The APK, moreover, embodied an open-minded attitude towards technology unusual in any European army of the post-Napoleonic period. No idea was too ridiculous, no invention too impractical, to be rejected without exhaustive study.[1]

The commission did not work in a vacuum. It supervised, for example, the introduction of percussion locks and an improved, finer-grained gunpowder for existing cannon. Its primary attention during the 1820s and 30s, however, was focused on a secret weapon with a reputation of being potentially among the most devastating innovations ever made in the art of war—shrapnel. For centuries field artillery had employed two basic forms of ammunition: round shot for long ranges, case shot for short. No continental army had developed an efficient method of dealing with a dispersed enemy at anything but point-blank ranges. The primitive explosive shells thrown by the howitzers, with their preset fuses and uncertain fragmentation, were almost worthless for this purpose. Their inaccuracy, moreover, was proverbial. In 1784, however, the British Lieutenant Henry Shrapnel had designed a hollow round shot with very thin walls, filled with bullets and with a bursting charge just sufficient to break open the casing and scatter the balls. Manufactured and widely used during the Napoleonic Wars, this "spherical case shot" made a deep impression on many Prussian observers, particularly veterans of Waterloo. They urged its adoption in Prussia, and the APK began testing it as soon as it obtained British models for study and analysis.

Initially this decision appeared sound. The results of the first series of tests convinced the APK of shrapnel's superiority to all other forms of fire at long range. General Braun, Scharnhorst's old collaborator and a difficult man to impress, declared that it would give artillery the power to decide a battle by itself. Another senior officer described shrapnel as seven times more effective than case shot and fifteen times better than round shot. The enthusiastic reception given to the new invention was also fostered by the profound secrecy in which the states of Europe shrouded their research on the subject. Armies tend to believe that anything which attracts the attention of other armies must be valuable; the veil of mystery which surrounded shrapnel contributed a good deal to the legends of its destructive potential. Since security measures in the 1830s were no better, relatively speaking, then in the 1970s, each country had a good idea of its neighbors' progress in designing a better shrapnel, but this information was usually kept secret from the men responsible for using the new invention in battle. Artillerymen who attempted to publish instructions on the use of shrapnel or to publicize the results of test firings found their work censored or suppressed. Such instruction as the junior officers and enlisted men received was vague and theoretical. Arguments that no weapon, no matter how devastating, was of any value if its use was not understood failed to impress the guardians of Prussia's military secrets. Not until 1837 did the War Ministry relax its internal security enough to permit—by special Cabinet Order—batteries to fire the new ammunition under field conditions. The official principles for use of shrapnel in wartime were only made generally available to artillery officers in 1856. And long before that time shrapnel itself had been revealed as just another tool of war— a tool, moreover, which had serious shortcomings.[2]

The first enthusiasm with which shrapnel was received was rapidly modified when the APK discovered that too many of the rounds fired either burst at the wrong time or not at all. The major problem lay in the fuses. Nineteenth-century soldiers knew two ways of detonating a shell. Its fuse could be designed to explode on contact with a target, or it could be preset for a certain time and distance. However, the erratic trajectory of a spherical shot fired from a smoothbore cannon, combined with the problems of designing a reliable detonator, made Prussian gunners reluctant to trust percussion fuses, particularly for shrapnel. The new ammunition's major theoretical advantage was its destructive power against enemy personnel at long range. This in turn would be considerably reduced if shrapnel rounds exploded only on impact. Too many balls would plow harm-lessly into the ground or be otherwise wasted. Prussian de-signers worked for three decades to develop a reliable time fuse which would detonate shrapnel at predetermined ranges. Bor-mann fuses, Bartsch fuses, Breithaupt fuses—the names of the designers read like a roster of artillery officers. Prussian fuses were among the best in Europe, widely copied by other German states and even across the Atlantic. Their superiority, however, was only relative. Even under the artificial conditions existing at maneuvers, the ratio of duds remained one in three—a per-centage so unacceptable that by 1866 shrapnel would be tempo-rarily abandoned for field service.[3] It may be true that this policy allowed the best to become the enemy of the good, that more effort should have been devoted to developing a functional percussion-fused shrapnel. But if the Prussian artillery failed to pursue this course, it nevertheless was hardly indifferent to the advantages of technical innovation.

This concern for innovation was equally apparent when artillerymen considered the guns from which shrapnel would be fired. Their initial situation was highly unfavorable. Losses during and after 1806 combined with the hasty rearmament of 1813 had forced the utilization of a wide variety of purchased, donated, and captured pieces. By the end of the War of Liber-ation the Prussian artillery was using equipment from every country in Europe. One of Prince August's first tasks when peace broke out was to establish uniform designs of guns and vehicles for the entire artillery. The *System c/16*, introduced in 1816, brought order out of chaos at the expense of quality. It included six- and twelve-pounder cannon for direct fire, with seven- and ten-pounder howitzers for high-angle fire. The new guns had been hastily designed. Despite iron axles, improved laying machinery, and lighter carriages, they remained inaccu-rate, slow-firing, and among the clumsiest in Europe—even the "light" six-pounder weighed well over two tons. When the Guard Artillery held firing exercises on the range at Wedding, sentries had to be posted to warn away sightseers and passers-by, because no one had any idea where the shot would fall.[4] But if most officers agreed that the existing cannon were unsatis-factory, the consensus went no further. For three decades after Waterloo, the Prussian artillery was racked by a conflict which foreshadowed one of the most consistent problems of modern military science—balancing firepower and mobility.

Since the days of Frederick the Great, Prussia's horse artillery had considered itself a *corps d'elite* whose mission placed it several levels above the rest of the gunners. The assumption was well-founded. The inefficiency of the fortress artillery and the pusillanimity of its officers had been such a byword during the campaign of 1806 that Prince August was determined never again to permit Prussia's fortresses to become refuges for the incompetent and the superannuated. Each of the nine corps of the Prussian army had an artillery brigade of fifteen companies. Three of them were horse artillery. Three were intended to man twelve-pounders on mobilization. The remaining nine changed functions and equipment annually, training with field guns, then in fortress service. The versatility, however, was superficial. Prince August's decision to avoid specialized functions meant that the officers and men of the foot companies never fully mastered either field or garrison service. Much of the apparent pedantry in artillery manuals of the period, the concern for technical minutiae, the endless listing of mathematical tables and formulae, can be explained by the burden of knowledge placed on the average officer. Not only were the men switched from one type of gun to another too often to learn anything; training facilities remained totally inadequate. A company expected to man light guns on mobilization was allowed less than a hundred rounds of ammunition for its annual target practice. As budget cuts and inflation ate into available funds, the artillery's peacetime establishment of teams was reduced until a foot company could move only two of its guns at one time.[5]

The horse artillery escaped this general cheese-paring. Unlike the foot companies, whose cannoneers walked behind their pieces, all horse gunners were mounted. Far from being specifically detailed to work with cavalry, as was the rule by the third quarter of the nineteenth century, the horse artillery was the only really mobile artillery in the army. Its status rose accordingly. During the War of Liberation the Prussian infantry, with its flexible tactics and its increased mobility, had often outrun the foot batteries ostensibly supporting them. The cavalry divisions and corps tested during post-war maneuvers also clamored for more mobile artillery. Veterans of the Peninsula and officers who served beside the British in the Waterloo campaign were particularly impressed by their six-pounder horse batteries, which could maneuver with the speed and precision of a cavalry squadron. Heavy guns, after all, were useless if they could not be moved where they were needed; increased mobility might be well worth a certain sacrifice of firepower.[6] The horse artillerymen made a strong case—so strong that in 1818 Prince August agreed to exempt them from the periodic changes in role and equipment which remained the lot of the other gunners. Instead the horse artillery concentrated on learning to move. Horse batteries were given the best men and the best teams; foot companies, often reduced to borrowing from cart and plow to take the field at maneuvers, were suitably envious.. The artillery was a middle-class arm; socially ambitious bourgeoisie who had virtually no chance of being commissioned in a cavalry regiment were able to find compensation by serving in the horse artillery. The combination of social pressure and difference in training made horse battery commanders increasingly reluctant to accept officers transferred from foot units. Some zealots even advocated establishing the horse artillery as a separate arm with its own promotion list. Horse artillery, they declared, had nothing more in common with foot artillery than guns and firing theories.[7]

The leader of the separatists during this period was Colonel Ernst Monhaupt, an opinionated officer with a sharp tongue and quick temper who was also the best horse artilleryman in Prussia. Commanding the 3rd Brandenburg Artillery Brigade, he was able to test and demonstrate his concepts under the direct observation of the King and the General Staff. The horse artillery, Monhaupt argued, must develop as an independent entity with its own *esprit de corps*. Dash, boldness, initiative—these were the main requirements of a gunner officer, and to inculcate them it was necessary to eliminate the farrago of useless information with which cadets were burdened. An artillery officer did not have to know how to make gunpowder any more than a hussar had to be able to make steel to use a saber. Whether a horse artilleryman could calculate a shell's trajectory was unimportant. Riding and driving, horses and harness—this was what gunners must master. Guns should be as light and mobile as possible, able to keep pace even with attacking cavalry, able to gallop to point-blank range of an enemy position and so overwhelm it with grape and canister that infantry or cavalry would only have to charge through the ruin made by the guns.[8]

Monhaupt's ideas were often criticized as impractical products of a hyperactive imagination; nevertheless he greatly influenced the development of the Prussian artillery in the 1820s. If he devoted most of his attention to improving his horse artillery, he was too efficient to neglect the foot companies entirely. His brigade marched well, maneuvered well, and was regularly praised in army orders. Other experts, unsympathetic though they might be to Monhaupt's flights of fancy, praised the quality of his horse artillery, describing it as a decisive weapon and occasionally grudgingly approving the suggestion that it should be given separate drill regulations. Prince August, still unwilling to divide his arm by function, even allowed the three horse batteries of each brigade to be combined under a staff officer during the annual maneuvers. But in the process the horse artillery tended to emphasize the adjective in their title at the expense of the noun. Monhaupt's original concept of delivering an overwhelming fire at short range was not without merit when infantry still carried smoothbore muskets, but the inadequate peacetime allowance of practice ammunition prevented its implementation. Increasingly the frustrated cavalrymen of the horse batteries tended to concentrate on rapid, precise maneuvering—dubbed "circus-riding" by the rest of the army. Executing the complicated maneuvers which impressed so many observers required emphasis on mobility and careful individual training, both useful in improving the artillery's status and efficiency. But by the 1830s the "cavalry spirit" had become so dominant that in some batteries, the guns were regarded as useless ballast and any suggestion that artillery should cooperate closely with other arms was treated as an impertinence.[9]

This attitude in turn influenced proposals for material innovation. When a Prussian horse artilleryman of the 1820s and 30s described his ideal gun, he spoke of a design which would combine maximum mobility with minimum effect. Range, weight of shot, number of slugs in a round of canister—these were relatively unimportant if a battery could keep pace with the tactical situation, if it could take position, open fire, and change position before the enemy artillery could find its range. It was an argument which was to be repeated many times under many circumstances in the emerging Age of Technology. The British battle cruisers of the Fisher Era emphasized speed and gun power at the expense of armor protection. The fast, light tanks so popular during the 1930s were produced in response to a doctrine emphasizing the importance of dodging antitank fire and overwhelming a position by numbers. Fighter pilots of all nations initially preferred the biplane's maneuverability to the speed and firepower of the low-wing monoplane. And in 1836 the APK began work on a series of new designs incorporating the horse gunners' demands for mobility. Three years later the prototypes were ready for testing—not only on the firing ranges, but in months of gruelling route marches over terrain from the swamps of East Prussia to the Silesian mountains. It required three more years to convince the War Ministry of the need to re-arm the artillery and to obtain the Finance Ministry's consent for the construction and introduction of the *System c/42* for the entire Prussian artillery.

Ballistically, there was virtually no difference between the new six- and twelve-pounder cannon and seven-pounder howitzers and those they replaced. The APK's major success had been in reducing weights. The six-pounder *c/42*, for example, weighed less than 3,600 pounds. The cumbersome heavy howitzers had been eliminated. Carriages were so designed that men could be mounted on the limbers and caissons without appreciably diminishing the pulling power of a six-horse team.[10] But if the *System c/42* was a major triumph for the advocates of a mobile artillery, even before its adoption critics were suggesting that the Prussian army was on a false course. An artillery which did not understand shooting was worthless, they argued, no matter how brilliantly it maneuvered. Artillery could neither ride nor drive an enemy to death.[11] The Prussian twelve-pounder of the Napoleonic Wars weighed over three tons. It was clumsy and slow-moving. Nevertheless it had proved indispensable against the superior French artillery. Moreover, the moral influence of the big guns was at least as significant as their actual effect; Prussian infantry always seemed to fight better when supported by a battery of twelve-pounders.[12] Some advocates of fire power went so far as to suggest that the six-pounder was too small to be useful under any conditions, and advocated its replacement by a nine-pounder, or even a short twenty-four pounder on a field carriage. Artillery taking the field with this weight of metal would have little need to worry about the mobility of its guns. The only time they might have to move quickly was in pursuit of a defeated enemy.[13]

This viewpoint had not influenced the design of the *System c/42*; nevertheless it could not be dismissed or ignored. Nor could the lines of demarcation between mobility and firepower be drawn as sharply as their respective advocates might wish. In the minds of an increasing number of designers, the real challenge lay in developing a gun firing a heavy round at long ranges, yet able to move nearly as rapidly as the existing light artillery.[14] And here metallurgy must join forces with ballistics. While much could be done to lighten carriages, the weight of an artillery piece essentially depended on the metal used in its manufacture. During the first quarter of the nineteenth century bronze had won general recognition as the best gun metal in existence. It was lighter and more durable than the cast iron it replaced. It was less likely to burst when overheated—an important factor in field operations. But bronze was also expensive. A state with an artillery park of bronze cannon had a relatively large amount of capital lying idle in the form of gun barrels. With military budgets curtailed everywhere in Europe after 1815, economy-minded generals and ministers began to investigate the possibility of reintroducing cast iron guns to the field artillery. Improved casting processes, it was argued, had eliminated much of the danger from bursting barrels, and the economic advantages of cheaper iron cannon would outweigh their technical deficiencies.

The Prussian artillery was not enthusiastic. As late as 1810 it had been unable to develop useful cast iron guns; both the c/16 and c/42 systems used bronze exclusively for the field artillery. Large numbers of iron six- and twelve-pounders, purchased, captured, or cast during the War of Liberation, were already stored in arsenals and fortresses. The weight of cast iron field guns, moreover, was a powerful argument against their adoption for officers concerned with improving the artillery's mobility.[15] Nevertheless, the combination of concern for improved firepower and interest in new metals prepared the artillery, and the army generally, for its first continuing exposure to the nineteenth-century entrepreneur.

2

Whether as symbol of an era, warning for the future, or source of evidence for preconceptions, the House of Krupp exercises an irresistible fascination for interpreters of the German condition and the German catastrophe. Though many merchants and manufacturers helped introduce the Prussian army to the Industrial Revolution, selecting the Krupps to illustrate the process is useful for a variety of reasons, not least because so many popular accounts agree that ". . . the way of this family and its industrial empire mirrors . . . the changing currents which have dominated the political nature of their country and the national aspirations of their society . . . the lifelines of Germany and of Krupp seem to run in parallel directions."[16]

Essentially only two books, though with many titles, have been written about this parallel. One presents the Krupp dynasty as merchants of death, conscious and willing partners in the fomentation of two world wars, or at best men interested only in their firm and its growth, indifferent to the wider implications of their work.[17] A contrasting—and smaller—school of thought describes patriotic German businessmen and industrialists, who cared for their workers, served their country, turned an honest profit, and suffered undeservedly for the crime of being on the losing side.[18] The rise of the House of Krupp has been explained in terms of parlor psychology, economic determinism, and influence peddling. Similarly, Alfred Krupp himself, founder of the family fortune, Europe's first cannon king, appears to his biographers as a stern, if somewhat eccentric, *Familienvater*, an unprincipled schemer, and a borderline psychotic.

If scholars have done little or nothing to modify these polarized interpretations, this is explainable by the nature of the material at their disposal. The firm has consistently refused to make its archives available for research. Particularly for the early years of the firm, the best sources remain the collections of correspondence and memoranda edited in the 1920s by Wilhelm Berdrow, the Arthur Schlesinger of the House of Krupp. These must be used with caution. Nevertheless, they offer useful insights into the nature of the relationship of soldiers and businessmen during the first half of the century—particularly when fitted into a military-technical rather than a social or economic context.

The name of Krupp appears for the first time in the municipal registers of the Free City of Essen in 1587. For over two hundred years the family followed a pattern common in German "home towns," rising and declining with successive generations, its sons making marks as merchants, officeholders, and moneylenders, or filing for bankruptcy as their interests and talents dictated. Its first contact with the steel business began with the Napoleonic Wars. For centuries swordsmiths and cutlers had converted wrought iron to steel by a process known as cementation: packing the iron in charcoal and heating it at around a thousand degrees. This blister steel, taking its name from the blistering of its surface during the heating process, was uneven in quality and uncertain in composition. Its successful production depended on lore and instinct as much as scientific method. Then in the 1740s an Englishman, Benjamin Huntsman, developed a process of melting blister steel in special crucibles, able to withstand great heat for long periods of time. The heat freed the molten metal from many of the impurities which resisted older methods of purification, while distributing carbon much more evenly than was possible in the blister process and its modifications. The result, called crucible steel or cast steel, was harder and more durable than anything in Europe. No continental manufacturers were able to imitate it by the end of the eighteenth century. After a series of expensive and embarrassing fiascoes, European smiths and craftsmen found it preferable to import tool steel and machine parts from England, even at a cost of £700 per ton, until the British blockade and Napoleon's continental system ended the trade and threw Europe on its own resources.[19]

Cut off from their primary sources of supply, industrialists and inventors everywhere in the Ruhr valley began once more to attempt the production of crucible steel, this time encouraged by Napoleon's offer of four thousand francs to anyone who could duplicate British methods. Friedrich Krupp, the current head of the house and a born gambler, was unable to resist the challenge. On September 20, 1811, he founded Fried. Krupp of Essen, a factory "for the manufacture of English cast steel and all articles made thereof." For the next five years the foundry devoured capital at an alarming rate, producing nothing but high-carbon blister steel by the time Napoleon's overthrow brought the return of British steel salesmen and their high-quality product.[20]

Friedrich Krupp died in 1826 without making good his boasts of having discovered the secret of cast steel. His fourteen-year-old heir, Alfred, found himself in a vicious circle. The new factories, the artisans and smiths of the Ruhr, purchased steel in small quantities at best. To improve his product he needed the kind of capital associated with large, steady orders—orders which in turn eluded him because of the uncertain quality of his product in comparison with its competitors. Inevitably Krupp turned to the Prussian government. Its requirements for steel were growing annually; the Berlin mint alone could absorb Krupp's entire annual output. A Prussian contract might also encourage orders from some of the smaller states as well. But government funds in the 1820s were being used to subsidize roads and canals. Industries which did receive assistance were old Prussian firms rather than concerns in the exposed and undependable Rhineland. English cast steel was dependable and cheap; government agencies saw no reason to break precedent and risk increased costs by placing orders with a small factory managed by an importunate adolescent.[21]

Not until 1830 was Krupp able to boast of success in producing "a completely weldable crucible steel."[22] If the finished product remained inferior to the best English steel, it was nevertheless marketable, and Krupp had developed a new method of using it. Rolling, the process of pressing hot metal into sheets, bars, or shapes by passing it through smooth or appropriately-grooved metal rollers turning in opposite directions had been a common technique in English mills for almost fifty years.[23] The resulting slabs and bars were sold all over the continent, in quantities and at prices Krupp had no chance of meeting. Nor had he been able to market his machine tools and dies against English competition. But the small quantities of high-quality cast steel his foundry was beginning to produce could serve another purpose. It could be made into small-sized precisely-manufactured rolls for sale to goldsmiths, watchmakers, and similar individuals who might be convinced that rolling their own stock would be cheaper in the long run than purchasing finished or semifinished English wares.

154

In the next decade the firm of Krupp of Essen moved slowly towards solvency. But the improvement was relative. Krupp steel was still inferior to its English competitors; Krupp's orders were those for which English firms did not seriously compete. And in the 1840s Krupp was the victim of economic growth. If this decade has been described as a time of "take-off" in Germany's economy, it was also a time of consolidation. Firms based on small-scale machine production were either expanding or being forced out of business, and Alfred Krupp was caught in the middle once more.[24] The goldsmiths and silversmiths, the watchmakers and manufacturers, who had purchased his small rolls were either closing their doors or producing goods on a scale requiring larger rolls than Krupp had previously been able to supply. In an effort to keep pace with the times Alfred expanded the scale of his operations, concentrating on developing complete rolling mills instead of individual rolls. This meant direct competition with British firms possessing years of experience and increasingly concerned with preserving their continental markets. Again Krupp began touring Europe's industrial and political centers, obtaining a few large orders, but more often finding himself underbid by English salesmen. In 1840 he landed the biggest contract of his career when the Vienna mint agreed to purchase a rolling mill for 5,000 florins, but the Austrian officials argued that the mill did not perform to specifications and refused payment. For almost two years the frantic Krupp attempted to obtain redress from Metternich's bureaucrats, finally accepting a token settlement which left the firm where it had been fifteen years earlier: on the edge of bankruptcy.

Alfred's routine request for aid from the Prussian government was just as routinely denied. He kept his doors open by taking in a distant cousin as a silent partner, and by concentrating once more on small-scale precision production. Krupp's spoon and fork rollers sold well on the continent and were good enough to patent in Great Britain. And cast steel could be used for other objects as well. The Berlin industrial exhibition of 1844 featured a large collection of Krupp steel products. One display, a set of chimes designed by Alfred's brother, Fritz, won for the firm a gold medal. Another remained virtually unnoticed—two musket barrels.

3

Krupp described his motives for dabbling in the arms trade in different ways on different occasions, sometimes speaking of instinct, sometimes of foresight, and sometimes of chance. But there is nothing surprising in the the head of a struggling firm desperate to sell steel to any buyer for any purpose considering the possibility of obtaining customers in a field where high-quality metal is vitally important. Moreover, the technical problems involved seem to have interested Alfred, becoming a kind of hobby which absorbed much of whatever spare time he had between 1836 and 1843. When existing machinery proved unable to bore out steel blocks satisfactorily, Krupp used his hard-won abilities as a blacksmith to produce hollow-forged musket barrels tougher and more durable than anything ever seen in Europe. Alfred sent samples to France, to England, to Prussia. He gave them to friends and visitors, to army officers of his acquaintance, even to other manufacturers. In itself a cast steel musket was like a solid-gold toothpick—interesting, but irrelevant. The metal was expensive. The hollow-forging process, by which Krupp hoped to gain an edge over possible competitors, was difficult to duplicate. The quality of the barrels far exceeded the ballistic demands of a smoothbore military musket. But despite his near-disaster in Vienna, Krupp was convinced that to survive his firm needed large orders. If he could sell cast steel rollers to governments, there was no reason why he could not try selling cast steel weapons to armies. And if initially steel muskets might be regarded as a novelty, so much the better. At least they would not be ignored.[25]

In July, 1843, Alfred Krupp embarked on another of his periodic sales expeditions through the Rhineland, hoping to market his new machine tools. One of his points of call was the royal Prussian armory at Saarn, near Düsseldorf. It was neither a casual nor an accidental choice. Established in 1817 as a source of small arms for Prussia's western provinces, staffed by a succession of more or less bored junior officers with varying degrees of technical competence, the Saarn arsenal had in recent years begun to take an increased interest in weapons technology. Its workshops were manufacturing the percussion muskets which the War Ministry had adopted in 1839. Its master gunsmiths talked of a revolutionary new weapon whose details were still kept a closely-guarded secret—a breechloading rifle developed by a locksmith named Dreyse. Even more important for Alfred's purposes, since his father's day the firm of Krupp had occasionally done business with the Saarn arsenal. Alfred had not been in Saarn for years, but he took advantage of the contact by requesting permission to send the armory a few of his cast steel musket barrels for testing.

The musket barrels were an entering wedge. Krupp himself did not believe the state would make small arms of steel; his expressed intention was that his sample barrels be regarded as a small-scale standard for judging the worth of cast steel cannon.[26] To the officers at Saarn the idea of constructing two-ton artillery pieces from a metal so expensive and difficult to produce that the arsenal purchased it by the pound appeared an interesting technical speculation—the sort of problem useful for banishing boredom during the long months of assignment to an unimportant arsenal in a provincial backwater. But there was no particular hurry about it. As soon as he returned to Essen, Krupp despatched two of his best creations to Saarn, then waited. The barrels first had to be made into muskets, then tested. Prussian thoroughness combined with lethargy to spin out the process over months.

In the meantime Alfred found another opening. The French War Ministry imported and tested two of his barrels, with results which amazed the experts. Krupp's work received the highest praise—and the French army continued to put its faith in iron. Cast steel was still too expensive for mass production weapons. If Krupp's Parisian adventure produced no orders, it did leave him with a sheaf of glowing adjectives to add to those contained in the reports from Saarn and the artillery workshop at Deutz, where Alfred also had acquaintances willing to test his invention. On March 1, 1844, Krupp wrote to the Prussian War Ministry announcing his success in making steel which was stronger, purer, and harder than any other metal, able to replace bronze cannon and wrought iron musket barrels. He forwarded two barrels which had been tested in government arsenals, and declared his willingness to supply any material and make any test the government might wish. Three weeks later he was officially informed that "the present method of manufacturing

157

[musket barrels] and the nature of the barrels so produced, at a cost not inconsiderably less, meets all reasonable requirements and leaves hardly anything to be desired."[27]

The War Ministry's reply has often been cited—not least by Krupp himself—as merely another example of the shortsightedness and technical ignorance often attributed to the nineteenth-century military mind.[28] In fact it was a clear and accurate evaluation of the situation. It was difficult to overstrain the barrel of a muzzle-loading smoothbore musket. Even the rapid-firing needle gun, which had been in production since 1842, performed quite satisfactorily under the most rigorous tests with a wrought iron barrel. The quality of Krupp's work was not at issue—only the use he had made of it. The second half of the War Ministry's reply, often overlooked, suggested that the production of cast steel cannon "must be the subject of further calculation," and promised to communicate with Krupp on the subject. At first glance this statement appears inconsistent. Proportionally a smoothbore cannon and a smoothbore musket were subjected to approximately the same stresses. Why should a metal deemed too expensive in one case be regarded as potentially useful in the other? The answer lay in the continued high price of bronze, combined with the continued inability of Prussian designers to develop iron guns which did not burst when overheated. Bronze might still be less expensive than steel, but the difference was far less than that between steel and iron. The cost of a bronze cannon barrel was already high enough to make its replacement by a better, though slightly costlier metal a possibility worth studying.[29]

To Alfred Krupp, however, the War Ministry's reply was another in a long list of polite refusals. His first reaction was to tear the letter to shreds. Three decades later the bitter memory remained, leading him to misquote the War Ministry as having proclaimed the smoothbore flintlocks of the Prussian army as "requiring no improvement."[30] His attitude was but little changed when the *Allgemeine Kriegsdepartement* sent him sketches and specifications for a cast iron six-pounder and requested him to use them as a model for casting a steel barrel— with the proviso that it be no lighter than its iron counterpart. Militarily the requirement was sensible. A light barrel meant excessive recoil when the gun fired, with corresponding difficulties bringing it back into position. Metallurgically, to Krupp at least, it was absurd. The main advantage of steel was its greater endurance. A cast steel gun weighing as much as an iron one would be too strong for any charge which could conceivably be fired from it. It would be so expensive that no army would be likely to pay for it. Finally, the forging of such a mammoth piece of metal, weighing over a ton, was beyond the capacity of his foundry. A three-pounder, he suggested, would be just as useful for testing purposes, and he could supply one within a few weeks.

The War Ministry did not in fact take delivery of its first cast steel Krupp gun until September, 1847. This three-year gap between promise and performance was only partly a result of technical difficulties. By this time Krupp's experience with assorted bureaucracies had taught him the vast gulf between expressed interest and signed contracts. Moreover, he had become deeply involved in the possibility of selling cast steel to the Prussian army in another form, one as far removed as possible from his image as Europe's cannon king.

In the first half of the nineteenth century Prussia, like most continental states, included in its army a number of cuirassier regiments. Big men mounted on big horses, they constituted a reserve force, thrown into battle at the decisive moment to settle the issue by shock action. Their kinship to the medieval knight went even further, however, and it was this which attracted the notice of Alfred Krupp. Prussia's cuirassiers wore metal breastplates. The idea was by no means anachonistic. A well-made breastplate could turn sword cuts, bayonet thrusts, even pistol and musket balls fired at anything but point-blank range. But they were heavy. The standard Prussian breastplate weighed almost twenty-five pounds. The Elberfeld firm of Wilhelm Jäger, which manufactured most of them, purchased some steel plates from Krupp in order to test their suitability for cuirasses. Alfred then approached the Prussian government directly with an offer of cuirasses weighing half as much as existing models, yet bullet-proof at twice the range. Prospects for a large and profitable order seemed excellent—until the War Ministry's purchasing department declared a requirement for ready-to-wear cuirasses instead of the semifinished steel plates which were all Krupp was able to deliver on a large scale. At the same time

Krupp's competitor took full advantage of his contacts in the offices and regiments to demonstrate the ability of his firm to meet all demands for cast steel cuirasses. Krupp abandoned the unequal contest, more than ever convinced that selling weapons to armies required the same kind of careful promotion and self-advertising as selling spoon rolls to cutlery manufacturers.

By the end of the cuirass controversy, Alfred Krupp's military acquaintances ranged from Carl von Reyher, a future Chief of Staff, to "a few majors and captains . . . who have a voice in affairs."[31] Soldiers were learning about the properties and potential of cast steel. They were beginning to exchange ideas with Krupp on the best way to produce the test gun which had been discussed for so long. Yet by his own account, at least, Alfred felt himself under no pressure to proceed with the casting. He had had enough experience both of the problems of making large-scale castings and the slowness of the Prussian military bureaucracy to waste no more time than necessary in the corridors and offices of Berlin. Not until the winter of 1846 did he again broach the subject of a steel cannon to the War Ministry. His proposal had changed but little since 1844: he offered a thin-walled cast steel three-pounder, to be cast at government expense and tested to destruction. This time, however, the War Department agreed virtually by return mail. This unheard-of rapidity for a government agency has led Krupp's official biographer to suggest that the soldiers had merely been awaiting Alfred's pleasure. Subsequent events would seem to put it in the category of bureaucratic accident.

Nor did Alfred himself give particularly high priority to the cannon. Casting did not begin until July 1847. The barrel was ready for shipment by September, but Krupp hesitated, fearing the Prussian military authorites would postpone taking action of any sort. With the reassurances of the War Ministry sounding in his ears, Alfred finally consigned his problem child to Berlin. A month later, however, he followed it with a series of importunate letters, describing in detail his efforts to utilize cast steel in arms construction, urging that his cannon be tested as rapidly and thoroughly as possible, and concluding, as usual with "my most obedient request for your gracious notice and favor for my zealously offered services."[32]

Chapter IX

Cast Steel Rifles

The learned gentlemen of the *Artillerie-Prüfungs-Kommission* were systematic rather than creative. They had seen and tested both blueprints and actual barrels and carriages by the dozen over the preceding three decades. Krupp's three-pounder lay for months in a Spandau arsenal, not forgotten, but given no special priority. It had not even been mounted on a carriage for testing when the March Revolution broke over Berlin and gave everyone something else to think about. Armies marched and countermarched; thrones wavered, men died in battle, in prison, or by firing squad. There was no time to spare for a few hundred pounds of steel. At the same time Krupp's interest was diverted, not so much by the revolution, which seems to have affected him only insofar as it threatened his plant or his customers, but by the prospect of an even better outlet for his product. The German railway network was expanding in all respects during the late 1840s. Not only were there more miles of track; the volume of traffic was heavier than ever before, with a corresponding increase in the demands made on rolling stock. Loads were heavier; trains moved faster; and the wrought iron wheels, springs, and axles of the cars were proving unequal to the new strains. For Krupp it was an article of faith that steel—his steel—could supply the deficiencies. His firm had come well through the revolution. Major orders for spoon-rolling mills from Russia and Britain, closer contact with banking houses newly

interested in making loans to promising firms, gave him the
capital he needed. The factory began to produce tires, springs,
and axles of high-grade steel. More significantly, the railroad
companies began to try them in hundreds, then in thousands.
Krupp remained an outsider among German industrialists. His
high-handed methods, his jealousy, his suspiciousness, were
subjects of humor only to those not directly affected by them;
nevertheless, he found himself in a classic seller's position. His
product was good; it met an increasing demand; and—for once
—he could deliver. During the revolution, Krupp had discharged
almost half his labor force. By 1849, so many orders were on file
in Essen that the works employed over 300 men. Eight years later,
four times as many employees responded to the early morning
bell and answered to the name of *Kruppianer*. If Krupp of Essen
is best known as a producer of armaments, it is no accident that
the firm's trademark, first adopted in this period, represents three
interlocking cast steel railway tires—the foundation of the firms
initial prosperity.

But Alfred's experiences with private contracts had made him
suspicious of their durability. They must be supplemented, he
reasoned, by sales to governments. Even a relatively small order
by the standards of a major state would probably far overshadow
the requirements of any number of individual firms. And German
ministries tended to remain loyal to firms with which they had
once dealt. In the fall of 1848 Alfred sought to goad the *Allgemeine Kriegsdepartement* into action by spitefully suggesting
that there was no need for them to hurry in testing his cannon;
his firm was at present too busy to accept orders which promised
no profit. The authorities took him at his word. Not until June 2,
1849, did the *Artillerie-Prüfungs-Kommission* seek to determine
the worth of Krupp's three-pounder. The results, as Krupp had
predicted, astonished the entire commission. In order to demonstrate how much stress a cannon could withstand, a major part
of any initial test involved the destruction of the barrel, after the
gun had demonstrated its durability. The cast steel, however,
refused to burst even when loaded almost to the muzzle with
black powder. Finally the officer in charge buried the gun in a
ditch, ordered everyone into a bombproof shelter, and fired the
charge with a time fuse. The cannon still held. Prince Kraft zu
Hohenloe-Ingelfingen, who in the next quarter-century was to

make a career as Prussia's most distinguished artilleryman, was one of the observers who discussed what to do next. Most of the officers were of the opinion that the barrel was indestructible, but it was decided to fire a last shot in order to fulfill the previously-determined schedule. The committee reentered the shelter, heard the noise of an explosion, and emerged to find no sign of the cannon. Suddenly a rain of fragments descended on the surprised officers. The barrel had not burst; it had been blown to pieces.[1]

Hohenloe recounted and embroidered the story many times in his long career. But an official report was not necessary for the Prussian government to admit that cast steel was superior in strength and durability to any material previously tested. It was also expensive. The artillery was sufficiently impressed by the durability of Krupp's railway axles to consider using steel axles for its gun carriages. But when Krupp offered the War Department a cast steel six-pounder for testing, he was kindly warned that orders for cannon might well depend on lower prices —a shrewd business measure generating a certain nostalgia in this era of cost overruns.[2]

Krupp's reaction was baffled rage tempered by sarcastic jibes at bureaucrats, generals and technicians. His acid criticisms, however, do not obscure the fact that the APK's response to the cast steel barrel was an accurate reflection of military and financial realities. Military budgets had been cut to the bone throughout Germany in the age of the Holy Alliance. The age of mass production was still in the future. The problems of introducing new weapons systems of any kind closely paralleled those of a modern state. The cost relative to available funds was so high, the time needed to complete the innovation so long, that there was no margin for error in making the initial decision. Breechloading rifles, cast steel cannon, or improved cuirasses—to be adopted, they must demonstrate beyond doubt that they represented more than a marginal improvement over their predecessors. They must also be as technically perfected as possible. The result of this attitude was an arms race in reverse. Neither the German states nor the continental powers which influenced their military thinking were particularly anxious to accept the risks of innovation. The advantages of being first were outweighed by the desire to have the best.

The Prussian artillery, moreover, was generally well satisfied with its bronze smoothbores. The campaigns and skirmishes of 1849-49 had shown the barrels and carriages of the *System c/42* to be sturdy and mobile, with no tendency to explode or collapse under field conditions. It was not the artillery's material which had provoked criticism during the revolution and its aftermath. It was its tactics, training, and command.

By the 1840s the ethos of the Prussian artillery reflected a unique combination of middle-class comfort, professional competence, and a deep, if limited, sense of duty. The officer corps included a disproportionate number of bourgeoisie. Even the Guard Artillery had thirty commoners to balance its fifty aristocrats. By and large the corps had made peace with slow promotion. Second lieutenants of twenty-five years' service were not unknown. Professional ambition was condemned as pushiness; an officer with time at the war academy was an object of suspicion to seniors and contemporaries alike. But there were compensations. The artillery carefully preserved its status as a learned arm. Every gun limber contained a small library of works on geography, history, and higher mathematics. Junior officers were solemnly warned not to betray the secrets of the gunners' guild. In conversation with their social superiors of the infantry and cavalry they cultivated an air of mystery, of initiation into technical complexities beyond the ken of ordinary mortals. The natural result was to give the artillery a collective image of pedantic stuffiness, which might be better than open contempt, but nevertheless was no substitute for professional respect.

An even more serious problem was posed by a combination of regulations and convention which made every artillery officer personally responsible for the fate of his guns, even if he lost or mishandled them by responding to orders. One result of this regulation was the training of junior artillery officers in evasion and indiscipline. Another was the operational isolation of the artillery from the rest of the army. Line and staff officers who attempted to give orders to gunner subalterns and were answered by formal protests tended to concede the issue rather than face angry generals. They also tended to have as little contact as possible with the artillery. The learned arm went its own way in garrison and on the maneuver grounds.[3]

The combination of slow promotion, guild spirit, and tactical independence fostered an officer corps of ill-tempered eccentrics, competent enough in the details of service, but whose skills seldom extended beyond handling a battery in the field. And the development of even this ability was handicapped by an increasing emphasis on precision drill, smart appearance, and the proper loading of wagons and limbers. Marksmanship was virtually ignored. Batteries fired their annual allowance of ammunition at previously measured ranges. At the end of the year, the results were posted without comment. If a unit failed to reach the army's average, it shot badly. That was that. No recognition was given to above-average performances, no criticism to substandard ones.[4]

2

With such preparation, it is hardly surprising that the Prussian artillery's record in Baden and Schleswig-Holstein was less than distinguished. Deployed in isolated batteries and single guns, it could neither shoot nor move effectively. Particularly in Baden, where the insurgents were seldom obliging enough to offer massed targets, the guns were often little more than a noisy burden. The artillery also suffered from the improved range of infantry weapons. The rifles developed during the 1840s were effective at three times the range of their smoothbored predecessors, and they were carried by a fair number of insurgent volunteers. On more than one occasion Prussian batteries were forced to change positions under the fire of a few riflemen—hardly a way to enchance the arm's reputation.

The Prussian artillery received a salutary shock. A future chairman of the APK, August Encke, summarized the obvious lessons of the revolution by declaring that the artillery must learn to move quickly and precisely. It must improve its coordination with other arms. Finally its senior officers must learn to maneuver formations larger than a battery.[5] The War Ministry cooperated by increasing the peace establishment of horses. During the summer and fall of 1849 the foot companies were given enough teams to move four guns at once. In the words of one regimental historian, seldom had an order been received with such rejoicing. The foot gunners' morale soared; at a stroke they felt themselves raised to equality with the horse artillery. But their optimism faded during the mobilization of 1850. Most of the new horses were still unbroken; many of their drivers were reservists who had not been on a horse since their discharge. When the Guard Artillery attempted to move its guns from Magdeburg to Berlin, for example, the resulting harness galls, saddle sores, and broken axles were incontrovertible proof of the need for improved training of men and animals alike.[6] They were also an indisputable embarrassment to artillerymen who had argued for decades that all they really needed were more horses.

Horses were only a beginning. In 1851 the artillery brigades of each army corps were reorganized as regiments, each including a horse battalion of three six-pounder batteries, two foot battalions with a total of four six-pounder, three twelve-pounder, and one howitzer batteries, and a fortress battalion. In order to increase efficiency it was decided to stop rotating the assignments of the foot companies. In future every company would perform the same mission in peace and war. Finally, the Prussian artillery began taking a second look at its weapons. Experience in Baden and Schleswig had shown that the artillery's most dangerous foes were skirmishers armed with modern rifles. But what was the most effective way of dealing with the problem? An obvious method of restoring the artillery's traditional mastery of the battlefield at long ranges would be to rifle *its* barrels. As early as 1817 General Rühle von Lilienstern had discussed with the APK the possibility of introducing breechloading rifled cannon. Initially technique did not follow theory. A cannon tested in Hanover in 1825 proved useless, as did a similar design offered to the APK two years later. A bronze breechloading rifle tested in 1836 was rejected on technical and financial grounds: its breech leaked gas and its ammunition was too expensive. However, in the same decade, Baron Wahrendorff, of the Swedish artillery, and a Piedmontese officer, Giovanni Cavalli, working independently, developed model breechloaders which were sufficiently advanced to attract widespread interest. As early as 1841 the Prussian War Ministry sent a purchasing agent to the Swedish ironworks at Åker to order three smoothbore breechloading cannon. Tested between 1843 and 1846, they were described as durable and easy to serve. But the APK suggested that because of their great weight, these guns were suitable only for siege trains and fortresses—particularly since Wahrendorff's breeches still leaked gas. For five years the APK abandoned its own fruitless researches to study and evaluate reports from foreign armies. By 1851 the verdict was apparently final. If the technical problems involved in designing a gas-tight breech were not entirely insoluble, a design suitable for military purposes remained to be developed.[7]

Should rifles be desirable, then, the obvious solution was to develop muzzle-loading designs. But were rifled cannon the best response to open-order tactics and rifle-carrying skirmishers? An increasing number of officers with battle experience suggested that the experimental muzzle-loading rifles under test in Europe's arsenals might be accurate enough, but their rate of fire was too slow to cope with modern infantry tactics. Their muzzle velocity, moreover, was so high that it unacceptably reduced the blast effect of individual rounds. Using them against skirmishers was like shooting pigeons with a big game rifle. What was needed to blow away skirmish lines were guns capable of firing shell, shrapnel, and canister horizontally at medium and short ranges. Since each round must have the greatest possible blast effect, the gun should be of fairly large caliber, probably a twelve-pounder. On the other hand, accuracy at long range was not particularly important. Therefore the muzzle velocity of these cannon could safely be reduced. Their barrels could be made shorter and lighter, thus enhancing mobility. Such a gun, it was argued, would be a true *Einheitskanone,* able to replace at least the howitzers and six-pounders presently assigned to the field artillery, and perhaps some of the heavy twelve-pounders as well.[8]

The idea was not original. For several years the Prussian artillery had been attempting to give its howitzers a more effective shell and improve the accuracy of their high-angle fire. It was also executing desultory research on a short twelve-pounder which was supposed to fire primarily shell and shrapnel and be nearly as mobile as the existing six-pounder. There had been no reason to expedite the program before 1849. No one seriously proposed replacing the new and expensive c/42 guns so quickly. But the lessons of the revolution were thrown into even sharper focus when the French army adopted a short bronze twelve-pounder in 1853 and the Saxon artillery began testing a similar design. Clearly the APK would have to act on the question of introducing shell guns to the Prussian army.

The commission's work was handicapped by a sharp difference of opinion between two of the most senior and influential officers in the artillery. In 1854 August Encke was promoted Lieutenant-General and assigned as chairman of the APK. Encke had made a reputation as an energetic, hard-driving soldier. A native of Hamburg, whose first military service had been in the military contingent of that city, he combined a Hanseatic patrician's dislike for aristocrats, especially inefficient ones, with a sharp tongue and a quick pen to sign transfers. Within months he had revitalized the commission and brought it to support his own enthusiastic advocacy of rifled cannon. On the other hand the Inspector-General of the artillery, General von Hahn, was convinced that Prussia needed shell-firing smoothbores. Hahn's historical image is that of a reactionary, bitterly hostile to rifled cannon.[9] Instead he seems to have combined an alternate view of desirable innovations with a reluctance to see effort, funds, and talent divided between two programs. As early as 1854 he urged the APK to resume the research abandoned a decade earlier, and in 1855, tests began on shell-firing cannon in competition with c/42 six- and twelve-pounders. At the same time, however, the APK continued evaluating designs and materials for rifled barrels.

3

Alfred Krupp had grown tired of attempting to convince the army directly of the value of cast steel. Twenty years' experience had made him one of Europe's master salesmen and promoters. He completed his steel six-pounder at his own expense, wrote in vain to the Prussian government requesting a patent on it, then shipped it to the London Exhibition of 1851. Displayed in a military tent, surrounded by Krupp's cast steel cuirasses, mounted on a base of polished ashwood, the cannon proved to be one of the exhibition's more sensational displays, attracting the attention of most of the London newspapers. But the real pride of the House of Krupp was a steel ingot weighing over two tons, nearly twice as much as its largest competitor. Queen Victoria herself was impressed; Alfred was awarded a medal and column after column of free publicity in the newspapers and journals of western Europe.

It was in part this publicity which encouraged Alfred to approach the Prussian government once more in the matter of his cannon. There were sound business reasons for his decision. The use of Krupp steel on railway cars was just beginning; as yet there was no guarantee that the railroads would provide the kind of market necessary to keep the expanding plant operating at capacity. The Olmütz crisis, with its accompanying demonstrations of Prussian military weaknesses, might well have softened the views of the War Ministry towards expensive technical innovations. Finally, Alfred's correspondence sounds unmistakable chords of pleasure at the thought of King Frederick William IV not only accepting a cannon, but displaying it for a month in the royal palace at Potsdam. It was the kind of advertising Krupp had learned to appreciate and use to best advantage. Czar Nicholas of Russia, who saw the cannon during his state visit in the summer of 1852, appears to have been more impressed by it than by the Prussian needle gun. His enthusiasm did not extend to placing orders; but another man, a Prussian prince with bitter memories of Olmütz fresh in his memory, also got his first look at Krupp's cast steel cannon. Prince William of Prussia was not struck by any intuitive flashes. Apart from any other considerations, his close connections with the British court had probably made him aware of Krupp's successes at the London Exposition, and the story of the indestructible cannon had spread far beyond the limits of the APK. Himself neither a designer nor a tinkerer, William was nevertheless interested in military weaponry. He had been among the leading advocates of breechloading rifles for the infantry; Krupp's gleaming cast steel cannon inspired the Prince at least to see the factory which produced it. In July, 1853, Prince William of Prussia became one of the few authorized visitors to the Krupp works in decades. He expressed his satisfaction by awarding Alfred the Order of the Red Eagle Fourth Class. It was the only order Krupp was to receive from the Hohenzollerns for several years—but it was the first link in a chain which would bind the two dynasties for over a half century.

The London Exhibition established a fashion for similar trade fairs and industrial exhibitions everywhere on the continent. Krupp ingots and Krupp machine tools became familiar and prize-winning sights outside of Essen; Krupp springs and tires were rapidly ousting their competitors on Europe's railways. But Alfred refused to abandon hope of making his fortune in artillery. He presented a cannon to the Russian army for testing, which survived over four thousand rounds without deteriorating. The committee was so impressed that it ordered the cannon preserved as a museum piece. Krupp sought orders among the states of the German Confederation. The Duke of Brunswick was ready to purchase a dozen cast steel cannon until the trunnion on the test piece broke. Another cannon sent to Hanover brought nothing but an unfulfilled guarantee to pay Krupp a thousand thalers. Württemberg was interested, but not interested enough to sign contracts. Krupp's first sale came only when the Khedive of Egypt ordered a handful of guns.

Yet behind a surface of empty promises, fruitless negotiations and burst barrels, Krupp's prospects were improving. In Germany, and particularly in Prussia, the suitability of steel as a material for field guns was becoming a major topic of discussion in military and ministerial circles. Artillerymen were reluctant to risk their reputations by relying on a metal never really tested under field conditions. Cast steel was still expensive, particularly in view of the fact that all German states possessed large parks of bronze guns which might perhaps be successfully updated by rifling the barrels. Moreover, the introduction of steel cannon would make the armies dependent for all practical purposes on the efficiency and good will of private entrepreneurs and industrialists. Casting steel was still almost as much art as science. No one seriously suggested that government arsenals, skilled though they might be at working with bronze and iron, could match the expertise of men like Alfred Krupp at anything but prohibitive costs in time and money.[10]

These and similar objections, however, were rapidly giving way before the results of the testing grounds. More and more books and articles suggested that bronze was no longer the best material for casting modern cannon—particularly rifles, which required heavy powder charges to reach their maximum ranges. Since the days of Wahrendorff and Cavalli it had been plain that bronze was not sturdy enough for a reliable breechloader. In particular, bronze breeches were too vulnerable to powder gases. After a few hundred rounds such cannon would be more dangerous to their crews than the enemy. Forcing powder and shot into a muzzle-loading rifle might damage the rifling if the barrel were bronze. Moreover, the capacity of bronze rifling to resist corrosion remained open to question. An increasing number of experts saw cast steel rifles as the only answer.[11] Wilhelm Rüstow suggested steel might replace bronze entirely in European artillery parks.[12] Even technical conservatives who felt there was "no particular want . . . for steel to constitute the entire body of the gun" debated the possibility of using it for those parts subjected to the greatest strain.[13] And in 1855 the APK officially concluded that bronze, while it might be an ideal metal for smoothbores, did indeed erode too rapidly to be useful for a rifle. Only with cast steel was it possible to produce a rifled barrel light enough for field operations and durable enough for years of service.

Encke wasted no time. He stretched his budget, ordered two six-pounder barrels from the firm of Alfred Krupp, rifled them in the Spandau arsenal, and began test firing. But Encke was almost as skillful a courtier as he was an artilleryman. Instead of challenging Hahn directly, he began testing the rifles as *fortress* artillery. Moreover, realizing the importance of royal support for such a drastic and expensive innovation, he began converting the king. Frederick William IV, with his facile enthusiasm for the new and different, was impressed by the test results. If such cannon were introduced, he declared, he would never go to war. The monarch even prepared his own design for a rifled barrel: a cast iron core hulled in bronze in an effort to combine the hardness of one and the durability of the other. Given the royal armorer's tendency to change his mind, Encke was not counting on his enduring support. Nevertheless, approached at the right time, he might be a useful ally.

By January, 1857, Encke's cast steel rifles were ready for testing under field conditions. Their performance was such that one member of the APK declared that a six-pounder rifle was necessary for the army no matter what it cost. Even skeptics agreed that a battery of such guns would be a useful addition to the corps artillery. Von Hahn, however, remained unconvinced. When the series of tests was ended, he sent the APK a memorandum declaring research into rifled cannon at an end and specifically forbidding the waste of time and funds on developing a rifled field gun. Encke did not disregard his superior's order. Like a good artilleryman he interpreted it. Working on a shoestring, with material on hand and funds from previous budgets, he continued testing the six-pounder. The original barrel, designed for fortress work, had been over eight feet long and was was far too clumsy for field service. A new design with improved rifling was only six and a half feet long, yet was as accurate as its predecessor. Moreover, it could be adapted to existing smoothbore carriages. By January 1859, the APK submitted a report praising the rifle's range and accuracy. It recommended pursuing research on a larger scale by ordering material for four experimental four-gun batteries.[14]

The APK had also decided that the rifles should be breechloaders. This represented a significant departure from its earlier reservations. It did not involve tactical considerations. Unlike small arms, breechloading cannon could not fire significantly faster than muzzle-loaders under most conditions. Since the entire gun carriage recoiled with every shot, by the time the piece was returned to battery, a reasonably efficient crew could have it reloaded from either end. The APK, however, believed that it had finally succeeded in developing a gas-tight, erosion-resisting breech. Whether pride in its technical skill would have been enough to overcome objections that breechloading cannon were too fragile and complex for field service may have been questionable.[15] But bureaucratic infighting was also involved. By the end of the decade it was plain that the question of rearming the Prussian artillery did not really involve rifles versus old-style smoothbores. It was generally agreed that the traditional artillery material had reached its apogee in the System c/42, and was obsolescent. The choice lay between alternate replacements. Would the cannon of the future be a rifle, or a smoothbore shell gun of the type advocated by von Hahn? The proposed Prussian shell gun, a bronze twelve-pounder, was demonstrating range and accuracy superior to any existing smoothbore gun when firing explosive shells. At last the Prussian artillery seemed to be developing a weapon able to counter modern small arms. Could the rifled cannon keep pace?

No one doubted that they could hit small targets at long ranges. But even their defenders accepted the argument that in order to compete with the new shell guns, the rifles must demonstrate reasonable efficiency firing shell and shrapnel. The fuses for these rounds remained fragile and unreliable. It was possible to argue that loading at the breech was less likely to damage their delicate mechanisms than the process of ramming them down the grooves of a muzzle-loader. And a reduced percentage of duds might in turn make rifles more acceptable to the War Ministry.[16]

4

In 1859, the Prussian field artillery was reorganized. In future each regiment would have three foot battalions, each with one battery of seven-pounder howitzers and two of old-pattern twelve-pounders. Only the three batteries of the horse artillery battalion retained the six-pounder. This armament was generally recognized as temporary, pending final decisions on the shell guns and rifles currently being tested. For Alfred Krupp, however, the government's delay was a bitter disappointment. For years he had given away guns freely yet had received no orders worth mentioning. Sheer stubbornness probably contributed as much to his decision to continue attempting to market his cannon as did the vague hope of lucrative government contracts.[17] Another economic factor increasingly influenced Krupp's relations with the Prussian government: the problem of securing patents on his steel products. Though Minister of Commerce August von der Heydt had little use for the uncouth, abrasive industrialist, his reluctance to grant or extend patents for the firm of Krupp was not motivated by personal dislike alone. Von der Heydt was dedicated to strengthening the economic role of the state, and was understandably reluctant to permit a single private firm to gain virtual monopoly of a new and increasingly important process such as the casting of steel. But this was small comfort to Krupp, who was ready to do virtually anything to secure extensions of the patents on which the prosperity of his firm depended.

In the spring of 1859 Krupp's concern for his patents and

the APK's interest in cast steel cannon increasingly focused on one person: William of Prussia—Prince Regent since November, 1858, following the physical and emotional collapse of his brother. Encke and General Constantin von Voigts-Rhetz of the *Allgemeine Kriegsdepartement* had immediately begun arguing the value of cast steel. Encke climaxed his sales program in May by inviting William to a test shoot on the *Jungfernheide*. Five days after witnessing the range and accuracy of breech-loading six-pounder rifles made from Krupp cast steel, the regent issued a Cabinet Order for the purchase of 300 of them, to be completed as rapidly as possible. The APK's original recommendation had been only a hundred; William made the change in his own handwriting, at the urging of Voights-Rhetz.[18]

In May, Krupp visited Berlin. This time he found all doors open—to the Minister-President, to War Minister Eduard von Bonin, to the Prince Regent himself. And when he left the capital, he was followed by a signed order for 312 steel castings suitable for boring into breechloading six-pounders. The government offered him an opportunity to deliver finished barrels, but Krupp refused. To retool his factory for this, he argued, was too expensive for such a small contract. He began designing a gun workshop. He ordered his engineers to expedite development of another of his projects: a breechblock which he described as twice as efficient as the government-designed competitor.[19] Yet initially Krupp's cannon were a means to an end. In the winter of 1859-60, barrels bored from his cast steel were passing every test with flying colors. Krupp took advantage of the situation to appeal to the Prince Regent, to the new War Minister, Albrecht von Roon, and to any military man with the slightest interest at court, not for larger arms contracts, but for an extension of the patents on his railway tires. He even ordered his Berlin agent to overlook the APK's criticism of the Krupp breechblock. Nothing mattered but the patents. Cannon might be the wave of the future, but present prosperity depended on railway contracts.[20]

Krupp's sycophantic recital of his patriotic and unrewarded service to the state was a farrago of special pleading and outright falsehood, but it impressed William. On March 19, he recommended to von der Heydt not only that Krupp's patent be extended, but that the state railways buy more Krupp steel. Von der Heydt, hoping for a change of mind, delayed his answer for a month, then refused to grant the extension. William overrode him. On April 25, the Ministry of Commerce was instructed to extend Krupp's patent another seven years.[21] This violation of the principle of free trade may have reflected William's growing disenchantment with his ministers. It may have indicated his willingness to take Krupp's assertions at face value.[22] In any case Krupp was sufficiently confident of royal favor to offer the War Ministry the patent for his new breechblock on the condition that for at least fifteen years all cast steel blocks for cannon be purchased from his company. He wished Prussia to benefit from his invention, Krupp declared. Should his offer be accepted, he was willing to refuse contracts from any country which might be Prussia's enemy.[23]

Krupp's offer was a bit too one-sided for the new War Minister. Albrecht von Roon had no control over the Ministry of Commerce, but he was unwilling to commit the state either to a single supplier of steel, or to a breechblock design that was widely criticized in official circles as being something less than gas-tight. He temporized while Krupp developed anxieties about competition and production details and vainly sought air-tight patents for his cannon and his breechblock. William and Roon visited his factory, sampled his hospitality, and refused to commit themselves. By the spring of 1862 Krupp had exhausted his power of persuasion. Then more bad news came from Berlin. During 1862 the Prussian government had requested prototype cast steel blocks and barrels from several other firms, tested them, found them suitable for military purposes, and was planning to issue future contracts on a competitive basis. Krupp's initial reaction was to blame his enemies at court, charge Prussia with collective ingratitude, and threaten to sell cannon to anyone who could pay for them if any other firm received a contract for cast steel. His Berlin representative could only repeat that the government continued to insist on preserving the principle of a free market economy. Even Krupp's supporters in the War Ministry and on the APK considered it irresponsible to abandon the principle of open testing and competitive bidding. Krupp was free to submit any designs of breechblocks and gun carriages that he wished. He was welcome to offer cast steel ingots and gun barrels to the state. He would receive no monopolies.[24]

Chapter X

Weapons and Techniques

If Krupp regarded his cannon as a means to a more profitable end, the Prussian artillery was more concerned with how to use its rifles than who should manufacture them. The Prince Regent's decision to order three hundred cast steel barrels at two hundred thousand thalers meant that they were not going to rust away in storage. On January 31, 1860, a Cabinet Order converted three batteries in each regiment to six-pounder rifles. Six months later the regiments were ordered to reorganize their foot battalions so that each included one battery of rifles, one of old twelve-pounder smoothbores, and one of howitzers. The horse batteries would retain temporarily the six-pounder smoothbores.

This plethora of models reflected the fact that rifled cannon still had numerous critics. It also reflected the shortcomings of the rifles coming into service. To date all efforts to design a workable time fuse for rifled shrapnel had failed. The problem was compounded because rifles had virtually no windage. Their elongated projectiles were indeed designed to fit the grooves of a rifled barrel as closely as possible. Experts suggested in turn that this meant when rifles fired shell or shrapnel the flame from the explosion could not ignite the fuse, which was at the point of the round, as readily as it did in smoothbores, with their spherical ammunition. Few Prussian artillerymen were as yet prepared to accept percussion fuses as a substitute. The canister round of a rifle was also proving less effective than that of a smoothbore, because the spherical rotation imparted by rifling gave the balls an irregular flight pattern. There was no doubt that rifles were accurate at longer ranges than smoothbores. But this was complicated by the small blast effect of a six-pound shell—less than that of a twelve-pounder at short and medium ranges, and less damaging than a ricocheting round shot at ranges over 750 meters. To compensate for this demanded observation and rangetaking more careful, systematic, and accurate than anything ever required of the Prussian artillery. And this, in turn, was likely to limit seriously the mobility of rifled batteries.[1]

The issue of firepower versus mobility was far from resolved within the artillery. In 1857 the General Inspectorate had issued a memorandum on the future of artillery suggesting that improved infantry weapons meant that artillery could no longer operate within 450 meters of the front line. But for those officers who believed in the close integration of artillery with the other arms, it was important to have guns able to change position rapidly, to keep pace with cavalry, to blow away skirmish lines with shrapnel and canister. The horse artillery, still an elite force, was particularly reluctant to abandon its fast-moving six-pounders. Its officers still dreamed of deciding battles by galloping to duelling range and spraying the enemy with canister. The notion of compensating for the limited effects of rifled shell and shrapnel by using rifles in masses had as yet made little headway. The thrust of Prussian military opinion still favored the use of guns a battery at a time.[2]

Advocates of this viewpoint were able to draw support from events in Italy. The close terrain of Lombardy offered little opportunity for the use of massed batteries. On the other hand, before the war the French artillery had been partly equipped with rifles, light muzzle-loading four-pounders. Boldly handled in battery strength, they proved their worth against Austrian smoothbores at Magenta and Solferino. But so, apparently, did the French shell guns. Everyone's prejudices were confirmed. Throughout Germany a flood of articles, essays, and pamphlets addressed themselves to the lessons of the Italian campaign and their implications for the future of artillery. Muzzle-loading rifles on the French pattern were defended as superior to breech-loaders on the grounds of robustness and simplicity of operation. Cast steel was described as too expensive to be practical. It was also evaluated as four times better than bronze, and governments were urged to finance it by selling their old bronze cannon. Rifles were recommended for the entire field artillery, for half of it, for a third of it. The twelve-pounder shell gun was described as the backbone of the artillery and as a useless compromise with no ballistic advantages.[3]

The Prussian government was as confused as the experts. The War Ministry made a general and a specific response by ordering the APK simultaneously to study the experience of foreign armies and to begin evaluating a light rifle on the French model. The project was an interesting combination of technical and political considerations. It called for an eight-centimeter rifle firing a four-pound shell and light enough to accompany cavalry. Most European states had a similar weapon, and a mobile rifle might help provide some common ground between horse artillerymen and the advocates of rifled cannon.

In a further effort to bring some order out of the intellectual chaos resulting from the Italian campaign, on December 27, 1860, Prince William created a special commission to determine the future organization and equipment of the Prussian artillery. It consisted of ten senior officers representing a broad spectrum of experience and opinion. Its recommendations were just as broad. It stated that eight-gun batteries were too large to be controlled by a single commander and favored reducing them to six guns apiece without reducing the existing number of ninety-six guns in a regiment. This meant reorganizing the regiments into sixteen batteries, and initially no two proposals for arming them were alike. The commission agreed that the proportion of rifles should be increased. It supported efforts to design a four-pounder rifle. But given the continued inferiority of rifled shrapnel and canister, the commission also favored retaining smoothbores: shell guns plus a few howitzers for high-angle fire. It settled the armament of the foot batteries by voting on one caliber at a time, finally recommending that the foot artillery of each regiment be organized in three battalions with a total of four batteries of six-pounder and four of four-pounder rifles, three of twelve-pounder shell guns, and one of howitzers. Re-arming the horse artillery was somewhat simpler. Since cavalry support required direct fire, howitzers were useless. Six-pounder rifles were too heavy. The commission was reluctant to issue four-pounders to the horse batteries until the design proved itself. By a process of elimination, therefore, the horse artillery was assigned twelve-pounder shell guns.

The commission's work represented a series of compromises. By rearming half the artillery with rifles and half with smooth-bores, advocates of both would be equally satisfied—or dissatisfied. The introduction of the twelve-pounder shell gun was intended to satisfy both those who believed artillery's major task in future would be firing shrapnel or canister at short ranges and those who wanted a highly mobile artillery. Advocates of mobility were further mollified by the commission's support for a lighter, handier rifle. On the other hand, the commission had gone on record as supporting rifled cannon, and recommended their increase.[4]

The situation was complicated by the fact that three of the four guns recommended were still on drawing boards or undergoing field trials. The short twelve-pounder, the least revolutionary of the new designs, was not ready for service until the end of 1861. Test reports praised its mobility and firing characteristics; improved fuses gave its shell and shrapnel the lowest percentage of duds in the Prussian artillery. On July 1, 1862, it was ordered issued to the foot artillery. The horse batteries, however,retained their six-pounders pending completion of the tests of the cast steel four-pounder—which was proving far from satisfactory.

The gun's problem began in the design stages. Initially the APK proposed to construct only the barrel from cast steel, then changed its mind and included the carriage as well. The commission also recommended that the gun be given only a four-horse team, and refused to alter this decision, even when informed that this would increase the weight drawn by each horse to the point where the four-pounder would actually be less mobile than its six-pounder counterpart. It did, however, agree to subsidize the construction of two test guns, one designed for four horses, one for six.[5]

Only one firm was able and willing to deliver finished test models at the government's price. In March, 1861, Krupp's delivered two four-pounders mounted on Krupp carriages, utilizing the new Krupp breechblock. Comprehensive tests began in May; by November the first reports were coming in. They were less than favorable. Troop units were having enough difficulty adjusting to the six-pounder. Unsure of the best way to use rifles in any case, commanders could see no use for what appeared to be merely an inferior copy of its predecessor. Horse artillerymen were particularly critical of the new gun. Its canister round was unsatisfactory even for a rifle. Its mobility was less than expected. Von Hahn, overjoyed at the apparent corroboration of his distrust of rifled cannon, submitted a questionnaire to senior regimental officers of the artillery. The answers confirmed his expectations. By an overwhelming majority the four-pounder was declared unsuitable for the horse artillery. It was approved for foot batteries by the narrow margin of ninety-eight to seventy-six, but almost all of the respondents qualified this by agreeing that the army needed only one type of rifle. Adding the four-pounder, they declared, would create needless duplication. One hundred seventeen of the officers polled—two-thirds of the total —favored maintaining an equal ratio between rifles and smooth-bores. Only eight were bold enough to declare unequivocally that smoothbores were obsolete.[6]

The APK was also unenthusiastic about the new design. Its initial report was not issued until December 30, 1862—almost eighteen months after the tests began. And the report itself was somewhat ambiguous. It praised the four-pounder as being more mobile than its heavy counterpart, yet having fire effect almost equal to the six-pounder. Its lighter ammunition, moreover, would place less strain on the supply services. But the report was extremely cautious when considering specific recommendations for the new rifle's use. It had proved, the APK suggested, superior to the old howitzers in delivering some types of high-angle fire. Therefore it might initially replace them in the corps artillery. Since an overwhelming majority of the officers polled in the summer of 1861 had also favored this replacement should the four-pounder be adopted, the commission was hardly taking an exposed position.

Von Hahn remained unconvinced. Mobility, he declared, was no proof of military effectiveness. Moreover, two so closely related types of cannon would be difficult to use effectively in war. If four-pounders could do the work of howitzers, would not the six-pounder be even more efficient in the high-angle role?

He recommended caution and further testing—particularly in view of continued complaints from the field. The four-pounder's breech mechanism was unsatisfactory. Its Krupp-designed carriages were too expensive and complex. It was not as accurate as the six-pounder at long ranges. Four horses could not move the weapon rapidly enough to take advantage of its lighter weight. But on the other hand the four-pounder was easy to serve and highly maneuverable. Its range and rate of fire exceeded those of any smoothbore. Admittedly, it required some adjustments in doctrine and practice. But should it be given an improved carriage, a gas-tight breech, and two more horses, technical experts and battery officers alike were beginning to believe the four-pounder had a future. An increasing number of enthusiasts went so far as to proclaim smoothbore cannon as obsolete as smoothbore muskets. The Prussian four- and six-pounders, they declared, were the best light and heavy guns for the future field artillery, and cast steel was the best material for their construction.[7]

As study of the four-pounder continued in the summer and fall of 1863, tensions within the German Confederation combined with the growing urgency of the Schleswig-Holstein question to make it increasingly possible that the Prussian artillery might be able to test its new guns on living targets. But whether they could hit the targets was open to question. The constant changes in armament meant that some batteries had had two or three different types of cannon since 1858. The lengthy technical debates over the artillery's armament had forced tactics into the background since the mid-1850s. The rifles in particular required careful training, especially in long-range firing, and might have inspired major adjustments in tactical thinking as well. Instead, they became another point of controversy in the old argument of firepower versus mobility. Officers who had had an opportunity to test the accuracy of the six-pounder at long ranges on the big new firing range at Jüterborg increasingly recommended that rifles be used *en masse* as position guns. Remaining in place during the course of a battle rendered possible the kind of precise observation enabling the rifles to sweep the field with accurate long-range fire. Through these techniques the artillery would recover the importance it had held in the days of Napoleon.[8]

In 1864, however, the interior organization of the Prussian artillery did not support such grandiose ideas. A regiment still had only four rifled batteries, and these were distributed among its three foot battalions, each of which had a different composition. Shell guns, rifles, and howitzers jostled each other in a tactician's nightmare.[9] It was possible, moreover, to argue that the range and accuracy of the new rifles meant they could best be employed as enlarged sniper's weapons, in small numbers against targets of opportunity.[10] This continuing material and doctrinal flux would severely handicap the Prussian artillery in the course of the Schleswig-Holstein campaign.

2

The two-division expeditionary corps which was Prussia's initial contribution to the Confederation army included a strong force of artillery—110 guns, 38 of them rifles. However the commander, Prince Frederick Charles, had no experience in handling artillery and was reluctant to interfere in its administration. He went no further than recommending that each division keep a battery in reserve and that corps artillery remain concentrated for use at decisive moments.[11] When the Prussian expeditionary force opened the campaign by attempting to force the Danish position at Missunde, the Prince proposed to use his guns in a traditional role: silencing the Danish artillery before the infantry stormed the enemy redoubts. But an all-day cannonade on February 2 failed to accomplish the mission. Twenty-eight Danish pieces kept firing in the teeth of sixty-four Prussian guns. Artillerymen blamed a heavy fog, which made accurate observation impossible. They blamed the technical ignorance of generals who assigned targets at impossibly long ranges even for rifles. But if the alibis were legitimate, the fact of failure remained.[12]

Despite the Missunde fiasco, the Schleswig campaign proved unexpectedly favorable to the cause of rifled cannon—and from an unexpected source: the army's siege train. Since 1850 the APK had been studying the possibility of replacing some smoothbore battering pieces by rifles, and a Cabinet Order of February 18, 1858, provided for their gradual introduction. The process was expedited when a series of tests held in Jülich in 1860 convinced the German Confederation to introduce rifles as part of the armament of its fortresses. Perhaps siege rifles could not as yet replace mortars and howitzers for high-angle fire; but for special purposes, such as breaching the walls of masonry fortifications, and for long-range bombardment during the opening phases of a siege, they would be invaluable.[13] By 1863 the Prussian siege train included 120 rifles, most of them twelve- and twenty-four-pounder cast-iron muzzle-loaders converted from existing stocks of smoothbores.

Like the field artillery, the siege gunners remained unsure of the best way to use their new rifles. But they were to gain experience in a hurry. As the Prussian troops struggled north from Missunde, Frederick Charles grew increasingly concerned at the prospect of dealing with the Danish fortifications around Düppel. Orthodox Prussian opinion regarded sieges as a waste of time and effort. Frederick Charles, however, was convinced that merely to bombard Düppel with field guns, whether rifles or smoothbores, would be a waste of ammunition. Even if the Danish guns were by a miracle silenced, the roads were too bad and the weather too cold to bring up an assault force sufficiently strong to carry the position by a *coup de main*. Instead he recommended a siege. And on February 21 he wrote to Berlin requesting eight or twelve twenty-four-pounder rifles in addition to the dozen he already had. They would, he declared, be indispensable in the next weeks.[14] He was not alone in his opinion. Crown Prince Frederick also warned against repeating the error of Missunde and attempting to do siege artillery's job with field guns. Artillery Colonel Graberg submitted a memorandum to the allied commander, Field Marshal Wrangel, suggesting that a siege would bring certain results with fewer casualties than a direct assault. Wrangel remained reluctant to lose time in a siege, but was overruled. On February 26, the War Ministry informed him that twenty-four siege guns were on their way to Denmark.[15]

Frederick Charles was in no particular hurry. Since the beginning of the campaign, subordinates had criticized him for being too cautious and unenterprising. Now he planned to wait until all the artillery he requested was on the ground and emplaced in batteries before commencing operations. Attempting to intimidate the Danes with the desultory fire of a few siege guns, he argued, would only waste ammunition and give the Danes time to rectify deficiencies in their works. The abortive bombardment of Fredericia, on the opposite side of the peninsula, by Prussian and Austrian field guns on March 20 and 21 appeared to support the Prince's viewpoint. Two thousand rounds set part of the city on fire and frightened some of the civil population into fleeing. They did not force a Danish surrender. On March 15, the first three batteries armed with twenty-four-pounder rifles opened the bombardment of the Düppel redoubts. Their accurate fire had an unexpected effect on the Danes, scattering working parties, destroying shelters, and demoralizing the garrison to a point where prisoners later suggested that an infantry assault on the heels of the bombardment might well have carried the works then and there.[16]

But the siege progressed by slow degrees. The first parallel was opened on the night of March 29, then proved to be too far from the Danish works for smoothbore guns to have any effect. A "half-parallel" 250 meters closer to the works was opened on April 7, but also proved unable to cover the smoothbores. Thus for the first weeks of the siege, the burden of artillery support fell on the rifles. As early as April 3, eight twenty-four-pounders and sixteen twelve-pounders were ordered north to reinforce those already in action. And in a matter of days battery commanders discovered that the error in siting the parallels worked to their advantage. Rifles actually were more effective at longer ranges; the reduced powder charges necessary for close-range shooting also reduced accuracy. Rifled guns destroyed blockhouses, breastworks, and palisades, dismounted Danish cannon, rendered battery positions untenable. By April 7, most of the guns in the Danish redoubts had been silenced. The artillery preparation had in fact outstripped the work of the engineers. Not until April 11 was a second parallel opened 250 meters in front of the half-parallel; this meant that the smoothbore mortars could finally be emplaced and add their fire to the rifles. But as yet the high command was unaware of how well the artillery had done its work. The King himself requested that a third parallel, only 250-300 meters from the Danish outposts, be opened. This would enable the infantry to emerge virtually under the Danes' noses, with a corresponding reduction in casualties. It cost a week to construct, but when put to the test, William valued blood more than time.[17]

The final assault on the redoubts of Düppel came on the night
184

of April 18. It proved anticlimatic, as the storming parties faced little serious opposition. Four field batteries, representing each type of gun in use, were detailed to follow the infantry into the works, and the much-criticized four-pounders proved particularly effective. But Danish prisoners and Prussian observers alike gave most of the credit for the low casualty list to the physical and moral effect of the siege rifles.

3

The siege of Düppel also marked the beginning of a new era in the artillery's high command. Much of the blame for the slow pace of the siege fell on Frederick Charles's senior artillery and engineer officers. The Crown Prince in particular described them as lethargic and superannuated, dominated by memories of 1814, and responsible for an unheard-of number of errors.[18] Finally William responded to the complaints. On April 8, General Gustav Eduard Hindersin arrived at Frederick Charles's headquarters with orders to take charge of the artillery and engineer operations in front of Düppel. Hindersin was the man for the job. Like Encke, he was of bourgeois descent, a second son whose father destined him for the artillery on the grounds that he could not afford to maintain both Gustav and his brother in the cavalry. But he did finance a private tutor, who convinced young Hindersin that he could make a future following the guns. At sixteen he was serving as a volunteer in the 3rd Artillery. Commissioned a second lieutenant in 1825, in succeeding decades he earned general recognition for his abilities in both staff and command positions. He also established a reputation as a hard-driving, humorless man, spare of speech and laughter. His behavior towards subordinates has been described as monstrous, even by the standards of the artillery. He praised them seldom, and when he attempted to do so, often managed to sound critical. Once he made an enemy, he pursued the luckless man with bitter hatred. Yet Hindersin's poisonous personality was a professional asset. Superiors avoided conflicts with him; subordinates did their utmost to keep him happy. This was all Hindersin wanted; a Prussian general was not a candidate for public office.[19]

Hindersin won no popularity contests in front of Düppel, but even his enemies could not deny the effect of his rough tongue and driving energy in expediting preparations for the assault. In these respects he contrasted sharply with von Hahn, whose increasing age was transforming him into a liability as Inspector-General. Hahn's continued opposition to rifled guns was not as significant as his refusal to adjust training to the changing conditions of war. He still insisted, for example, that target practice should be rigidly controlled, that each battery should fire a set number of rounds at set targets at predetermined ranges. He refused to alter the regulations to take account of the increased range of rifles. He was reluctant even to issue telescopes to battery commanders, so that they could observe the fall of their shot. In any case, most of the existing firing ranges were too small to permit the rifled batteries to practice at long ranges, and Hahn refused to allot funds for their expansion. As a result, even during the Danish War, batteries remaining in their peacetime garrisons continued to emphasize complicated parade-ground evolutions. And some of them were unable to do these circus acts satisfactorily. The Guard Artillery, for example, had been revitalized in the 1850s by its close contact with the intellectual currents sweeping the artillery. Stationed as it was in Potsdam and Berlin, the regiment's batteries tested new equipment. Its officers were kept aware of the progress of the APK's experiments. Yet its annual parade in the spring of 1864 was so unsatisfactory that King William was finally convinced of the necessity for a change in command. On April 22 he appointed Hindersin as the Second Inspector-General of the artillery. When Hahn retired in December, Hindersin took his place.

As soon as his appointment was announced, Hindersin began lobbying for an increased number of rifles in the field artillery. His experience at Düppel had convinced him that smoothbores were obsolete. Their continued presence in the Prussian army, he declared, kept him awake nights. He found a loyal supporter in Hohenloe, whose developing abilities as a gunner were matched only by his skills as a courtier. If he was honestly convinced the army needed more rifles, he also believed his career would advance rapidly by following Hindersin's star. Hohenloe's principal task was to use his position as a royal adjutant to discuss rifled cannon with the king, to invite him to test firings, to urge the obsolescence of smoothbores. On July 25,

1864, he received his reward: promotion and command of the field artillery of the Guard.[20] When Hindersin and Hohenloe discussed increasing the army's rifled artillery, they had a specific weapon in mind—the four-pounder. The design might not be perfect. The breech might still leak gas. But on balance, both men believed that the rifle offered a reasonable compromise between mobility and firepower. Both believed the four-pounder's performance in Denmark warranted its adoption as a replacement, not only for the howitzers, but the twelve-pounder shell guns as well.

This decision to adopt a weapon not yet technically refined represented a major departure from Prussian tradition. It was an expensive risk, and faced determined opposition. Horse artillerymen in particular had been consistent foes of the light rifle, regarding its weight and its inferior canister round as a threat to their traditional role. There had even been some regrets when in 1863 the six-pounders finally gave way to twelve-pounder shell guns. But by 1864 an increasing number of authorities suggested that the horse artillery was giving itself airs out of proportion to its military value. The elaborate, high-speed maneuvers of the horse batteries were useless under fire. Given enough horses, foot batteries could keep pace with cavalry under campaign conditions. No valid reason remained for maintaining horse artillery as an independent entity. Gracious acceptance of the inevitable seemed the best way of ensuring continued existence—especially when the King himself spoke of arming the horse artillery with four-pounders. By January, 1865, the royal wish became an order that one horse battery per regiment be rearmed as soon as possible. In June a Cabinet Order also reorganized the three howitzer batteries of the field artillery regiments into four batteries each of six four-pounders. In the interests of increased mobility, the guns were given six-horse teams.[21]

Reorganization, however, preceded rearmament. As early as April 1864, the King had decided to order 300 cast steel four-pounders, to be produced and delivered as soon as possible. He favored giving the contract to Krupp. For a decade hardly a trade fair or international exposition had not featured Krupp steel castings, Krupp cannon barrels, and Krupp salesmen to stress their virtues. Belgium and several south German states were placing orders with the firm. The Russian government had ordered a hundred twenty steel breechloaders for their fortress artillery. Krupp was well aware that the Prussian army was on the verge of deciding whether to adopt the four-pounder—and that since 1862 the Prussian parliament had refused to approve the military budgets. The constitutional and political implications of this refusal meant little to him. What mattered was the possibility of another lucrative contract, perhaps a series of them. A decisive move on his part, demonstrating confidence in the state and willingness to do business on favorable terms, might be all that was required. On January 26, 1864, Krupp wrote to Roon offering long-term credit to the Prussian government. Roon was unwilling to commit himself as long as the military budget remained unsettled, but he did ask Krupp for a price list. Alfred responded by repeating his offer, this time sweetening it with a statement of readiness to deliver a dozen batteries of four-pounders—without a down payment.[22]

As Prussian and Austrian rifles demonstrated their worth in Schleswig-Holstein, Alfred travelled to Berlin. This time he had headlines as a background when he told Roon he was ready to deliver up to two million thalers' worth of cannon on credit. It was an unheard-of offer—and even Krupp's official biographer admits it contained elements of bluff. Krupp probably did not believe that Roon would commit the government to such an amount of long-term indebtedness. He was, however, convinced that Prussia could not avoid buying more rifles, and hoped to influence Roon by his generous offer. He failed. Roon had never been particularly impressed by Krupp. Like an increasing number of officers, he admitted the quality of cast steel, but thought Krupp placed too high a value on his product. The Prussian army had done quite well before Krupp; it could survive without him. He rejected the offer of credit. But this time his "no" meant "maybe."

As the war wound down, the King and the War Minister put together the terms of an order, not for cannon, but for 300 cast steel four-pounder gun barrels. The cannon were to be completed by the state arsenal in Spandau. Krupp was bitterly disappointed. The contract was not negotiated; it was offered him on a take it or leave it basis. The price per barrel was unsatisfactorily low. Moreover, it reduced his status once more to a jobber. The government was indifferent. If Krupp refused the terms, he was informed Prussia would either make the new guns of bronze or do business with his competitors.[23]

Alfred accepted the contract. Production and delivery of the new guns progressed slowly enough to hamper training programs and keep artillerymen from gaining confidence in the new weapon. Nevertheless by the spring of 1866 Hindersin convinced the War Ministry that the short twelve-pounders should be entirely withdrawn at least from the foot artillery. The pressure of time prevented the rearming of more than two of the four twelve-pounder batteries in each corps by the outbreak of war. More seriously, men who had spent their active service learning to handle twelve-pounders or howitzers were expected to take unfamiliar weapons into action against a powerful and efficient Austrian artillery. For Hindersin, however, this was an acceptable risk. Even the most efficient smoothbore battery, he believed, was useless under modern conditions.

The new guns were accompanied by a refurbished image. Hindersin encouraged senior officers to transfer some of their zeal for parade-ground evolutions to field work during the annual maneuvers. Men, animals, and material were expected to earn their pay. If exalted personages happened to observe these new bursts of energy, so much the better. It contributed to a general reevaluation of the Prussian artillery's mobility and efficiency, which in turn helped improve its officer corps. An increasing number of aristocrats and *Abiturenten* were willing to seek glory by following the guns. Regimental selection boards had a wider choice of candidates than at any time in their history. Hindersin took particular interest in the careers of some of these promising young men. A future Chief of Staff, Alfred von Waldersee, began his service in the artillery, caught Hindersin's eye, and was transferred to the APK as the first in a long list of preferred appointments which carried him to the highest posts in the army. Of course not every new officer was so talented or so fortunate. Nevertheless this improvement of the arm's social status made no small contribution to improving the artillery's relations with infantry and cavalry officers.[24]

This process did not immediately alter the tendency of many senior officers to regard field artillery as ballast, particularly in view of the successes won by the needle gun in Denmark. Infantry fire, they argued, could prepare attacks even more effectively than smoothbore shell guns. Rifles were certainly useful against targets of opportunity at extreme ranges, but the kaleidoscopic structure and fast pace of the modern battle had rendered obsolete the employment of massed batteries in the Napoleonic fashion except in emergencies: to decide victory or to cover a retreat, in both cases only when all other means had been exhausted. The result of such thinking as reflected in maneuvers was a continuing tendency for corps and division commanders to hold a disproportionate number of their guns as a reserve which often never came into action. Direct infantry support was furnished in traditional style, by single batteries chivied about the field.[25]

The artillery did little to alter these patterns. First Hahn, then Hindersin, had bent every effort to make the artillery part of the army, to eliminate the kind of crusty independence which two decades earlier led subalterns to instruct generals in the proper use of cannon. But for fifteen years most forward-looking Prussian gunners had been concentrating on technology. The controversies over steel versus bronze, rifles versus smoothbores, time fuses versus percussion fuses, had absorbed everyone's attention. Even Hindersin had been too busy getting rifles adopted to develop a tactical doctrine for them. The artillery drill regulations had been unrevised since 1812. Nor were battery and battalion commanders able to profit from the kind of perceptive articles and pamphlets which helped their comrades of the infantry adjust to the needle gun. One typical manual, written in 1865, seldom achieved greater profundity than encouraging gunners to hold their positions until their mission was fulfilled, even if this involved the risk of being put out of action by enemy fire.[26] General von Hahn died in 1865. Hohenloe, placed in charge of the funeral, was informed that according to the general's will no rifles, and specifically no four-pounders, be used to fire the last salutes. At first he thought it was a bad joke. When he learned otherwise, he scoured Berlin and escorted Hahn to his grave with a force of shell guns, howitzers, and old twelve-pounder cannon salvaged from the arsenals.[27] Yet the war of 1866 was to suggest that the last laugh might have been Hahn's after all.

Chapter XI

Action Front!

The role of the Prussian artillery in the campaign of 1866 reflected its shortcomings in armament, training, and doctrine. The War Ministry's belated decision to adopt the four-pounder meant that almost half the batteries of the main army—54 out of 144—took the field still equipped with the obsolete smoothbores. Even where four-pounders were available, senior artillery officers and battery commanders alike were often legitimately reluctant to embark on a campaign with material in whose use their men were untrained. Thus an average of six batteries per corps would be going into action with guns completely useless at ranges of over 1500 meters, and whose effective range was only a little over half as great. In itself, the short range might not necessarily make the batteries ineffective. Advocates of the twelve-pounder had long insisted that daring and skillful officers could achieve telling results by shifting positions and ranges before enemy rifles or rifled cannon zeroed in on them. But given the Prussian artillery's almost total lack of practice in firing on moving targets at unknown ranges, combined with the fact that relatively few artillery officers had been trained in selecting and assuming battery positions quickly, the Prussian twelve-pounders would have to struggle to escape the role of sacrificial lambs.

The tactical organization of the Prussian artillery further compounded its problems. In both peace and war each field regiment had twelve foot batteries—six of four-pounders, four of six-pounders, two of twelve-pounders. As a rule, by the start of the campaign they were organized into two battalions each of one twelve-pounder, one six-pounder, and two four-pounder batteries, and one battalion of two six-pounder and two four-pounder batteries. The former were intended as divisional artillery, the latter as corps reserve. In peacetime, the horse artillery consisted of a battalion of three batteries. On mobilization it formed four batteries, one or two assigned to the independent cavalry and the others to the reserve. A Prussian corps, therefore, could have as many as seven batteries in reserve, as compared to eight assigned to its infantry divisions. And since the First and Elbe Armies took the field with only one corps headquarters between them—the army commanders handled their other seven divisions directly—the artilleries of their inactive corps were also concentrated under army headquarters, forming reserves of ninety-six and eighty-four guns, respectively.

No one was quite sure how to use these masses of guns. Prince Frederick Charles, commanding the First Army, regarded them as a decisive instrument, able to turn the tide of battle by their fire power alone. But no senior artillery officer had practiced controlling a hundred guns even at maneuvers. On the march, moreover, twelve or fifteen batteries together required a large amount of road space. This problem was exacerbated by the fact that throughout the campaign of 1866 the Prussian artillery's usual march pace was a walk. Once the First Army left its railheads the Prince's victory weapon became a roadblock. Staff officers fearing traffic jams tended to push it to the rear of the infantry, the cavalry, and their essential supply columns. In the Second Army, even corps artillery reserves fell two or three days' march behind when the army entered Bohemia.[1]

The Prussian artillery faced an adversary whose status and equipment had benefited appreciably from the campaign of 1859. The Austrians had fought that war armed with old-style smoothbore cannon which were consistently outranged and outshot by the rifled batteries of the French. This fact led to a decision to rearm the entire Austrian artillery with rifles. Despite the Finance Ministry's objections to the cost of the project, by 1863 the army had accepted designs for muzzle-loading four-pounder and eight-pounder rifles; by the end of 1864 the changeover was virtually complete.

There was nothing remarkable about the new Austrian guns. Neither soldiers nor bureaucrats saw any need to innovate in materials or design. Bronze was proved and tested. Its theoretical weaknesses as material for rifled cannon did not justify accepting the risk and expense of adopting cast steel. Similarly, the problems of erosion and gas leakage were considered to outweigh the potential advantages of loading field guns at the breech. The ammunition of these rifles was equally conventional: percussion-fused shell, time-fused shrapnel, and case-shot. Their maximum ranges—2,000 paces for shrapnel, 4,000 for four-pounder shell, 5,000 for eight-pounder shell—were about the same as their Prussian counterparts. But if Austria's guns might not receive high marks in a theoretical treatise on cannon construction, they were sturdy, durable, and reliable in action. Above all, there were enough of them. The Austrian *Nordarmee* took the field with seven hundred rifled cannon—over half again as many as the Prussians. The rapid introduction of the rifles, moreover, meant that by 1866 officers and men had had time to become acquainted with the strengths and weaknesses of the cannon they served. And the relatively long term of color service in the Austrian artillery—four to six years—meant that the batteries had strong cadres of experienced soldiers.[2]

Austrian doctrine for the organization and employment of their artillery was a logical corollary of their revised infantry tactics. The notion that victory depended essentially on the shock power of closed columns made the gunners entirely responsible for preparing the way for the decisive bayonet charges. There was no question of holding masses of guns to the rear. Austrian doctrine called for the formation of corps and army artillery reserves, but it also demanded that these guns be deployed and sent into action as rapidly as possible. Unlike their Prussian counterparts, Austrian artillery officers were indoctrinated with the idea that it was no disgrace to lose guns to the enemy while closely supporting one's own infantry. After 1859, artillery and infantry were increasingly trained together—particularly in Italy during Benedek's tenure as commander.

The organization of Austrian higher formations further aided these developments. Each of the four or five brigades of an Austrian corps had a battery of four-pounders directly assigned to it. Corps artillery usually consisted of five batteries, three of four-pounders, two of eight-pounders. Thus the infantry could count on immediate direct support, while even a cautious corps commander would be encouraged to commit his reserve artillery in support of guns already in action.[3]

In the opening combats of the war the Austrian gunners did nothing extraordinarily well. There were no Drouots or Sénarmonts, no Henry Hunts or William Pegrams among their leaders. But in offensive battles like Nachod and Trautenau, the brigade batteries supported the infantry's bayonet charges effectively and aggressively. Corps commanders employed their reserve artillery from the first, whether to support offensive operations or, as at Skalitz and Gitschin, as a main prop of a defensive position. Against Austrian gun lines of from forty to sixty barrels, the Prussians deployed batteries by ones and twos. At Nachod the Prussian commander kept over half his cannon in reserve, so far to the rear that they did not come into action until the Austrians were already in retreat. At Soor, the Prussian Guard put only eighteen guns into action all day. At Trautenau, sixty-six of I Prussian Corps' ninety-six guns never fired a round, and after eight hours of fighting the Prussians could pit only twelve guns against thirty-six supporting the attack of a single Austrian brigade. At Skalitz, not until the end of the action was the fire of as many as nine batteries concentrated against a single target—and by that time the Austrians were in the midst of breaking off the action. At Gitschin, the gunners of the Prussian First Army were somewhat more successful in massing their fire early in the day, but were still unable either to silence the enemy artillery or force its withdrawal.

Accounts of these opening battles are replete with details of Prussian batteries brought into action at excessive ranges, then being outshot or overpowered, forced into precipitate withdrawals, or such constant changes of position that their fire was rendered ineffective.[4] And if, as Hohenloe suggested, the Prussian rifles were so technically superior to the Austrian that ten of them should be able to cope with sixteen Hapsburg cannon, this superiority existed only on the firing ranges and in the test halls of government arsenals.[5] The slightly longer maximum ranges of the Prussian guns were difficult to utilize effectively on the battlefield. Too many crews, particularly in the newly-equipped four-pounder batteries, expected the gun to do all the work, with a corresponding loss of morale when their Austrian targets stubbornly refused to be blown away. The twelve-pounders were excess baggage. In the closing years of the American Civil War, particularly during the Wilderness Campaign, smooth-bores had been extremely effective close-support weapons in wooded, broken ground that put a premium on point-blank rapid fire. But the Bohemian countryside was gentler, its terrain more open. As a result, the twelve-pounder batteries, many of them commanded by officers who sincerely believed in the value of the weapon, found themselves without a role. When they attempted to join gun lines and participate in artillery duels, they were almost always outranged. Rather than leave them there as helpless targets, commanders withdrew them, with obvious effect on the morale of the rifled batteries which remained under fire. When the smoothbores tried to provide close support for their own infantry, Austrian rifle and artillery fire soon forced them out of action. Nor did this reflect lack of either courage or professional competence in the Prussian ranks. Saxon smooth-bore batteries spent a similarly frustrating day at Gitschin, vainly seeking a role.

Battery and battalion commanders seemed bewildered in the first encounters. In 1846 gunner subalterns might have argued with infantry generals; in 1866 few artillery officers seem to have objected when told the terrain was unsuitable for guns or ordered into action a battery at a time. But neither did they display an attitude of "ours not to reason why." Austrian bayonet charges intimidated Prussian artillery far more than Prussian infantry. When battery commanders were allowed to choose their own positions, fear of losing guns kept them from pushing close to the firing line and contributed to a tendency to retreat to new positions whenever an Austrian attack seemed to be drawing too close. Another peacetime custom reducing the artillery's battle efficiency was the practice of withdrawing batteries which exhausted their ammunition. Theoretically, the units replenished their limbers from the combat train, then resumed their original positions. This was supposed to save casualties and reduce the risk of accidental explosions. In practice it proved difficult to get a battery to resume its position quite as quickly or quite as eagerly as doctrine prescribed.[6]

It is readily understandable, then, that the Prussian infantry tended to ignore their supporting artillery. Units which suffered most of their casualties from Austrian shell fire might well be pardoned for paraphrasing that common taunt of the American Civil War: "Who ever saw a dead gunner?" Regimental and battalion commanders increasingly relied on the needle gun to support their movements rather than wait for artillery fire which was all too likely to be ineffective. At Skalitz and Gitschin, Prussian infantry silenced their own guns even more effectively than the Austrians did by advancing through their fields of fire. And on several occasions, particularly at Skalitz and Soor, Prussian skirmishers were able to come to close quarters with their tormentors, silencing Austrian guns or forcing them to withdraw by their heavy, accurate rifle fire. It was more than the Prussian artillery was able to do.

The Prussian guns were crewed and officered neither by poltroons nor by incompetents. As Hohenloe correctly suggested, the officers and enlisted men of the artillery were on the whole the same in 1866 as in 1870, when the arm was to play such a decisive role in overthrowing France.[7] The artillery's role in the initial battles had been humiliating to say the least, and in the days before Königgrätz, battery and battalion commanders earnestly discussed past errors and future roles. Senior officers too debated better ways of using their artillery. The staff of the Second Army drew the obvious conclusion that if too many guns were not coming into action, the way to remedy the situation was to encourage the corps commanders to keep their reserve artillery closer to hand. The suggestion was generally ignored; encouragement was no substitute for precise orders. Nor could improvisation and enthusiasm, particularly in the first days of a major war, replace coherent prewar doctrine. The Guard Artillery offers a useful illustration. On the morning of July 3 the commander of one of its battalions, grimly determined that *this* time his cannon should come into action, requested permission to mass his guns separately from their ammunition wagons at the head of his march column, so that they could move more quickly if needed. Hohenloe agreed, but both men were to rue this unconsidered decision during the day as more and more of the Guard's guns lost contact with their caissons and ran out of ammunition in the midst of battle.[8]

2

More than good will and eagerness were necessary against
the Austrian guns moving into position along the Bistritz river.
On July 1, Benedek's Chief of Artillery, the Archduke William,
had been assigned the task of surveying and constructing positions on the high ground east of the river, the heights of Lipa
and Chlum. The Archduke's name has been lost even to military
history. Quiet, methodical, uninspired and uninspiring, he was
nevertheless deeply committed to the welfare of the arm in which
he served. Like Prince August of Prussia a half-century earlier,
he had lent the prestige of a ruling house to the artillery, but
unlike the Prince, he possessed considerable ability as an ad-
ministrator.[9] He had spent years helping to train his gunners for
the test they would face on July 3, and two days establishing a
series of mutually supporting redoubts which commanded the
Bistritz valley and offered protection against the even higher
ground to the north over which the Second Prussian Army would
advance. Austrian officers had time to construct earth and log
shelters for the guns, to measure ranges and select aiming points,
to establish magazines, to supervise the construction of trenches
and earthworks for infantry supports. It was work demanding
application rather than genius, and on the morning of July 3,
450 Saxon and Austrian guns rolled into the batteries or took up
supporting positions. Three hundred twenty more were in reserve. Benedek expected them to be the rock on which the Prussian infantry attacks would shatter, opening the way for a decisive
Austrian counterattack.[10] In the center, at least, his prognostica-
tions proved almost accurate. For here the First Prussian Army
was under orders to cross the Bistritz, clear away the defenders
of the river line, and proceed to storm the Lipa heights overlooking the valley.

The Prussians had learned something in a week. This time the
guns of all three assaulting divisions, plus the II Corps reserve,
were promptly committed in support of the infantry. If as usual
the twelve-pounder batteries had to be promptly withdrawn
because of their short range, at one time the Prussians were able
to mass seventy-two guns against the thirty-two supporting the
Austrians along the river. Despite the impossibility of observing
fire accurately in a combination of river mist and powder smoke,

Prussian artillery fire contributed appreciably to their successful—and relatively inexpensive—crossing of the Bistritz. But by
10 AM the situation had altered. Beyond the villages of Mokrow-
ous, Dohalitz, and Unter-Dohalitz, beyond the *Holawald*, the
ground sloped upward, with no cover save a few bushes between
the Prussian infantry and the Austrian artillery massed on the
Lipa heights. One hundred thirty-six guns from two corps laid
down an impenetrable curtain of shellfire to their front. Their
fire was so intense that as early as 10:30, several batteries had
exhausted their ammunition and were replaced from the army
reserve and the artillery of the 1st Light Cavalry Division. By
11 AM, 160 guns were pounding the three Prussian divisions
which had crossed the river. Isolated attempts to rush the gun
line collapsed almost as soon as they began; Prussian commanders
at all levels could do no more than order their men to take cover,
hold on, and hope that their own artillery could reduce the
pressure.

The Prussians tried, but old patterns died hard. Of the eight
batteries assigned to the 3rd and 4th Divisions, only one remained
in action after the infantry crossed the river. The two smoothbore
batteries could not reach the Lipa heights; five of the rifled batteries either failed to cross the river altogether or were forced
back by Austrian fire. Initially they were replaced only by the
rifles from II Corps reserve. Not until 11 AM did Frederick Charles
authorize the commander of the artillery reserve to move his guns
forward. Half of them—eight batteries of smoothbores—were useless, but before noon, his rifles were in action on both sides of the
Holawald. Shortly after 1 PM the Prussian gun line was further
reinforced by batteries from the 5th and 6th Divisions, whose
infantry simultaneously moved into the fighting line.

The extra barrels added firepower but multiplied confusion.
South of the *Holawald*, batteries from five separate formations
jostled for positions and competed for targets. North of the woods,
where batteries from the reserve initially reinforced only the
rifles of the 8th Division, the command situation was somewhat
more favorable. But fire control was just one aspect of the Prussian problem. They were heavily outnumbered, yet trying to
silence entrenched guns on high ground. Austrian gun teams,
limbers, and caissons could withdraw behind the crest of the
heights and remain safe from any but chance hits; the flat tra-

jectory of the Prussian rifles made it virtually impossible to search reverse slopes effectively even under ideal conditions. And conditions were far from ideal. The Austrians time after time forced Prussian batteries to change positions, making impossible the kind of long-range, precision marksmanship discussed by early advocates of rifled cannon. If batteries abandoned this concept to bombard the Austrian positions more or less at random, they soon faced another problem: ammunition supply. The fords of the Bistritz were under heavy Austrian fire. Battery commanders who sent messengers ordering their ammunition wagons forward were informed instead that the caissons could not force their way through the mass of men, horses, and wagons blocking the crossings. A single *Feldwebel* managed to resupply his guns. The other batteries had to abandon their positions, cross and recross the river, and usually take up new positions at new ranges once they returned.

Despite these handicaps the Prussian batteries did some damage, dismounting guns, decimating crews, and igniting ammunition. But they were unable either to silence the Austrian artillery or draw its fire away from the hard-pressed infantry. By noon, the demoralization among the Prussian riflemen was serious enough to make the King and his senior officers wonder whether the First Army could withstand a determined Austrian attack. The Hapsburg artillery by itself had won a significant local victory.

Just to the north, in the *Swiepwald*, the Prussian 7th Division was somewhat more fortunate. Initially this was an infantry battle on both sides, but when the Austrian IV Corps commander, Count Festetics, decided to mount a massive counterattack to drive the victorious Prussians out of the woods, he supported it with most of his corps artillery. When it failed, the next one was prepared by fourteen batteries from IV and II Corps. The 7th Division was supported by only four batteries, too few either to maintain an artillery duel or provide fire support to help repel the desperate Austrian bayonet charges. The 7th Division's infantry were on their own.

On the basis of events along the Bistritz, the Austrian guns should have shattered the Prussians in short order. The situation in this part of the field, however, was different. The Austrian artillerymen were not an elite armed with super-weapons. They

were simply good, competent gunners, and around the *Swiepwald*
their competence lagged somewhat. In particular, the gun crews
seem to have been careless in setting fuses. Too many shrapnel
rounds failed to explode, or burst harmlessly in midair instead of
among the trees. Too many percussion-fused shells failed to
burst on impact with the soggy ground. When they did explode,
their blast effect was often reduced by the *Swiepwald*'s tangled
underbrush. The 27th Infantry, the first Prussian regiment to
enter the *Swiepwald* and the last to leave it, suffered 473 casualties
on July 3. Only sixty-one were inflicted by artillery fire. One
man was killed by a falling tree; two casualties are listed as
"contusions"; nine are not described. If all of these are counted
as coming from wood splinters or falling branches, a maximum
total of only seventy-four men were put out of action by the artillery.[11] This ratio of losses reflects another aspect of fighting
in the *Swiepwald* which reduced the effect of the Austrian fire.
The commanders on the spot were blindly determined to clear
the woods and smash the First Army's left flank as rapidly as possible. Instead of giving their overwhelmingly superior artillery
time to wear down Prussian strength and Prussian morale, as it
was doing just to the south, they used their guns merely to provide overtures to the series of abortive infantry attacks which
collapsed under the fire of the needle guns. They also failed to
provide liaison between the Austrian infantry and the Austrian
battery positions. As more and more Austrians became entangled
in the *Swiepwald*, the artillery gradually ceased fire rather than
risk shelling their own men.[12]

On the Prussian right, the three divisions of the Elbe Army
began their advance around 8:30. At the beginning of the action,
the Prussian artillery had a chance to do what it did best: fighting
small-unit actions. A four-pounder battery of the advance guard
silenced and drove off a Saxon battery covering the only bridge on
the army's front passable for guns and wagons. Another battery
commander kept so close to the infantry that his rifles were able
to harass Saxon cavalry in reserve. But the dash and daring ended
there. The Prussians gradually built up a gun line east of the
river and began a noisy duel with a few Saxon and Austrian batteries, but the range of over 3000 meters meant that the adversaries
bombarded each other with virtually no result. One Prussian battery engaged in the fight from beginning to end suffered the loss
of two men and two horses!

Around 12:30 the four batteries which had formed the original
gun line were joined by two more from the 14th Division. Five
batteries from the army reserve finally managed to cross the Bistritz and take firing positions after 1 PM. But this mass of sixty-
six guns was little more than useless metal. It was unable to support the Prussian infantry in Stezirek Wood because they were
too intermingled with the Austrians. It failed to shake the Saxon
artillery between Problus and Nieder-Prim because the range
remained at 3,000 meters. Not until reinforced by three additional
batteries did the Prussians risk closing the range, and then only
to 2,300 meters. By that time the Prussian infantry, deployed in
open order, were advancing through the Saxon fire, forcing their
infantry out of the two villages, coming within rifle range of the
guns themselves. And at last one battery did something besides
waste ammunition at long ranges. Six twelve-pounder smoothbores of VII Corps galloped through their own infantry to blast
the garrison of Problus with shrapnel at point-blank range. It
was a last hurrah for the smoothbores—but an exception which
only proved a rule.

3

As the Second Army began its march on the morning of July 3,
it seemed that its gunners would have even less chance than their
comrades to the south of restoring their shaken reputations. All
three of the forward corps commanders initially ordered the bulk
of their artillery to march at the rear of the infantry; only a few
batteries were to accompany the advance guards and main bodies.
This was too much for Hohenloe. His impassioned arguments
finally won his guns a place behind the leading infantry division
of the Guard. And ironically, this change in orders seemed initially to demonstrate that artillery *was* more of a nuisance than a
support. It had rained all night. It was raining as the Second
Army moved forward. Unpaved country roads began disintegra-
ting under the pressure of boots, wheels, and hooves. Infantry
columns took on an accordion-like appearance as men and units
stuck in the mud; time and again the guns were ordered to make
their way cross-country and leave the roads free for the riflemen.
Wet grain clogged wheels already hub-deep in the rich Bohemian
soil. Horses dropped in their traces, and cannoneers dismounted

to lend their strength to overexerted teams. But Hohenloe and his subordinates kept their guns moving—around, through, and sometimes over the infantry. By 11 AM the reserve artillery had reached the village of Chotoborek—just about the time when Second Army Headquarters, which had marched with the Guard, was deciding that First Army was decisively engaged with the Austrians. When the Crown Prince determined to push forward against the Austrian flank and rear instead of sidestepping to the south and reinforcing Frederick Charles directly, Hohenloe was on the spot to receive his orders: form a gun line as rapidly as possible; open fire on the heights of Horenowes which formed the Austrian right flank; and announce the Second Army's arrival on the field.[13]

In light of the Prussian artillery's previous performances, it might be questionable whether the Crown Prince really expected his guns to do more than encourage the hard-pressed First Army by making noise. But orders were dispatched to the Guard and VI Corps: guns to the front. Two rifled batteries of the Guard were first into position, unlimbering around the village of Wrchnowitz to cover the infantry advancing on Horenowes. Around noon they were reinforced by four batteries of the 11th Division; a half-hour later, nine more batteries from the Guard and the 12th Division had moved into position. If the range was somewhat long even for rifles—about 2,500 paces—for once the Prussians had a clear field of fire and overwhelming numerical superiority. Ninety guns opposed sixty-four Austrian—forty on Horenowes, sixteen to the west of the heights, and eight around the village of Trotina. But the brunt of the struggle was borne by the five batteries of II Austrian Corps on the heights of themselves.

Since morning these guns had been bombarding the *Swiepwald*, but they changed fronts and targets with remarkable precision and intimidating accuracy. From the first they put round after round into the Prussian position; the batteries of the 11th Division, in the center of the gun line, were particularly hardpressed. The Prussian artillery might have been silenced altogether had it not been for two facts. The terrain was open enough that the guns could be deployed at wider intervals than usual. More important, however, was the failure of as many as threefourths of the Austrian shells to burst because of defective or improperly set fuses. Conceivably the Austrians' discounting of the possibility of damaging fuses in the process of ramming home shells in muzzle-loading rifles had been misplaced common sense.[14]

The shells that did explode were more than enough to keep the Prussian artillery at a distance. The Prussians forced a few Austrian gun teams out of range. They blew up a few Austrian caissons. But if by 1:15 the Austrians abandoned the fight, this was due primarily to the steady advance of the infantry of the Prussian Guard. Opposed only by remnants of units already shaken by the fighting in the *Swiepwald*, the Prussians drove forward rapidly. Under the threat of their needle guns, the Austrian batteries fell back to the heights of Nedelist. They had gained their army sixty minutes—time to at least begin evacuating the hard-pressed infantry from the *Swiepwald* and establishing new defensive positions against the growing threat from the north.

By 2 PM the Austrians had managed to withdraw most of their troops in the *Swiepwald* to the high ground between Chlum and Nedelist. If the infantry was disorganized and demoralized by their morning's experiences, they were falling back on a formidable position. Between the two villages Austrian engineers had constructed three strong redoubts, as well as smaller works. But the core of the defense would once again be the artillery—seven batteries in and around the villages and redoubts; ten, including eight from the army reserve, on the heights themselves; two more available if necessary: a total of one hundred fifty-two rifled cannon. Against this force the Prussians could muster at 2 PM only a single division. The 2nd Guard Division had not yet reached the field. The two divisions of VI Corps, aiming at the villages of Nedelist and Lochenitz, the flank and rear of the Austrian position, were not yet in position. In view of this situation, it was hardly remarkable that the 1st Guard Division and its supporting artillery were ordered to halt once they occupied Horenowes. But the division commander refused to abandon the initiative. Acting on his own responsibility, he sent his infantry forward against the heights of Chlum.

A good sign both of the haste with which this decision was made and the disregard of many Prussian generals for the artillery is the fact that initially the riflemen advanced with no artillery support whatever. The Prussian artillery which had occupied

Horenowes after the Austrians withdrew was not informed of the proposed advance. Indeed, the 1st Guard Division's own batteries were so thoroughly ignored that they were given no orders even to advance to Horenowes, to say nothing of taking the Chlum positions under fire.

Logically the Prussian advance should have been hopelessly pinned down almost as soon as it began. But a series of coincidences favored the Guard. At first the very absence of artillery support seemed to keep the Austrian gunners from taking the attack seriously. Since Austrian tactics stressed charges delivered by massed battalions, it is hardly surprising that artillery and infantry officers who had never been in action against the Prussians might fail to be suitably impressed by the loose skirmish lines and small company columns which began working towards the heights. Moreover, the terrain around Chlum was irregular enough to screen the Prussian advance periodically. But even the desultory fire which a few batteries directed on the ground to their front was inflicting casualties on the Prussians and disrupting their organization when the Austrian artillery caught sight of a more inviting, apparently far more profitable, target.

The hard-driving Hohenloe was not the man to see his infantry once more go forward without artillery support. On impulse, he limbered up his own four batteries, drove forward down the Horenowes heights, and unlimbered only 1,300 paces from the Austrian positions. In German military argot, it was a *Himmelfahrtskommando*, a suicide mission. Hohenloe was firing uphill from an exposed position. Even when the batteries of the 11th and 1st Guard Divisions joined him, he was outgunned two or three to one. But by utilizing the broken terrain and high grain to conceal his guns, and by changing position frequently, he hoped to attract Austrian attention and distract Austrian marksmanship.[15]

The daring maneuver succeeded on both counts. In particular the Austrian batteries in the forward redoubts, tired of apparently wasting ammunition on wheatfields, eagerly opened fire on the Prussian guns. But while they were conducting an artillery duel in approved textbook fashion, Prussian riflemen emerged from nowhere and began pouring rapid fire into Redoubt III, just east of Chlum. The Austrian infantry ostensibly covering the guns panicked and ran for their lives. An Austrian battery tried briefly to stop the Prussians with case-shot fired over open sights, but its horses were shot down by Prussian riflemen; its guns stuck fast in the soft ground behind the redoubt. A similar fate overtook a neighboring unit; only two of its eight guns escaped. Of the three batteries in and around Redoubt IV, just to the right of Redoubt III, one had previously been withdrawn when it ran out of ammunition. One was able to limber up with a loss of two guns. The third was initially able to retire, then forced to unlimber once more when charged by Prussian cavalry. Before the Austrians had time to move again, Prussian skirmishers shot most of the horses and men and captured six of the guns. Almost simultaneously, other units of the 1st Guard Division overran the village of Chlum.

In the interval between their deployment and the infantry attack on the redoubts, the Prussian batteries had been subjected to such a punishing fire that they were able to return only a few hasty salvoes. Nevertheless when they saw Austrian limbers exploding and Austrian guns withdrawing, their first reaction was a burst of cheers and a round of mutual congratulations. It was only later that they discovered that the infantry had done the work of silencing the guns.[16] And while the artillerymen patted themselves on the backs, the Prussian skirmishers kept driving forward. In a heroic attempt to check the Prussian advance, a single Austrian battery galloped to within 200 paces of Chlum, unlimbered, and opened fire on the guardsmen. It got off only ten rounds before the needle guns destroyed it. Other Prussian units occupied the villages of Lipa and Rosberitz, scattering the Austrian infantry, threatening to cut off the two corps still facing the Bistritz. The Austrian artillery was called upon to stem the tide. Batteries from brigades and army corps, from the artillery reserve and the cavalry divisions, were thrown into action without regard to their parent formations, unlimbering to screen the infantry retreating from east of Chlum and the Lipa heights, firing a few rounds, then crumbling under Prussian rifle fire. There was irony in the fact that this was exactly the kind of fighting for which advocates of the smoothbore shell gun had declared that weapon best suited, while the Austrians had nothing but rifles, whose shrapnel and canister rounds were not enough by themselves to keep the Prussians at bay. But the gunners fought it out to the muzzle, time and again holding their ground until the Prussians were in their battery positions, then withdrawing as best they could. They did not always succeed, but they traded guns for time—time for Benedek to concentrate his reserves for a final counterattack.

When VI Austrian Corps was ordered to retake the heights of Chlum, its commander refused to send his infantry forward against the needle guns without artillery support. By 3 PM, 120 cannon were shelling the heights and the villages of Chlum and Rosberitz. The guardsmen had captured the heights without artillery. To hold them they too would need guns. The 1st Guard Division's batteries led the way, followed by Hohenloe's reserve battalion, which went into line on the plateau south of Chlum. The Prussians had excellent observation, a clear field of fire, and ranges of from eighteen hundred to a thousand paces—no problem for rifled guns. One Austrian column carried Rosberitz at the cost of heavy casualties, but got no farther. A six-pounder battery opened fire to their front; a battery of four-pounders took them in flank. A series of desperate charges brought the Austrians almost to the muzzles of the four-pounders, but a combination of case-shot at a hundred paces and the needle guns of the battery's supporting infantry proved too much for Austrian courage.

The Austrians delivered a series of even more desperate attacks on the village of Chlum. But here the guns belonged to the battalion whose commander had separated them from his caissons. By 4:30 they were almost out of ammunition, and Hohenloe grudgingly ordered their withdrawal. His disappointment was compounded when a quarter-hour after his guns left the infantry to its own resources, the artillery of I Prussian Corps moved into the position he had abandoned, and played a major role in repelling the final Austrian attacks.[17]

By this time units of VI Prussian Corps had occupied Nedelist and threatened to cut the Austrian lines of communication. Prince Albert's troops were retreating in disorder from the Problus position; III and X Austrian Corps had abandoned the heights overlooking the Bistritz. With the Prussians in hot pursuit, Benedek sacrificed his last reserves of infantry and cavalry in a desperate effort to keep the army's escape route open. But once more the real work of screening the withdrawal fell to the Austrian guns. Lieutenant-Colonel von Hofbauer, commanding the two battalions of the army's artillery reserve originally on the Chlum heights, had withdrawn southeast to a position between the villages of Sweti and Wsestar when the Prussians broke through the redoubts. From there he had supported the Austrian counterattacks; now he covered the Austrian retreat. Except for isolated companies and battalions, his guns had no infantry support; Austrian riflemen in this sector refused to stand before the needle guns. Batteries fired shell or shrapnel as long as possible, then switched to case-shot to hold off Prussian skirmishers, then withdrew to the next high ground and began the process over again.

Late in the afternoon Benedek visited the gun line and received Hofbauer's assurance that the artillery would fight to the last round. The Colonel kept his pledge. As Austrian resistance collapsed elsewhere and targets became more difficult to find, batteries from almost every unit of the Prussian army moved into position against Hofbauer's gun line. Over 250 cannon, from first to last, took the Austrians under fire. Yet it was not artillery, but infantry, which finally forced the Austrians to retreat. Troops of I Corps and the Guard pressed forward despite Austrian fire. By 4:30 both Wsestar and Sweti had fallen to VI Corps. It was time to go. One after another the Austrian batteries retreated, abandoning over twenty guns whose teams had been shot, or which became mired without enough hands to free them. But they did not abandon the fight. Throughout the final hours of the struggle for central Europe, Hofbauer only permitted his batteries to leave the field when they had nothing left to shoot. He remained himself until severely wounded, and as his hard-hammered gunners withdrew from their original positions they were joined by others—batteries whose infantry had retreated or fled, batteries which still had a few rounds and some fighting spirit remaining. Between 5 and 6 PM the final Austrian gun line formed on both sides of the highway leading to Königgrätz. Thirty-one batteries from five corps, three cavalry divisions, and the army reserve, shot it out with thirty-three batteries from three Prussian armies until the late July night fell and the main army had crossed the Elbe.

Their fire inflicted heavy casualties on Prussian infantry already disorganized by hard marching, hard fighting, and victory. Perhaps more importantly, it helped to convince the Prussian high command not to pursue their enemy too closely. Not one

Austrian infantry brigade was combat-effective; all that remained intact was a single cavalry division. But the thick clouds of powder smoke thrown up from the guns effectively camouflaged the Austrian weakness. Even Moltke could be pardoned for his reluctance to take risks against an enemy which could screen his retreat with such a heavy curtain of fire. The smoke might well conceal an army corps. Even if it did not, troops and commanders who had spent the day under the terrible fire of the Austrian guns were understandably reluctant to advance against them once more.[18]

By 7 PM the Austrian batteries began evacuating their positions and withdrawing over the Elbe. They had lost a total of over thirteen hundred officers and men, and 187 guns destroyed or captured. They had saved an army. If Königgrätz was not a crowning mercy, a Jena or a Sedan, disproportionate credit must go to the cannoneers, who on every sector of the front did more than their duty on July 3.

Even in the final stages of the battle the Prussian artillery was unable to get out of its own way. As late as 3 PM, in the First Army's sector, batteries of II Corps were reported limbering up to facilitate quick retreat in case of an Austrian counterattack. Other batteries were retiring to replenish their ammunition. Still others were attempting to extricate guns stuck in the river. Not until the Austrian withdrawal was beyond doubt did First Army's batteries begin a careful advance towards the Horenowes heights. Similarly the guns of the Elbe Army did little to obstruct the withdrawal of the Austrians and Saxons in their sector, contenting themselves with long-range interdiction fire which did little more than empty caissons. As for the Second Army's batteries, most of them were caught up in the general confusion accompanying the repulse of the final Austrian counterattack around Chlum and Lipa. By the time they sorted themselves out, their infantry had done most of the work. A set of inferior and ephemeral verses written in the aftermath of victory glorified various elements of the Prussian army and their respective claims to honor: the heights of Chlum for the Guard, Langensalza for the Landwehr, Gitschin, Skalitz, and Nachod for the line.[19] No one wrote poems to the artillery.

4

The artilleries of the German Confederation offer little more than an extended footnote to the preceding discussion. They reflected the problems of the Prussian artillery on a reduced scale and with few significant variations. All of them were affected by successive economy drives of the 1820s and 30s, which reduced cadres of men and horses to a minimum, cut terms of color service to a point where artillery drivers were barely able to learn the rudiments of handling a team, and all but eliminated target practice. Most of the German states eventually modified, then abandoned, their Napoleonic-era cannon in favor of lighter, more mobile equipment broadly similar to the Prussian *System c/42*. Like their Prussian counterparts, during the 1850s the Confederation's artillerymen focussed their attention simultaneously on two new developments: rifles and shell guns. The advantages of both were generally recognized. Their adoption was another matter. Not every German state had a soldier-king, or a military budget large enough to support expensive experiments. When economy-minded assemblies and bureaucracies were willing to make additional funds available, the money was more likely to be spent on increasing the terms of service for the conscripts, on improving barracks accommodations, or on Minié rifles for the infantry.

The problem of rearmament was further complicated by the increasing willingness of France and Austria, particularly Austria, to make their muzzle-loading rifles available to the south German states at favorable prices. The deepening political gulf between Prussia and Austria in the 1860s encouraged south German governments to place orders with at least partial intention to avoid overt commitment to either party. This tendency was reflected even in battery organization. Prussian batteries had six guns, Austrian eight, and the German states were uncertain whom to emulate.

This combination of factors resulted both in a multiplicity of gun models in the south German contingents and in continually postponed rearmament. By 1866 Bavaria, the largest of the middle states, had only eighteen field batteries. Saxony had ten, Württemberg six, Baden and Hanover five apiece. From there the number declined to one or two in the smaller principalities.

Bavaria began introducing rifles as early as 1860, but five years later had only five batteries armed with Krupp six-pounders. Three-fourths of the Bavarian Corps' reserve artillery consisted of twelve-pounder shell guns. The Baden and Nassau contingents each included a battery of elderly six-pounder smoothbores. Hanover took the field with a battery of twenty-four-pounder howitzers, a design obsolete for two decades. The Grand Duchy of Hesse's horse battery had four six-pounder smoothbores and two muzzle-loading rifles. Its three foot batteries were armed respectively with twelve-pounder shell guns, Prussian six-pounders, and muzzle-loading rifled six-pounders from the La Hitte foundry of France—a collection whose coordination would challenge the best of artillerymen.[20]

The clearest indication of the problems posed by this lack of commonality is offered by the table of organization of VIII *Bundeskorps*. As mobilized in 1866, it included troops of four states. Its artillery was a combination museum and showcase of calibers and organizations. Smoothbore six-pounders, twelve-pounder shell guns, Prussian, French, and Austrian rifles stood hub to hub in the same gun lines. Six-gun and eight-gun batteries participated in the same fire missions. Even words of command varied from contingent to contingent. If individual batteries might be as good as any in Europe, the artillery as a whole did little to alleviate Prince Alexander of Hesse's frustration with his improvised formation.

Initially seventeen Prussian batteries were mobilized for the campaign against Austria's German allies. Almost half their guns were twelve-pounder smoothbores. Six batteries were equipped with four-pounders, but some of these units had been rearmed only weeks before the outbreak of war. There were only three batteries of the proved and tested six-pounders. This disproportionate number of smoothbores can be ascribed partly to the fact that the southern theater was a sideshow, partly to the mobilization of a number of reserve batteries whose gunners had never seen a rifled cannon. But whatever the reason for their presence, they placed a heavy burden on the rifles.

On June 27, at Langensalza, the Prussians brought twenty-four guns, including only six rifles, into action against almost twice that number of Hanoverian guns, including twenty-two Krupp six-pounders. The results parallelled those in Bohemia.

The Prussian artillery performed one role effectively. By maintaining its positions throughout the day, it functioned as a target for the Hanoverian guns and correspondingly reduced pressure on the infantry.

Nor did the situation improve when the *West-Armee* turned against the states below the Main. At Hammelburg on July 10, a single battery of four-pounders duelled fruitlessly with twice its number of Bavarian guns, while three batteries of twelve-pounders brought up in support were unable even to reach the Bavarian positions. Four days later at Aschaffenburg, a twelve-pounder battery proved helpless against twenty-two Hessian and Austrian rifles. At Tauberbischofsheim on July 24 a four-pounder battery stood for two hours under fire from sixteen, then thirty-two south German guns, accomplishing nothing. By this time Prussian officers had learned that it was impossible to engage smoothbores in a duel with rifles; the twelve-pounder battery originally involved in the action was mercifully withdrawn.

The Main Army formed no artillery reserve. Its batteries were all directly assigned to its three divisions. But instead of taking advantage of this to deploy large numbers of guns early in the action, Prussian commanders tended to decentralize control even further and commit their artillery to battle in traditional style, with batteries and sections supporting regiments and battalions. On several occasions these isolated units were surprisingly effective in supporting Prussian attacks. On July 4, at Rossdorf, for example, a four-pounder battery of the 7th Artillery contributed to the disorderly retreat of three Bavarian battalions from a strong defensive position. On the same day, well-aimed fire from a Prussian four-pounder, culminated, according to one account, by a shell bursting on the helmet of a Bavarian cuirassier, sparked the panic-stricken flight of a squadron, then a regiment, then an entire cavalry division.[21] As a general rule, however, the lessons of Bohemia proved equally valid in Bavaria: to be effective under modern conditions guns must be brought into action early, and in large numbers. It was perhaps fortunate for the Prussians that both the Bavarians and the composite VIII *Bundeskorps* also tended to fight their guns by batteries. The Bavarians had too many short-ranged smoothbores.[22] The south Germans had too many units unused to cooperating. While a battery from one contingent might empty its caissons supporting its own infantry, guns from another state would fire a few rounds and remain silent. It was a problem not of incompetence, but of inexperience.[23] The result, however, was the same: the Prussian infantry was usually able to go about its work of smashing south German bayonet charges relatively undisturbed.

Conclusion

Portents

Statesmen and soldiers throughout Europe were stunned by Königgrätz and its aftermath. Expert opinion in most capitals had predicted either an Austrian victory or a campaign of mutual exhaustion. Instead the Prussian army was dictating peace terms at the gates of Vienna, and the question dominating newspapers, cabinets, and officers' messes alike was "how did it happen?" The correspondents and observers who had participated in the campaign on both sides provided the initial answer. Almost with one voice, they proclaimed the needle gun as the key to Prussian victory. Most of Europe's major newspapers featured eyewitness accounts of the terrible effect of Prussian infantry fire and the desperate valor of the Austrians in their hopeless charges. Other journals picked up the theme, sometimes presenting wildly exaggerated narratives in an attempt to boost circulation. In the first days after Sadowa, both the French ambassador and the French military attache at Vienna declared that the Austrian defeat could be explained solely by the needle gun.[1] Austrians not primarily concerned with finding scapegoats in their own high command also joined the ranks of the needle gun's admirers. It was easier to accept defeat by superior machinery than to admit having been outgeneraled or outfought; a half-century later, the most distinguished Austrian historian of the war still described Prussian firepower as a decisive element in their victory.[2]

The reaction to this oversimplified adulation of the needle

gun began immediately. Writing on July 6, Friedrich Engels declared that "the immense and rapid success [of the Prussians] could not have been obtained without such superior fire. . . . But there were other circumstances cooperating." Breechloaders were useless without "stout hearts and strong arms to carry them" and cool heads to direct their action. All of these the Prussians had, and in a single week "the Prussian army has . . . conquered a position as high as ever it held."[3] The elderly Jomini declared that in view of Prussia's superior strategy, thirty thousand Tyrolean marksmen would not have changed the war's outcome.[4] By mid-July the French attaché had changed his mind so drastically that he was willing to say that the needle gun had contributed nothing to the Austrian defeat.[5] This argument was repeated in the report submitted on September 8, 1866, by the new French military attaché in Berlin. Baron Stoffel had been sent to Bohemia at the end of July to determine the causes of the Prussian victory. He concluded that Prussia's true strength lay in the fact that its army was the nation in arms, whose ranks were filled with educated patriots fighting for their homes. Superior weaponry was "only a secondary advantage . . . the Austrian army would have succumbed even had its infantry carried the same rifle as the Prussian infantry."[6]

The Prussian army itself did much to de-emphasize the role of the needle gun in 1866. Vanity was a contributing factor. If the Austrians preferred to attribute their defeat to weapons, the Prussians sought to give all the credit possible to men. Not for fifty years would military men willingly share the spotlight with scientists, engineers, and factory workers. The Seven Weeks' War had been won by the Prussian soldier, and poems, addresses, and monuments everywhere in the new North German Confederation testified to that fact. This process, however, involved much more than simple ego-gratification. It was generally recognized that after Königgrätz, every major military power in Europe would adopt breechloading rifles as rapidly as possible. This in turn meant that the technical superiority Prussia enjoyed in 1866 was likely to be transformed to inferiority within a few years. The needle gun was twenty-five years old, the basic design a decade older. New developments on both sides of the Atlantic had eclipsed it. Magazine rifles had been used in the American Civil War. French arsenals were beginning to produce the Chassepot, a weapon more reliable and with a longer range than its Prussian counterpart. Prussian military authorities generally admitted the need to improve or replace the needle gun. King William was extremely interested in the French Chassepot, and in 1868 Dreyse's factory at Sömmerda presented a new model of the needle gun for testing. A new cartridge and an improved firing chamber, however, represented at best marginal improvements of an obsolescent design, and even these modifications were not introduced before the outbreak of war in 1870. Prussia had reaped the advantages of being first in the field. Now it was beginning to suffer the consequences as the first state in Europe to face the problems of technological obsolescence.

This loss of superiority in infantry armament might be lamented but it was also accepted as inevitable. Once Prussia was no longer the only state in Europe with rapid-firing rifles, the best that its designers were likely to achieve were marginal improvements, important but not in themselves decisive.[7] Breechloader against breechloader presented an entirely different set of tactical and operational problems than breechloader against muzzleloader. Even if the needle gun had won the war in 1866, this fact was irrelevant to the future challenges facing the Prussian army. Accepting it might well lead to the kind of resting on past laurels which had proved fatal in 1806. Prussia's future opponents would obviously hardly be as willing as the Austrians had been to present mass formations as targets for the breechloader, or to pit bayonet charges against rapid fire. The campaign of 1866 had also demonstrated more clearly than ever the problem of maintaining effective control of skirmish lines and company columns. Prussian officers eagerly accepted the praise heaped on their infantry by foreign observers, but did not overlook the prevalence of straggling and shirking at Königgrätz, particularly around the *Holawald* and the *Swiepwald*, where even men willing to fight had simply become lost. The Austrian weaknesses in skirmishing and marksmanship had prevented them from taking full advantage of this situation. What would be the result against an enemy which regarded the rifle as something more than an inferior pike and had some skill in open-order combat—the French, for example?

In answering this question the Prussian infantry focussed on tactics rather than weapons. Some officers advocated stressing close order and limiting subordinates' independence; others proclaimed swarms of skirmishers as the only really effective formation on a modern battlefield. Moltke still denied that a skirmish line alone could drive an enemy from a reasonably favorable position. He favored the use of company columns and half-battalions, which in 1866 "repeatedly marched across open ground through the fire of numerous rifled cannon without losing all too many men."[8] Even more than his Chief of Staff, King William emphasized the value of the discipline and order conferred by closed formations and rejected all proposals to change the existing infantry drill regulations. Neither man really comprehended the effect of breechloader fire at close range. Neither had experienced the powerful urge to get out of the mass and *act*, to do anything which would restore some control over one's own destiny.[9] This emphasis on mass formations continued to influence the conduct of maneuvers. Open-order tactics, however, were hardly neglected. Company officers put greater emphasis than ever on fire discipline, on controlling skirmish lines, on indoctrinating their men to push forward independently should they lose contact with their units. Terrain exercises absorbed more and more training time; parade drill became secondary in more and more regiments.[10] But proponents of columns and skirmishers, mass formations and open order, alike believed that morale, training, and discipline were more important than armament. Prussian spirit, Prussian fire discipline, and Prussian tactical skill would outweigh the technical advantages of the Chassepot—as in fact they did in 1870.

2

This attitude did not imply a general indifference to material. The Prussian artillery was the center of two technical controversies in the months after 1866. The first involved the final replacement of the smoothbore twelve-pounders. Isolated critics might suggest that rifled cannon were overrated. The Saxon artilleryman Woldemar Streubel listed twenty-three separate points in favor of the smoothbores, and predicted that the bitter experience of war would send armies crawling back to them like a man longing for a rejected lover.[11] But the overwhelming weight of professional opinion was that the twelve-pounders had not performed well enough in either Bohemia or south Germany to justify their retention. Their short range, the irregular trajectory of their shells, and the continued problem of fuse damage made the smoothbores expendable. The south German states began replacing them as fast as their parliaments made funds available, while a Cabinet Order of November 6, 1866, eliminated them entirely from the Prussian field artillery.

But if rifles had finally become the sole armament of Prussia's field artillery, the metal for their construction was again a subject for debate. At various times before the war a half-dozen steel cannon had exploded without warning. In the course of the campaign five more had burst, and senior officers and battery commanders alike were growing nervous.[12] Rifled cannon might indeed be an extraordinary weapon, but safety factors could not be completely disregarded for the sake of range and accuracy. Alfred Krupp's desperate offer to replace several hundred cast steel barrels at his own expense might have a suspicious aura.[13] Nevertheless test showed that poorly-constructed breechblocks rather than defective barrels were responsible for four of the five explosions. This offered some support to postwar critics of breechloaders as too complex and unreliable to be useful outside of proving grounds and firing ranges. The factors which contributed to the breechloader's initial adoption in Prussia were still operative, however. From the battery level upwards no serious advocacy of muzzle-loading designs emerged. Instead professional opinion favored repairing or replacing the inferior breech mechanisms.[14] The army's primary criticism was directed rather against the metal used in the breechloaders' construction.

This continued distrust of cast steel reflected a continuing technical problem. If finished cannon barrels were not cooled evenly, they devloped flaws which tests seemed to indicate could not be detected until the cannon burst. The difficulty was compounded by the fact that each barrel cooled individually; thus no general conclusions could be drawn about the durability of any given production run.[15] Despite Krupp's repeated protests that his firm manufactured reliable cannon steel and had learned how to cool it properly, government inspectors continued to express their doubts. Even wooden guns, some junior officers reportedly declared, were better than undependable ones.[16] Hindersin took the problem seriously enough to order, in October, 1866, the construction of experimental four- and six-pounder bronze rifles. Tests began the next year, with surprisingly favorable results. The barrels proved far stronger, the rifling wore much more slowly, than expected. Best of all, when tested to destruction, bronze barrels gave clear warning before bursting. Arguments that bronze was not sufficiently durable to withstand existing blast effects without either increasing the weight of the barrel at the expense of mobility, or decreasing its length, with corresponding reductions in muzzle velocity and therefore accuracy, were not enough to offset growing support for the reintroduction of bronze to the Prussian artillery. The French military attaché's report of August 31, 1868 that this had been actually decided may have been premature. Four months later, however, the King ordered bronze four-pounders issued to a battery of the Guard and summoned a council of senior officers to deliberate the wider adoption of the new design. By November, 1869, the *Allgemeine Kriegsdepartement* recommended the purchase of three hundred bronze guns and proposed to use bronze for all new construction.

William was reluctant to make such a drastic decision. Admittedly Prussia had large stocks of bronze smoothbores which could be recast. Admittedly the reintroduction of bronze would free the state from its dependence on a private manufacturer. But complete rearmament twice in a decade appeared an extreme response to a dozen burst guns—particularly since the modified breechblocks and replaced barrels were withstanding the most rigorous tests the APK could devise. The outbreak of war with France resolved the issue, as the cast steel breechloaders of the Prussian artillery played a key role in crushing the Second Empire without the technical problems which had emerged in Bohemia. The few bronze rifles which took the field showed no special deficiencies, but neither did they display any marked advantages over their steel rivals. On October 31, 1870, the King declared that he could see no reason to replace Krupp steel with government bronze.[17]

What is significant about the issues of rifles versus smoothbores and steel versus bronze in the postwar years is their failure to arouse anything like the interest of similar controversies in the 1850s and early 60s. This in part reflected the army's earlier commitment to cast steel breechloading rifles—the kind of fundamental decision which once made precluded for a time anything but total rejection on one hand or minor modifications on the other. But it was an even clearer reflection of a drastic change in the climate of opinion in the Prussian artillery. Wartime experiences had shown that its critical weaknesses were in method, not material. Ineffective smoothbores and defective rifles had not handicapped the arm nearly as much as inability to use the weapons it possessed.

At regimental levels this meant training gun crews in something more than mechanical "service of the piece." It was no longer enough to execute a firing mission; future cannoneers must be able to determine why the mission failed and correct their errors. Techniques of observation must be improved. Officers must be trained to utilize to the full the potential of their weapons.[18] Hindersin fostered these developments by a series of lectures for senior officers, and in 1867 obtained funds to establish a gunnery school for the entire artillery. The experience gained at this school furnished the basis for new firing regulations. By 1869 in Berlin at least, the artillery was firing at unknown ranges, not at black bullseyes, but on targets made and painted to resemble bodies of troops—and hitting the targets. Baron Stoffel reported in amazement that battery commanders would estimate a range of 1,500 meters, range their guns at 1,400, 1,500, 1,600, and so on, and adjust their fire accordingly. Only a few minutes were required to bring an entire battery on target. Provincial gunners might not do quite as well as the elite marksmen of the Prussian Guard, but their skills were also vastly developed over 1866.[19]

Improving the quality of individual batteries was only part of the problem. The Prussian artillery in 1866 had neither decided battles by itself nor supported its infantry effectively. Their failures considerably diminished the gunners' sense of superior isolation. After all, in Hohenloe's sarcastic words, what would happen to an army corps composed entirely of artillery?[20] The fate of Austrian batteries abandoned to their own resources at König-grätz offered a vivid warning of the perils of excessive self-reliance. But how could artillery best be integrated into a combined-arms team? The experience of the Seven Weeks' War suggested that the essential responsibility of modern artillery lay in *preparing* decisive attacks. This did not involve bombarding hostile positions at 3,000 meters. Nor did it mean engaging in an artillery duel and leaving the rival infantries to fight it out by themselves. The prewar notion of infantry providing their own fire support might have some merit, but only at ranges under 500 meters. At a thousand meters, short range for a rifled cannon, a six-gun battery was thirty times as effective as a war-strength rifle company against infantry targets. But softening determined infantry took time, particularly since the introduction of rifled small arms prevented cannon from coming to close quarters. Guns held in army reserve until the last minute would be of little use in this process. The experiences of the First and Elbe Armies demonstrated that such forces would seldom be at the right place at the right time, particularly in offensive operations. Nor was it lost on Prussian gunners that the Austrian artillery reserve might have kept defeat from becoming disaster, but had done little to support infantry attacks during the war. On the other hand, since one's own artillery would probably be a primary target, enough guns must be available to divide the enemy fire and sustain the bombardment despite losses. Decentralization, employing artillery by sections and batteries, would render this kind of concentration difficult.

If tactical considerations made it imperative to deploy the greatest possible number of guns at the earliest possible moment, this departure from tradition was made earlier by the technical characteristics of rifled cannon. Their long range meant that they never really left the control of senior officers. Even after once opening fire, they could change positions and be directed against new targets almost at will. And experience suggested that rifles massed in a central location, taking full advantage of improving techniques of observation and fire control, could cover a good portion of the normal front of an army corps in combat. Thus no drastic changes in organization were necessary to implement the new approach. After 1866 each army corps retained its field artillery regiment, with a battalion assigned to each division and the remaining units held under corps control. What altered were methods and attitudes. In orders of battle the "reserve artillery" became "corps artillery"—a semantic gesture indicating to gunners and senior officers alike that artillery now belonged to the main fighting force instead of the baggage train. Regulation orders of march were altered to make the normal position of artillery close to the head of the column instead of at its rear. Corps maneuvers emphasized aggressive use of guns from the beginning, with batteries instructed to hold their positions to the last man even if they had nothing to shoot. The primary loyalties of the field artillery increasingly focussed on the army corps to which the regiment belonged rather than the arm as a whole. If by 1870 the Prussian artillery had not completely digested the lessons of Königgrätz, it was nevertheless ready and able to play a decisive role in the war with France—a reversal of form which depended on technique rather than weapons.[21]

3

To contemporary analysts of the Seven Weeks' War, the railroads were a far less controversial subject than either rifled cannon or needle guns. Baron Stoffel spoke for the majority when he warned against exaggerating the influence of the railway on Prussian concentration.[22] A few writers suggested that the maps and proposals of the modern strategists must have a different emphasis than those of a decade ago, that the railway network had become the most important factor in strategic planning. Railway lines, these men argued, determined the direction of a campaign, how it would begin, and how the troops would be concentrated; possession of an important railway center could be far more important than the capture of a fortress.[23] In general, however, military thinkers remained reluctant to accept the notion that the principles of strategy could be altered or modified by something as ephemeral as a steam engine.

This did not mean that railroads had not demonstrated beyond doubt their ability to expedite Moltke's strategy or any other by moving troops and supplies, by shortening the time required to carry out deployments, and—to some extent at least—by increasing the options available to the high command. At the same time, the Prussian experience demonstrated the necessity for careful planning and even more careful regulation if the railway network was to be of any value at all. Stoppages, bottlenecks, accidents in one area could influence the entire transportation system to an extent unknown in the age of fixed magazines and horse-drawn wagons. In the years after 1866, the European powers paid increased attention to their railroads, to constructing new lines with possible strategic value and to organizing existing ones for war.

In this area Prussia retained the pride of place it had lost in weapons technology. Utilizing and improving existing methods and material presented a different set of challenges than introducing something new, and the structure of Prussia's military railway administration was basically sound. Between 1866 and 1870, the railway system of the North German Confederation was integrated into mobilization plans. Transport schedules were constantly revised to incorporate new construction, new army corps, and new political situations. Cooperation between the General Staff and the civil-military Central Commission, now a permanent organization, also remained at a high level—a sharp contrast to the situation in France. Finally, the entire system of command and control of the lines of communication was reorganized In future field operations, each army and independent corps was to have its own Lines of Communications Inspectorate, responsible for controlling the flow of supplies and reinforcements in the army's rear, with full authority over all subordinate Inspectorates. A *General-Intendant* assigned to GHQ was given general responsibility for supply, communications, and security in the rear areas.

The system was not perfect. Military railway units were still too weak for the tasks assigned them; during the Franco-Prussian war, not only German, but French civilians were used to keep the railroads operating. The mobilization and concentration of the Prussian army was completed with only minor delays, but the supply system broke down in the same way and for the same reasons as in 1866. In the first weeks of the campaign the railways were blocked with tons of supplies which could not be moved forward because of a shortage of wagons and teams. In several cases, only the capture of French depots kept advanced Prussian units from going hungry. Experience showed that the *General-Intendant* had been given too many duties, that regulating and controlling railway transport required a separate central administration. When the Central Executive Commission at GHQ was made completely responsible for the railway services, the situation improved rapidly.[24]

The shortcomings of the organization of the Prussian railroads did not affect the fact that they fulfilled their most important mission. They brought the Prussian army into position when and where Moltke wanted it; they unloaded men and animals who were ready to go to war. The challenge of the machine is not to use it perfectly, but to make it perform the work desired. If in 1866 and 1870 the Prussian General Staff and the Prussian railway administration did not pass the test with full marks, at least they passed it, which is more than can be said for their opponents. By 1914 the German railway network was as well organized for war as the army itself, and functioned with the same efficiency until almost the end of the war—an efficiency which was the final fruit of a half-century's work.

4

In determining how and why the stream of time followed a given channel, the writer of a monograph faces the constant temptation to exaggerate the contribution of his particular subject to the general picture. In evaluating the influence of technology on Prussian and German military development between Waterloo and Königgrätz, the factors of balance and perspective are particularly crucial. To say, for example, an army's position in the state, its relationship to the society of which it is a part, depends in part on the ability to win wars, is not to say that there is a necessary relationship between military influence and victory. The ability to meet the challenges of the industrial revolution was an important indication of the efficiency of a nineteenth-century army. It was not the only one. Superior material, or superior ability to use approximately equal material, are important factors in warfare. They are not inevitably decisive, as the example of the Prussian artillery in 1866 clearly indicates.

Nevertheless, the ability of the Prussian army to use the inventions of its century exercised a wide-ranging influence on the development and outcome of the Seven Weeks' War. Prussia's victory was not accidental, but neither was it inevitable.[25] It is certain that without the railroads the course of the campaign would have been far different; it is equally certain that events would have taken another course had the Bohemian railway network been as complete as that of Silesia and Lusatia. Gordon Craig gives much of the credit for Prussia's victory to "Moltke's operational plan and his strategic sense . . . which took account of . . . the new conditions of warfare."[26] But Prussia's railroads and the well-developed plan for using them not only influenced Moltke's planning and enabled him to compensate for King William's continuing reluctance to declare war; they were in a sense the immediate cause of the war itself. For over two years Bismarck had been advancing Prussian interests in Germany by taking advantage of Austria's desire for peaceful cooperation. In the winter of 1865, however, he finally "reached the line of hard resistance. What he could not achieve through . . . further capitulation in Vienna, he now resolved to acquire through violence." His first tack was to find "a *casus belli* which would place Austria in the wrong" before Europe, the Prussian people, and most importantly King William himself. The Austrian government obliged by moving troops into Bohemia—a decision made essentially because the Austrian generals knew that they could neither mobilize nor concentrate large forces with anything like the speed of the Prussians. It was this decision which "properly exaggerated," gave Bismarck the weapon he sought "to justify himself before Germany and Europe, and to wind up the royal clock once more . . ."—one of the first examples of the interrelationship of technology and diplomacy which is among the distinctive characteristics of modern history.[27]

The Seven Weeks' War also pitted breechloader against muzzleloader, and Austrian tactics compounded the discrepancy. Whether Moltke's strategy and the superior quality of Prussia's rank and file would have ensured victory, whether the weaknesses of the Austrian military system would have meant defeat, had both armies or neither carried breechloaders, will never be known. If the lessons of the American Civil War and the experience of the Saxon Corps at Gitschin and Königgrätz strongly suggest that revised Austrian tactics might have compensated for inferior armament, suggestion is not proof. Gordon Craig argues that "the experience of Königgrätz stood, and still stands, as a warning against the danger of overvaluing technical superiority."[28] Baron Stoffel offered perhaps the best contemporary statement of this thesis. His detailed analysis of the needle gun stresses the calm, the steadiness, the fire discipline of the Prussian infantry as the real reasons why the Austrians were unable to get to close quarters. Yet at the same time he describes these qualities as being nurtured by confidence in the needle gun which had been developed over twenty years. Even men without experience of war trusted their weapons enough to fire "calmly and surely" under the most extreme stress—hardly a clear-cut example of the triumph of the moral over the physical.[29]

Since the beginning of history fighting men have made good the errors of their commanders and the deficiencies of the social and political systems which send them into battle. Prussian rifles and Prussian tactics helped their infantry to overcome uninspired leadership through the campaign. And on July 3, if the Austrian rank and file did not reverse a decision predetermined in so many ways, they came closer than is generally realized. Like Waterloo, Königgrätz was a near-run thing. As late as 3 PM the corps commanders of Frederick Charles's army were debating the wisdom of retreat; Royal Headquarters too was displaying signs of nervousness. The decisive attack on Chlum came "not a moment too soon."[30] What might have happened had the Austrian attack on the *Swiepwald* been successful? Would the Prussian Second Army have arrived only in time to cover the retirement of the First? What would have been the result had the garrison of the Chlum positions been armed with breechloaders? If the destiny of central Europe was decided on the field of Königgrätz, the nature and the extent of Prussia's victory was determined at three points: the *Swiepwald*, the heights of Chlum, and Problus. At all three points the needle gun played a decisive role. Its fire drove the Austrians from their position at Chlum and enabled Prussians disorganized by victory to repel the desperate Austrian counterattacks, often without artillery support. Its fire smashed the Austrians in Stezirek Wood, driving them into the flank of the Saxon corps and setting the stage for the retreat of the allied left. Finally, its fire enabled Fransecky's men to hold the *Swiepwald* for four crucial hours against a brave and determined enemy. If the needle gun did not win the war by itself, it did indeed prick Austria to the heart.[31]

The needle gun also illustrated a fact too often misunderstood or ignored by the soldiers of the nineteenth century. During the long peace that followed the Treaty of Frankfurt, even the German army did no more than keep pace with developments in weapons technology. It neither made nor sought drastic breakthroughs in this area. German martial virtues on one hand, abstract strategic considerations on the other, tended to dominate the thinking of regimental officers and *Generalstäbler* alike. The Schlieffen Plan, in so many ways the culmination of the military tradition of the Second Reich, took virtually no account of the effect of improved firepower on tactics, or the problem of keeping the massive right wing supplied.[32] During World War I the Germans described the allied offensives in the west as "battles of material," with "the sarcastic interpretation that they were battles fought by the enemy with material, but without brains."[33] But Ludendorff in his report to the Reichstag on October 2, 1918, declared that the tanks were one of the main reasons why Germany could no longer compel its enemies to make peace.[34] It is not necessary to accept Ludendorff's statement at face value to suggest that German overcompensation for the tactical shortcomings of the Prussian artillery in 1866 and German readiness to accept the kind of technological superiority represented by the needle gun as an isolated phenomenon may have contributed indirectly but vitally to shaping the world of the twentieth century. Modern technology had gone to war for the first time in 1866, and nothing would ever be quite the same again.

Notes

INTRODUCTION

1. Michael Stürmer, "Bismarck in Perspective," *Central European History*, IV (1971), p. 301. Cf. Karl-Georg Faber, "Realpolitik als Ideologie: Die Bedeutung des Jahres 1866 für das politische Denken in Deutschland," *Historische Zeitschrift*, 203 (1966), pp. 1-45.

2. Otto Pflanze, "Another Crisis Among German Historians? Helmut Böhme's *Deutschlands Weg zur Grossmacht*," *Journal of Modern History*, XL (1968), pp. 118-129.

3. Excellent examples of this technique are Michael Howard, *The Franco-Prussian War* (New York, 1962), pp. 1-39; and Gordon Craig, *The Battle of Königgrätz* (Philadelphia and New York, 1964), pp. 1-25.

4. Leopold von Ranke, *Englische Geschichte*, ed. by Willy Andreas, 3 vols. (Wiesbaden, 1957), I, p. 5.

5. Theodore Ropp, *War in the Modern World*, rev. ed. (New York, 1962), p. 13.

6. Lewis Mumford, *Technics and Civilization* (New York, 1934), p. 95.

7. R. H. Tawney, *Land and Labour in China* (London, 1932), p. 88.

8. For three widely-divergent corroborating examples, see Charles de Gaulle, *The Edge of the Sword*, tr. by Gerard Hopkins, (New York, 1960), pp. 16ff.; Quincy Wright, *A Study of War*, Vol. I (Chicago, 1942), p. 291; Wilhelm Rüstow, *Militärisches Hand-Wörterbuch*, Vol. I (Zürich, 1858), pp. 473ff.

9. "The Secret of Victory," published in *Weekly Tank Notes*, January 25, 1919, quoted in J. F. C. Fuller, *Armament and History* (New York, 1945), p. 18.

10. Kenneth Macksey, *Tank Warfare* (New York, 1972), p. 224.

PART I

CHAPTER I

1. For general accounts of railway development during this period, see G. Fleck, "Studien zur Geschichte des preussischen Eisenbahnwesens," *Archiv für Eisenbahnwesen*, XIX (1896), pp. 858ff.; *Hundert Jahre deutsche Eisenbahnen*, ed. by *Reichsverkehrsministerium* (Berlin, 1935), pp. 20ff.; Max Hoeltzel, *Aus der Frühzeit der Eisenbahnen* (Berlin, 1935); and Hans Nordmann, "Die Frühgeschichte der Eisenbahnen," *Abhandlungen der Deutschen Akademie der Wissenschaften zu Berlin: Mathematisch-natürwissenschaftliche Klasse, 1947/1948*, pp. 1-14. For the nature of the German money market cf. Knut Borchardt, "Zur Frage des Kapitalmangels in der ersten Hälfte des 19. Jahrhunderts in Deutschland," *Jahrbücher für Nationalökonomie und Statistik*, 173 (1961), pp. 401-421; and Richard Tilly, *Financial Institutions and Industrialization in the Rhineland, 1815-1870* (Madison, Wisconsin, 1966), pp. 96.

2. Camphausen's views on the military use of railways are included in *Zur Eisenbahn von Köln nach Antwerpen (Erste Eisenbahnschrift)* (Cologne, 1833), printed in M. Schwann, *Ludolf Camphausen als Wirtschaftspolitiker*, 3 vols. (Essen, 1915), III, pp. 287-305. A *Zweite Eisenbahnschrift* with the same title was published in 1835 and printed in *ibid.*, pp. 306-362. Cf. the narratives in Schwann, I, pp. 95ff; A. Bergengrün, *David Hansemann* (Berlin, 1901), pp. 192ff; and Klara von Eyll, "Camphausen und Hansemann: Zwei rheinische Eisenbahnunternehmer," *Tradition*, X (1966), pp. 218-231.

3. For List's life and work see Carl Brinkmann, *Friedrich List* (Berlin, 1949); Hans Gehrig, *Friedrich List und Dutschlands politisch-ökonomische Einheit* (Leipzig, 1956); and the correspondence in Erwin von Beckerath, *et al.* (eds.), *Friedrich List. Schriften, Reden, Briefe*, 10 vols. (Berlin, 1927-1935), I and II, *passim*. (Hereafter cited as List, *Schriften*). The quotation is from E. M. Earle, "Adam Smith, Alexander Hamilton, Friedrich List: the Economic Foundations of Military Power," in E. M. Earle (ed.), *Makers of Modern Strategy* (Princeton, 1943), p. 141.

4. "Deutschlands Eisenbahnsystem in militärischer Beziehung," List, *Schriften*, Vol. III, Part I, p. 260.

5. For List's views of the military uses of railways see the "Schriften zum Verkehrswesen" in List, *Schriften*, Vol. III, Part I, pp. 81ff., especially "Aufruf an unsere Mitbürger in Sachsen, die Anlage einer Eisenbahn zwischen Dresden und Leipzig betreffend;" "Über ein deutsches Eisenbahnsystem als Grundlage eines allgemeinen deutschen Eisenbahnsystems;" and "Deutschlands Eisenbahnsystem in militärischer Beziehung." The quotation is from "Deutschlands Eisenbahnsystem in militärischer Beziehung," p. 267.

6. See the general discussion in Bernhard Meinke, "Die ältesten Stimmen über die militärische Bedeutung der Eisenbahnen," *Archiv*

NOTES TO CHAPTER I

für Eisenbahnwesen, XLI (1918), pp. 921-934; and XLII (1919), pp. 46-74.

7. The quotation is from Heinrich von Treitschke, *Deutsche Geschichte im neunzehnten Jahrhundert,* 3rd ed., Vol. IV (Leipzig, 1890), p. 590. Cf. also W. O. Henderson, "Rother and the Seehandlung," in *The State and the Industrial Revolution in Prussia, 1740-1870* (Liverpool, 1958), p.˙130; Albert Fricke, *Die Anfänge des Eisenbahnwesens in Preussen* (Berlin, 1912); and Dietrich Eichholtz, *Junker und Bourgeoisie vor 1848 in der preussischen Eisenbahngeschichte* (East Berlin, 1962).

8. "Die Entwicklung des Militäreisenbahnwesens vor Moltke," *Militär-Wochenblatt,* 1902, *Beiheft,* pp. 237-238; Meinke, pp. 929-930.

9. Typical are such essays as "Über Eisenbahnen in Beziehung auf den Krieg," *Allgemeine Militär-Zeitung,* 1836, Nos. 14 and 18; and "Über die Verwendung des Militärs zur Herstellung von Eisenbahnen und Kanalen," *ibid.,* No. 96. (Hereafter cited as *AMZ*).

10. Major du Vignau, "Über die Anwendbarkeit der Eisenbahnen mit Lokomotivmaschinen zu militärischen Zwecken," *Zeitschrift für Kunst, Wissenschaft und Geschichte des Krieges,* II (1837), cited in Meinke, pp. 47ff.

11. *Über die militärische Benutzung der Eisenbahnen* (Berlin, 1836); *Darlegung der Technischen-und Verkehrsverhältnisse der Eisenbahnen, usw.* (Berlin, 1841); *AMZ,* 1841, No. 71; Meinke, pp. 61ff.

12. *AMZ,* 1839, No. 82.

13. *Ibid.,* 1836, No. 44; Meinke, pp. 51-52.

14. Cf. "Pz." [Karl Eduard Pönitz], *Die Vertheidigung von Süddeutschland gegen die Französen, mit Zuziehung der Eisenbahnen, usw.* (Stuttgart and Tübigen, 1844); and *Die Eisenbahnen und ihre Benutzung als militärische Operationslinien,* 2nd ed. (Adorf, 1853), pp. 22-23. The first edition was printed in 1842, and excerpts of it appeared in the *AMZ,* 1840, Nos. 61-63.

15. Eichholtz, p. 139.

16. The definitive biography is Eberhard Kessel, *Moltke* (Stuttgart, 1957). Wilhelm Bigge, *Feldmarschall Graf Moltke: Ein militärisches Lebensbild,* 2 vols. (Munich, 1901); and Max Jähns, *Feldmarschall Moltke,* 3 vols. (Berlin, 1894-1900), are the best of the hagiographical studies produced in the last century.

17. For example, the decision to run the Magdeburg-Wittenberg railway directly into the fortress at Magdeburg was postponed time after time over the objections of the directors, and the War Ministry's conditions for permitting it at all would have cost the company at least a half-million thalers if adopted in full. Cf. Eichholtz, p. 104; and List's essay "Die thüringische Eisenbahn," written in 1840. List, *Schriften,* Vol. III, Part I, pp. 294-306. For similar problems in the Rhineland, see Ludolf Camphausen's letter of September 16, 1838, in Schwann, II, p. 440.

18. Friedrich Meinecke, *Das Leben des Generalfeldmarschalls Hermann von Boyen,* 2 vols. (Stuttgart, 1895-1899), II, pp. 530ff.

19. Pierre Benaerts, *Les origines de la grande industrie allemande* (Paris, 1933), p. 319.

20. The problem of training competent officials is summarized in *Hundert Jahre deutsche Eisenbahnen*, pp. 466-477

21. Pönitz, *Eisenbahnen*, pp. 53ff: *Vertheidigung*, pp. 37ff.

22. Cf. A. Bergengrün, *Staatsminister August von der Heydt* (Leipzig, 1908), pp. 51ff.; A. von der Leyen, "Die Verhandlungen der vereinigten ständigen Ausschüsse über die Eisenbahnfrage in Preussen im Jahre 1842," *Archiv für Eisenbahnwesen*, V (1881), pp. 1-21; and Kurt Born, "Die Entwicklung der Königlich-Preusssichen Ostbahn," *ibid.*, XXXIV (1911), pp. 878-939, 1125-1172, 1431-1461.

23. The *AMZ*, 1842, No. 61, reported the transport of a battery of 12-pounders between Berlin and Zehlendorf on the Berlin-Potsdam line. The 21-car train covered the 12 kilometers in 20 minutes each way with no difficulty. Similar movements are discussed in Meinke, pp. 64-65.

CHAPTER II

1. O. von der Osten-Sacken, *Preussens Heer von seinen Anfängen bis zur Gegenwart*, 3 vols. (Berlin, 1911-1913), II, p. 308; Hanns Martin Elster, *Graf Albrecht von Roon, sein Leben und Wirken* (Berlin, 1938), pp. 211-212.

2. Reyher's policies are summarized in "Die Entwicklung des Militäreisenbahnwesens vor Moltke," pp. 243-245; and F. E. A. von Cochenhausen. *Von Scharnhorst zu Schlieffen, 1806-1906. 100 Jahre preussisch-deutscher Generalstab* (Berlin, 1933), p. 146.

3. Osten-Sacken, II, pp. 320-321, 370-371. For the Austrian transport see *Regierungsrat* Wernekke, "Die Mitwirkung der Eisenbahnen an den Kriegen in Mitteleuropa," *Archiv für Eisenbahnwesen*, XXXV (1912), pp. 930-931.

4. For von der Heydt's railway policies see Bergengrün, *von der Heydt*, chapter VII, *passim*. General discussions of the evolution of Prussia's railway network include T. S. Hamerow, *The Social Foundations of German Unification, 1858-1871* (Princeton, 1969), pp. 25-26; *Hundert Jahre deutsche Eisenbahnen*, p. 33; and Henderson, *State and Industrial Revolution in Prussia*, pp. 173-174.

5. Cited in *AMZ*, 1855, Nos. 5-6.

6. Bigge, II, pp. 98-99.

7. Kessel, pp. 234ff; [F. von Schmerfeld] "Moltke in der Vorbereitung und Durchführung der Operationen," *Kriegsgeschichtliche Einzelschriften*, ed. by *Grossen Generalstab*, XXXVI (Berlin, 1905), pp. 6-7. The "Reglement der französischen Armee von November 1855 über den Transport der Truppen aller Waffengattungen auf Eisenbahnen" appeared as a *Beiheft* to the *Militär-Wochenblatt*, 1855.

8. General Thoumas. *Les transformations de l'armée française*, 2 vols. (Paris, 1887), I, pp. 537ff; Major Millar, "The Italian Campaign

of 1859," *Journal of the Royal United Services Institution*, V (1861) pp. 269-308; E. A. Pratt, *The Rise of Rail Power in War and Conquest, 1833-1914* (London, 1915), pp. 9ff. For the use of railroads by the Austrians see Wernekke, pp. 932ff.; and "Unsere Eisenbahnen im Kriege," in *Geschichte der Eisenbahnen der oesterreichisch-ungarischen Monarchie*, ed. by Herman Strach, 6 vols. (Vienna, 1908), II, pp. 127ff.

9. Bonin to Moltke, February 1, 1859, and Moltke to Bonin, with accompanying memorandum, February 7, 1859, in Helmuth von Moltke, *Militärische Werke*, 1. Abt., *Militärische Korrespondenz*, ed. by *Grossen Generalstab, Kriegsgeschichtliche Abteilung*, 4 vols. (Berlin, 1892-1902), IV, pp. 1ff. (Hereafter cited as *MMW*).

10. "Denkschrift betreffend den etwaigen Einfluss der neuen Eisenbahnbauten und Projekte auf künftigen Truppenkonzentrationen gegen Westen," *ibid.*, pp. 67-74.

11. Moltke to Bonin, April 16, 1859; von der Heydt to Moltke, April 23, 1859, *ibid.*, pp. 74, 77-78, "Moltke in der Vorbereitung und Durchführung der Operationen," pp. 9ff.

12. Kessel, p. 275; "Moltke in der Vorbereitung und Durchführung der Operationen," pp. 11-12. The protocols of the conferences on the subject held in Berlin on June 25 and 28 are reprinted in *MMW*, 1, IV, pp. 146-47.

13. Moltke to Bonin, July 6, 1859, *MMW*, 1, IV, pp. 161-163.

14. Cf. Moltke's memoranda on the subject written in the spring of 1860 and June, 1863, *MMW*, 1, III, pp. 16ff. and pp. 43ff; and his outline for the General Staff Ride of 1861, *ibid.*, 2. Abt., *Die Thätigkeit als Chef des Generalstabes der Aimee im Frieden*, ed. by *Grossen Generalstab, Kriegsgeschichtliche Abteilung*, 3 vols. (Berlin, 1892-1906), III, pp. 148ff. General discussions include Kessel, pp. 289ff; and "Moltke in der Vorbereitung und Durchführung der Operationen," pp. 14-15.

15. Cf. the fragment "Bedeutung der Eisenbahnen für die Kriegführung," written sometime in 1861, *MMW*, 4. Abt., *Kriegslehren*, ed. by *Grossen Generalstab, Kriegsgeschichtliche Abteilung*, 3 vols. (Berlin, 1911-1912), I, pp. 204-205; and Kessel, 298ff.

16. Cf. "Die Militärischen Interessen des Bundes bei den Eisenbahnen," *AMZ*, 1855, No. 15; "Kriegsbereitschaft der deutschen Eisenbahnen," *ibid.*, 1861, Nos. 18-19; Kessel, pp. 306-307.

17. Heinz Helmert, *Militärsystem und Streitkräfte im Deutschen Bund am Vorabend des preussisch-österreichischen Krieges von 1866* (Berlin, 1964), pp. 37-38; Wolf D. Gruner, *Das Bayerische Heer 1825 bis 1864*, Vol. XIV of *Militärgeschichtliche Studien*, ed. by *Militärgeschichtliches Forschungsamt* (Boppard, 1972), pp. 269, 278-279; Enno E. Kraehe, "A History of the German Confederation, 1850-1866," (Ph. D. dissertation. Minnesota, 1948), pp. 241-242; "Ueber die militärische Benutzung der deutschen Eisenbahnen," *AMZ*, 1861, Nos. 13-14.

18. For the composition and work of the commission see Wilhelm Ritter von Gründorf von Zerbégeny, *Memorien eines österreichischen Generalstäblers 1834-1866*, ed. by A. Sanger (Stuttgart, 1913), pp. 158-166; Kraehe, pp. 243ff; and the comprehensive *Bericht über die*

Leistungsfähigkeit der Deutschen Eisenbahnen zu militärischen Zwecken erstattet durch die . . . Specialcommission (Frankfurt, 1861).

19. Cf. esp. the *Instruktion für den Transport der Truppen und des Armee-Materials auf Eisenbahnen* (Berlin, 1861), and the analysis in F. Jacquemin, *Les Chemins de fer pendant la guerre de 1870-1871* (Paris, 1872), pp. 62ff, 91ff.

20. Cf. the discussions in Reinhard Höhn, *Verfassungskampf und Heereseid: Der Kampf des Bürgertums um das Heer (1815-1850)* (Leipzig, 1938), pp. 261ff; Erich Marcks, "Albrecht von Roon," in *Männer und Zeiten*, Vol. I (Berlin, 1922), pp. 341-380; esp. pp. 348-353; Gerhard Ritter, *Staatskunst und Kriegshandwerk*, 4 vols. (Munich, 1954-1968) I, Chapters 5 and 7, *passim*; Friedrich Meinecke, "Boyen und Roon, zwei preussiche Kriegminister," *Historische Zeitschrift*, 77 (1896); Alfred Vagts, *A History of Militarism*, rev. ed. (New York, 1959), pp. 187ff; and Gordon A. Craig, *The Politics of the Prussian Army* (Oxford, 1953), pp. 140ff.

21. Richard McKenna, *The Sand Pebbles* (New York, 1962), p. 46.

22. Hajo Holborn, "Moltke and Schlieffen," in Earle, *Makers of Modern Strategy*, p. 177.

23. H. von Boehn, *Generalstabsgeschäfte: Ein Handbuch für Offiziere aller Waffen* (Potsdam, 1862), pp. 141ff, 313ff; Emil Demarteau, "Ideen über die rasche Erbauung neuer und die Benutzung bestehender Eisenbahnen zu militärischen Zwecken," *Österreichische Militärische Zeitschrift*, 1861, IV, pp. 26-38.

24. Jay Luvaas, *The Military Legacy of the Civil War: The European Inheritance* (Chicago, 1959), pp. 122, cites this reference from Pratt, p. 104. I have found no other evidence supporting this conclusion.

25. Moltke to Roon, December 6, 1862, *MMW*, 1, I, pp. 1-6.

26. Kessel, p. 362; Cochenhausen, p. 153.

27. For the planning and execution of these operations cf. Wernekke, pp. 934ff; Hermann Graf Wartensleben-Carow, *Erinnerungen des Generals der Kavallerie Grafen Wartensleben-Carow, während des Kriegszeit 1866 Major im Grossen Generalstabe* (Berlin, 1897), p. 1; Prince Kraft zu Hohenloe-Ingelfingen, *Aufzeichnungen aus meinem Leben*, 4 vols. (Berlin, 1897-1907), III, pp. 11-12; Moltke to Roon, December 8, 1863, *MMW*, 1, I, pp. 56ff; Gründorf, pp. 175ff; Kessel, p. 371; *Der Deutsch-Dänisch Krieg 1864*, pub. by *Grossen Generalstab, Abteilung für Kriegsgeschichte*, 2 vols. (Berlin, 1886), II, pp. 758-759.

28. Moltke to War Ministry, October 23, 1864, *MMW*, 1, I, pp. 224ff.

CHAPTER III

1. Cf. Wilhelm Rüstow, *Die Lehre vom Gefecht, aus den Elementen neu entwickelt für die Gegenwart und nächste Zukunft* (Zürich, 1865),

pp. 490ff; and *Der italienische Krieg 1859, politisch-militärisch Beschrieben* (Zürich, 1866), p. 346.

2. Cf. particularly Moltke's "Bemerkungen vom Jahre 1865 über den Einfluss der verbesserten Feuerwaffen auf die Taktik," first published anonymously in the *Militär-Wochenblatt* for July, 1865, and printed in *MMW*, 1, II, pp. 49ff; and "Ueber Marschtiefen," dated September 16, 1865, *ibid.*, pp. 235ff.

3. *Ibid.*, p. 227.

4. For a summary of Prussian planning prior to 1860 see *Moltke in der Vorbereitung und Durchführung der Operationen*, pp. 39ff; Wolfgang von Groote, "Moltkes Planungen für den Feldzug in Böhmen und ihre Grundlagen," in *Entscheidung 1866*, ed. by Wolfgang von Groote and Ursula von Gersdorff (Stuttgart, 1966), pp. 78ff.

5. "Aufmarsch der Preussischen Armee in einem Krieg gegen Oesterreich," *MMW*, 1, II, pp. 1-16.

6. Gordon A. Craig, *The Battle of Königgrätz* (Philadelphia and New York, 1964), p. 28.

7. Printed in *MMW*, 1, II, pp. 21-45. Cf. the analyses in Kessel, pp. 437ff; Bigge, II, pp. 195ff; and Craig, *Königgrätz*, p. 28.

8. *MMW*, 1, II, p. 36.

9. Cf. the memorandum "Vorgehen gegen Sachsen," written in 1862 and printed in *MMW*, 1, II, pp. 26ff; and the memorandum of April 2, 1866, emphasizing the necessity of concentrating against Austria no matter what course of action Bavaria followed in *ibid.*, 2, II, pp. 74ff.

10. *MMW*, 1, II, pp. 74ff.

11. Cf. Moltke's memoranda of April 9, 10, and 12, in *ibid.*, 1, II, pp. 106ff.

12. The text of the memorandum is printed in *ibid.*, pp. 119ff. See particularly the accompanying "Justification" and the discussions in *Moltke in der Vorbereitung und Durchführung der Operationen*, p. 50; and Kessel, pp. 446-447.

13. *MMW*, 1, II, p. 130.

14. "Vortrage bei Seiner Majestät dem Könige am 27. April, 1866," in *ibid.*, pp. 134-136; Kessel, p. 447.

15. Cf. particularly Moltke to Roon, April 23, in *MMW*, 1, II, pp. 148-149.

16. Moltke to Stosch (Chief of Staff, IV Corps), April 24, *ibid.*, pp. 150-151; Hohenloe, III, p. 224.

17. Cf the summary in Curt Jany, *Geschichte der Preussischen Armee vom 15. Jahrhundert bis 1914*, 4 vols., 2nd ed. rev. (Osnabrück, 1967), IV, pp. 236-237; and Moltke to Roon, May 1, in *MMW*, 1, II, pp. 151-152.

18. Moltke to Wilhelm, May 4, *MMW*, 1, II, pp. 153-154.

19. Cf. Moltke's correspondence of May 7-11 in *ibid*; pp. 156-167.

20. Moltke to Steinmetz, June 1, *MMW*, 1, II, pp. 186-187. He had said almost the same thing at the conference on May 25. Cf. Karl Leonhard Graf Blumenthal, *Tagebücher des Generalfeldmarschalls Graf von Blumenthal aus den Jahren 1866 und 1870/71*, ed. by Albrecht

von Blumenthal (Stuttgart and Berlin, 1902), p. 12.

21. Cf. the correspondence between Moltke and Blumenthal between June 8 and June 11, in *ibid.*, pp. 200-208; the orders to 1st and 2nd Armies and the Guard, *ibid.*, pp. 210-213; and Blumenthal's diary entries for June 6, 10, 11-12, 15, and 17 in *Tagebücher*, pp. 19-23. Blumenthal had been willing to sacrifice "all of Silesia, even Breslau" as late as May 21—a fact which made his call for reinforcements weigh more heavily with Moltke than might otherwise have been the case.

22. H. Bonnal, *Sadowa* (Paris, 1901), pp. 19-20, 184-186.

23. Kessel, pp. 455-456.

24. Groote, pp. 100ff; Craig, *Königgrätz*, p. 36.

25. Cf. Kessel, p. 455.

26. Craig, *Königgrätz*, pp. 176-177.

27. These two headings, discussed in Bigge, II, pp. 164 ff; summarize the position of Moltke's critics reasonably well. Of the many studies of the strategy of 1866, the best are Bonnal, *Sadowa*, and General S. von Schlichting, *Moltke und Benedek: Eine Studie über Truppenführung* (Berlin, 1900). Heinrich Friedjung, one of Moltke's more judicious critics, summarizes the debate and the relevant literature in *Der Kampf um die Vorherrschaft in Deutschland 1859 bis 1866*, 2 vols., 10th ed. (Stuttgart and Berlin, 1917), II, pp. 8ff.

28. Cyril Falls, *A Hundred Years of War* (London, 1953), p. 76.

29. Craig, *Königgrätz*, p. 177.

30. "Uebersicht des Verlaufs der preussischen Truppen-Transporte auf Eisenbahnen im Mai und June 1866," Appendix 2 of *Der Feldzug von 1866 in Deutschland*, ed. by *Grossen Generalstab, Kriegsgeschichtliche Abteilung*, 2 vols. (Berlin, 1867). See also E. Schäffer, *Der Kriegs-Train des Deutschen Heeres* (Berlin, 1883), pp. 73ff; and Wernekke, pp. 942ff.

31. For Moltke's orders transferring the Guard, see *MMW*, 1, II, pp. 210-213. The movement itself is discussed in Hohenloe, III, pp. 225ff.

32. Craig, *Königgrätz*, p. 177.

33. For Krismanic and his plan of campaign cf. Friedjung, I, pp. 235ff., 294-295, 483ff., and II, 31ff; [E. Steinmetz], *Die Kritischen Tagen von Olmütz im Juli 1866. Vom Eintreffen des Hauptquartiers der Nordarmee in Olmütz am 9. bis zum Abend des 15. Juli.* (Vienna, 1903); E. von Glaise-Horstenau, *Franz Josephs Weggefährte: Das Leben des Generalstabschefs Grafen Beck* (Vienna, 1930), pp. 94ff; and Johann Christoph von Allmayer-Beck, "Der Feldzug der österreichischen Nord-Armee nach Königgrätz," in *Entscheidung 1866*, pp. 112ff. For the railroads see Wernekke, pp. 933-939; and "Die militärische Eisenbahn-benutzung in Österreich im Feldzuge 1866," *Österreichische Militärische Zeitschrift*, 1867, II, pp. 395ff.

34. O. von Lettow-Vorbeck, *Geschichte des Krieges von 1866*, 3 vols. (Berlin, 1892-1899), I, pp. 129ff., II, 66ff; Wernekke, pp. 945-946; Pratt, pp. 123ff; H. M. Hozier, *The Seven Weeks' War*, 2 vols. (London, 1867), I, pp. 166-167.

35. Kessel, pp. 456ff.

36. *Heeresverpflegung*, Vol. VI of *Studien zur Kriegsgeschichte und Taktik*, ed. by *Grossen Generalstab, Kriegsgeschichtliche Abteilung* (Berlin, 1913), pp. 100ff; Pratt, p. 105. For the evolution of the military intendance service after 1815 see the comprehensive account in Hans Helfritz, *Geschichte der Preussischen Heeresverwaltung* (Berlin, 1938), pp. 320ff. Representative contemporary accounts include L. A. W. Froelich, *Die Militärökonomie im Frieden und im Kriege* (Stettin, 1858); and G. Messerschmidt, *Die Verwaltung des Militärhaushalts in Presussen* (Berlin, 1853); and *Die Militärökonomie. Handbuch für Militärverwaltungs-Beamte* (Berlin, 1854).

37. Wolfgang Foerster, *Prinz Friedrich Karl von Preussen. Denkwürdigkeiten aus seinem Leben*, 2 vols. (Stuttgart, 1910), II, p. 109.

38. Cf. Moltke to Roon, July 4, and his orders of July 5 to the 1st, 2nd and Elbe Armies, in *MMW*, 1, II, pp. 248-250.

39. Wartensleben, pp. 52-53; *Heeresverpflegung*, pp. 124ff.

40. For the Prussian security system see Captain Webber, "Notes on the Campaign in Bohemia," in *Papers of the Royal Engineers*, XVI (1868), cited in Pratt, pp. 55-56.

PART II

CHAPTER IV

1. Sigurd Rabe, *Das Zündnadelgewehr greift ein* (Leipzig, 1938), p. 18.

2. Kraft Karl zu Hohenloe-Ingelfingen, *Aus meinem Leben*, 4 vols. (Berlin, 1897-1907), I, p. 335.

3. W. Eckardt and O. Morawietz, *Die Handwaffen des brandenburgisch-preussisch-deutschen Heeres, 1640-1945* (Hamburg, 1957), p. 105; Curt Jany, *Geschichte der Preussischen Armee vom 15. Jahrhundert bis 1914*, 4 vols., 2nd ed. rev. (Osnabrück, 1967), IV, p. 199.

4. The description is from Dudley Pope, *Guns* (Verona, Italy, 1965), pp. 171-172.

5. Rabe, pp. 23ff.

6. Eckardt and Morawietz, pp. 104-105.

7. Jany, IV, p. 199.

8. Friedrich Meinecke, *Das Leben des Generalfeldmarschalls Hermann von Boyen*, 2 vols. (Stuttgart, 1895-1899), II. pp. 527-528.

9. "Wilhelm von Plönnies, Grossherzoglich Hessischer Major a.D.," *Militär-Wochenblatt*, 1889, *Beiheft* 2, p. 66. Wilhelm Rüstow also discusses the ability of a few good marksmen armed with modern rifles such as the Minié and Thouvenin to endanger the enemy's artillery, but says nothing about the needle gun. *Der Krieg und seine Mittel*

(Leipzig, 1856), p. 305.

10. Hans Busk, *The Rifle and How to Use It* (London, 1862), p. 40-41.

11. Constantin von Altrock, *Geschichte des Königin Elisabeth Garde-Grenadier-Regiments Nr. 3. von seiner Stiftung 1859 bis zum Jahre 1896* (Berlin, 1897), p. 26.

12. F. von der Wülbe, *Das Garde-Füsilier-Regiment* (Berlin, 1876), p. 51. It is characteristic of an enduring school of thought in all armies that when the commander of the 2nd Company reported that the needle gun did not require cleaning as often as the Thouvenin, it was believed in higher quarters that this would seduce the soldiers to carelessness.

13. Cf. the definitive analysis by Peter Paret, *Yorck and the Era of Prussian Reform* (Princeton, 1966), especially pp. 117ff., 208ff.; and the older, less comprehensive narratives by R. Sautermeister, *Die taktische Reform der preussischen Armee nach 1806* (Tübingen, 1935); and W. O. Shanahan, *Prussian Military Reforms, 1786-1813* (New York, 1945), pp. 109 *passim*.

14. Walter von Bremen (ed.), *Denkwürdigkeiten des preussischen Generals der Infanterie Eduard von Fransecky* (Berlin, 1913), pp. 63 *passim*; D. Paulus and A. von Woedtke, *Geschichte des 4. Rhenischen Infanterie-Regiments Nr. 30, 1815-1884* (Berlin, 1884), pp. 99 *passim*.

15. Wilhelm Rüstow, *Geschichte der Infanterie*, 2 vols. (Nordhausen, 1862), II, pp. 338.

16. See, for example, the arguments in J. Niedermayr, *Ansichten über leichte Infanterie und Bildung der Jäger-Truppen* (Munich, 1830).

17. Cf. "Chasseurs à pied oder Fusiliere," *Allgemeine Militär-Zeitung*, 1856, Nos. 79-83; Carl Eduard Pönitz, "Auch eine Ansicht über leichte Infanterie und ihre hauptsächlichste Bestimmung," *ibid.*, 1857, Nos. 1-4 (Hereafter cited as *AMZ*); Rüstow, *Der Krieg und seine Mittel*, p. 352.

18. The best and most consistent expression of these views was embodied in the work of Wilhelm Rüstow. See particularly *Geschichte der Infanterie*, II, pp. 336ff, and *Der Krieg und seine Mittel*, pp. 350ff.

19. Before the reorganization of 1860, a Prussian corps included only four active infantry regiments.

20. Major von Ollech, *Carl Friedrich Wilhelm von Reyher*, Vol. IV (Berlin, 1879), p. 143; Meinecke, II, p. 529.

21. Thilo Krieg, *Constantin von Alvensleben, General der Infanterie: Ein militärisches Lebensbild* (Berlin, 1903), pp. 18-19.

22. [Frederick Charles], "Einfluss des Zündnadelgewehrs auf das Gefecht," *Deutsche Wehrzeitung*, No. 71 (April 22, 1849), summarized in Wolfgang Foerster, *Prinz Friedrich Karl von Preussen, Denkwürdigkeiten aus seinem Leben*, 2 vols. (Stuttgart and Leipzig, 1910), I, pp. 75-76.

23. Reyher to Strotha, February 19, 1849, in Ollech, IV, pp. 150ff.

24. Printed in *Militärische Schriften weiland Kaiser Wilhelms des Grossen Majestät*, ed. by Kgl. Preuss. Kriegsministerium, 2 vols. in 1 (Berlin, 1897), II, pp. 86ff.

25. An opinion also shared by Prince Radziwill, an influential member of the royal entourage. Hermann Witte, *Die Reorganization des preussischen Heeres durch Wilhelm I* (Halle, 1910), pp. 38-39.

Chapter V

1. O. von der Osten-Sacken, *Preussens Heer von seinem Anfängen bis zur Gegenwart*, 3 vols. (Berlin, 1911-1913), II, pp. 249, 349; Jany, IV, pp. 138-139, 201; S. A. Callerström, "Muss die Anfertigung der Infanteriewaffen ausschliessend ein Gegenstand der Privatindustrie sein, oder kann sich damit die Regierung befassen und für das eigene Bedürfniss Waffenfabriken betreiben," *AMZ*, 1840, Nos. 6-8.

2. *Das Preussische Zündnadelgewehr, seine Bestimmung und Bedeutung* (Berlin, 1852).

3. For contemporary descriptions of the Minie and its evolution see Julius Schön, *Das gezogene Infanterie-Gewehr* (Dresden, 1854), pp. 37ff; Caesar Rüstow, *Das Miniê-Gewehr und seine Bedeutung für den Kriegsgebrauch* (Berlin, 1855); and Friedrich Engels, "The History of the Rifle," in *Engels as Military Critic*, ed. by W. H. Chaloner and W. O. Henderson (Manchester, 1959), pp. 48-59. In 1852, the Austrian Captain Lorenz designed a bullet which instead of expanding to fit the grooves of the rifle was compressed horizontally when fired. This variant of the Minie system was adopted by Austria and several other German states. The Austrian version is evaluated in Anton Dolleczek, *Monographie der k. und k. osterr.-ung. Blanken und Handfeuer-Waffen*, reprint ed. (Graz, 1970), pp. 95ff.

4. Eckardt and Morawietz, pp. 95 *passim*. But cf. Caesar Rüstow, *Die Kriegshandfeuerwaffen*, 2 vols. (Berlin, 1857-1864), *passim*.

5. Cf. Engels, "The History of the Rifle," in *Engels as Military Critic*, 55 *passim*; Rüstow, *Das Minie-Gewehr*, pp. 40ff. "Betrachtungen über den gegenwärtigen Stand der Bewaffnung der deutschen Infanterie," *AMZ*, 1858, Nos. 19-26; and *ibid.*, 1860, No. 15; B. Jacobi, *Das zehnte Armee-Corps des deutschen Bundesheers*, 2nd ed. rev. (Hanover, 1858); and Max Ebell (ed.), *Wilhelm Mauser, ein deutscher Erfinder. Sein Leben an Hand seiner Briefe* (Munich, 1921), pp. 16 *passim*.

6. Albert Pfister, *Pfarrers Albert, Fundstücke aus der Knabenzeit* (Stuttgart, 1901), p. 172; and *Deutsche Zwietracht, Erinnerungen aus meiner Leutnantszeit* (Stuttgart and Berlin, 1902), pp. 36-37; Paul Sauer, "Das Württembergischen Heer in der Zeit des Deutschen Bundes," (Ph. D. dissertation, Freiburg, 1956), pp. 260-261, 271.

7. It had proved impossible to convert percussion smoothbores to needle guns. Not only would it be necessary to design an entirely new cartridge for the large-bored musket, but the production and fitting of

needle gun locks would take as long as the manufacture of an entirely new gun. Eckardt and Morawietz, pp. 94-95.

8. The text of the report is in *Militärische Schriften Kaiser Wilhelms*, II, pp. 91-99.

9. See the narrative account in *ibid.*, II, pp. 82ff; and Prince William's letter of February 20, 1856 to the King, in *ibid.*, pp. 103-107. The long-debated proposal to increase the number of fusilier battalions bore some fruit when the army was reorganized in 1860. In 1820 the independent garrison companies of the guard and line had been consolidated into nine reserve regiments of two battalions, one for each corps. Since 1833 they had been used as garrison troops for the Rhineland fortresses; now they were given a third battalion, entitled "Fusiliers," and ordered to train as light infantry. Reassigned to their parent corps, each regiment was to draw its recruits from the entire district in the same way as the *Jäger*. They seemed to have been initially regarded as a potential elite force in the pattern of the *chasseurs à pied*. However, there was little distinction in practice between the newly-baptised fusiliers and the rest of the army. Cf. Jany, IV, pp. 130-131, 231; "Die leichten Fusstruppen der k. preussischen Armee und deren Verwendung im Gefechte," *Österreichische Militärische Zeitschrift*, 1866, I, pp. 377-397.

10. "Einige Betrachtungen über den gegenwärtigen Krimfeldzug," *AMZ*, 1855, Nos. 97-102; "Militärische Betrachtungen in Beziehung zur Gegenwart," *ibid.*, Nos. 7-10.

11. *Vom Kriege*, Vols. I-III of *Hinterlassenes Werk des Generals_ Carl von Clausewitz* (Berlin, 1833-1834), I, pp. 2, 101, 339.

12. Michael Howard, "Jomini and the Classical Tradition in Military Thought," in Michael Howard (ed.), *The Theory and Practice of War* (New York, 1966), p. 17.

13. Carl von Clausewitz, *On War*, trans. O. J. Matthys Jolles (New York, 1943), pp. 172-173.

14. C. S. Forester, *The General* (Boston, 1967), p. 161.

15. As an article in the *AMZ* suggested, the adoption of the so-called *Laufschritt* would have little effect as long as the infantryman still carried a pack and wore boots. Ordinary soldiers could not run fast enough to neutralize the longer ranges of small arms. "Ueber den Angriff der Infanterie gegen Infanterie," *AMZ*, 1855, Nos. 57-58.

16. Cf. Prince Frederick Charles's essay of December. 1855, "Einige Einflüsse jener Bewaffnung auf der Strategie," discussed in Foerster, I, pp. 179-180; and Rüstow, *Der Krieg und seine Mittel*, pp. 474ff.

17. Cf. among many examples Wilhelm Rüstow, *Untersuchungen über die Organization der Heere* (Basle, 1855), p. 187; "Ueber die neuesten Fortschritte im Kriegswesen," *AMZ*, 1855, Nos. 55-56; and "Streifereien auf dem Gebiete der modernen Taktik," *ibid.*, 1857, Nos. 5-10, 29-32, 57-58, 79-80, 83-88, 93-104.

18. Cf. Prince William's letter of October 30, 1853, and his memorandum of January 25, 1855, to the *Generalkommando* of the III Corps, and of August 25, 1855 to Frederick William IV in *Militärische*

NOTES TO CHAPTER VI

Schriften Kaiser Wilhelms, II, pp. 203ff., 210ff., and 233ff. For discussions of these orders and their implementation, see *ibid.*, pp. 199ff, 238; Osten-Sacken, II, pp. 376-377; Jany, IV, pp. 204-205.

19. "Das gezogene Gewehr als Hauptwaffe der Infanterie," *AMZ*. 1856, Nos. 25-32; "Pz." (Karl von Pönitz), "Betrachtungen über die allgemeine Bewaffnung der Infanterie mit gezogenen Gewehren," *ibid.*, Nos. 33-36; and "Zum Zündnadelgewehr," *ibid.*, Nos. 53-54.

20. "Pz." (Karl von Pönitz), *Taktik der Infanterie und der Kavallerie zum Gebrauche für Offiziere aller Grade und Waffen*, 2nd ed. rev., Vol. I (Leipzig, 1847), pp. 126-127.

21. "Einige Betrachtungen über den gegenwärtigen Krimfeldzug," *AMZ*, 1855, Nos. 97-192.

22. Frederick, Charles, "Einflusses den die Bewaffung der Infanterie mit gezogenen Gewehren auf die Taktik im nächsten Krieg aussern wird," in *Was sich das Bornstädter Feld erzählt*, a collection of essays published in 1855 and discussed in Foerster, I, pp. 174ff.

23. Antoine Henri Baron de Jomini, *Précis de l'Art de la Guerre*, rev. ed., 2 vols. (Paris, 1855), II. pp. 233-234.

24. *Ibid.* 2nd Appendix, pp. 376 *passim*. The quotations are from pp. 376 and 400.

CHAPTER VI

1. Quoted in Charles Thoumas, *Les Transformations de l'armée française*, 2 vols. (Paris, 1887), II, p. 97.

2. "Rapport du maréchal commandant en chef le 4ᵉ corps," in A. Duquet, *La Guerre d'Italie (1859)*, (Paris, 1882), p. 288.

3. In the spring of 1859 the army still lacked over 100,000 guns, and parts were still being largely produced by small independent firms and individual gunsmiths, then delivered to Vienna for assembly. One regiment, for example, was not rearmed until the end of April; two months later it lost over six hundred men at Solferino. Franz Herzmann, *Geschichte des k. und k. 52. Linien-Infanterie-Regiments, Erzherzog Franz Carl* (Vienna, 1871), pp. 472, 517; Heinz Helmert, *Militärsystem und Streitkräfte im deutschen Bund am Vorabend des preussisch-österreichischen Krieges von 1866* (Berlin. 1964), p. 146. For Austrian tactics see Andres, "Vergleichende Übersicht des französischen und österreichishen Tirailleursystems." *Österreichische Militarische Zeitschrift*, 1860, II, pp. 193-199 and the summary in Heinrich Friedjung, *Der Kampf um die Vorherrschaft in Deutschland, 1859 bis 1866*, 2 vols., 10th ed. (Stuttgart and Berlin, 1917), II, pp. 358 *passim*.

4. Cf. among many examples J. Schweinitz, *Entwurf einer Reorganization der Österreichischen Armee* (Vienna, 1862); and "Ansichten uber ein neues Manövrierreglement der k. k. österreichischen Infan-

terie," *Österreichische Militärische Zeitschrift*, 1862, II, pp. 46-50.

5. Cf. "Einiges über das Feuergefecht der Infanterie," *Osterreichische Militärische Zeitschrift*, 1863, III, pp. 377-383; "Über Jägerwesen," *ibid.*, pp. 113-120, 169-181; and the *Exerzier-Reglement für die Kaiserlich-Königlichen Fusstruppen 1862* (Vienna, 1862).

6. M. v. B., "Reflexionen über das zerstreute Gefecht der Infanterie, vornämlich mit Hinblick auf den letzten Krieg in Italien," *AMZ*, 1860, No. 15; [Roth], *Betrachtungen über die französische und österreichische Armee und deren Gefechtsweise im Feldzuge von 1859* (Munich, 1862).

7. [Frederick Charles], *Eine militärische Denkschrift (Über die Kampfweise der Franzosen)* (Frankfurt, 1860), *passim*.

8. *Militärische Betrachtungen über einige Erfahrungen des letzten Feldzugs und einige Zustände deutschen Armeen* (Darmstadt, 1860), pp. 10-12, 81-82; F. G. von Waldersee, *Die Methode zur kriegsgemässen Ausbildung der Infanterie und ihrer Führer im Felddienste* (Berlin, 1861), pp. 18-19. Cf. also "Der Ruf nach einer verbesserten Truppenausbildung," *AMZ*, 1858, Nos. 95-98; "Die preussische Heeresreform beim Eintritt ins neue Jahr," *AMZ*, 1862, Nos. 1-2, 5-6, 9-10; "Wie sieht es mit unserer Taktik für den Fall eines Krieges mit den Franzosen aus?" *ibid.*, Nos. 23-24; and Otto Graf Baudissin, "Die organization der deutschen Armeen," *Die Grenzboten*, 1862, III, pp. 449-461.

9. Hohenloe, I, p. 263.

10. "Das System der Compagnie-Colonnen als Grundlage der Elementärtaktik," *AMZ*, 1861, No. 5; A. von Boguslawski, *Die Entwicklung der Taktik seit dem Kriege von 1870/71*, 2nd. ed., Vol. I (Berlin and Leipzig, 1878), pp. 9-10; Jany, IV, pp. 204-205. The company column, used by the fusiliers since 1812, was made optional for the entire infantry in 1847. The structure of the Prussian infantry battalion— four companies each of over 250 men—seemed better adapted to the use of company columns than that of most of the other states, where battalions normally consisted of five or six companies each around 150 strong. Even critics who believed battalions of a thousand men too clumsy to handle as a unit often regarded these small companies as too weak to be viable tactical units. Cf. d-V, "Die günstigste Organization der Infanteriebataillone," *AMZ*, 1857, Nos. 53-56; Thoumas, I, pp. 45 ff; "Die Compagnie-colonne als Grundlage der Infanterietaktik," *AMZ*, 1862, No. 43.

11. "Vorschrift für den Unterricht in der geöffneten Gefechtsordnung in der k. bayerischen Armee," *Österreichische Militärische Zeitschrift*, 1863, IV, pp. 255-264; *Suddeutsches Heerwesen und suddeutsche Politik, von einem Norddeutschen* (Berlin, 1869), pp. 24-25; von Zimmerman, *Der Antheil der Grossherzoglich Hessischen Armee-Division am Kriege 1866*, Vols. XXII-XXIII of *Kriegsgeschichtliche Einzelschriften*, ed. by *Grossen Generalstab, Kriegsgeschichtliche*

Abteilung (Berlin, 1897), pp. 274ff; Oskar Bezzel, *Geschichte des Königlich Bayerischen Heeres von 1825 mit 1866*, Vol. VII of *Geschichte des Bayerischen Heeres* (Munich, 1931), pp. 117-118.

12. Foerster, I, pp. 176-178, 230.

13. E. Höfler, *Gedanken über die taktische Ausbildung der Truppen überhaupt, zunächst der Infanterie* (Augsburg, 1861).

14. W. von Plonnies, *Neue Studien ueber die gezogene Feuerwaffe der Infanterie* (Darmstadt, 1861), pp. 259ff; Caesar Rüstow, *Die neueren gezogenen Infanteriegewehre. Ihre wahre Leistungsfahigkeit und die Mittel, dieselben zu sichern* (Darmstadt and Leipzig. 1862), pp. 3-4, 61ff.

15. Foerster, I, pp. 180ff.

16. "Bemerkungen vom 12. Juli 1858 über Veränderungen in der Taktik infolge des verbesserten Infanteriegewehrs," in Helmuth von Moltke, *Militärische Werke*, 2. Abt., *Die Thätigkeit als Chef des Generalstabes der Armee im Frieden*, ed. by *Grossen Generalstab, Kriegsgeschichtliche Abteilung*, 3 vols. (Berlin, 1892-1906), II, pp. 7ff. (Hereafter cited as *MMW*).

17. *MMW*, 3. Abt., *Kriegsgeschichtliche Arbeiten*, ed. by *Grossen Generalstab, Kriegsgeschichtliche Abteilungen*, 3 vols. (Berlin, 1893-1904), III, pp. 62ff., 136ff., 256ff.

18. See his comment on a lecture delivered by Major von Doering of the General Staff, quoted in *MMW*, 2, II, p. 24; "Bemerkungen vom April 1861 über den Einfluss der verbesserten Feuerwaffen auf die Taktik," in *ibid.*, pp. 29ff.

19. *Allerhöchsten Verordnungen uber die grösseren Truppenübungen* (Berlin, 1861). This so-called "green book," originally so top-secret it was only issued to officers, was translated into French in 1868 as *Ordonnance Royale sur les grandes manoevres de l'armée prussienne 29 Juin 1861*, trans. Eugene Pitois (Paris, 1868). For comments see Jany, IV, pp. 231-232; and Boguslawski, *Taktik*, I, pp. 33ff.

20. "Bemerkungen vom 5. Januär 1860 zu einem Berichte des Oberstleutnant Ollech über die Französische Armee," in *MMW*, 2, II, pp. 16-24. Italics added.

21. See Friedrich III, *Tagebücher 1848-1866*, ed. by H. O. Meissner (Leipzig, 1929), pp. 109-110, 214-215; "Die preussische Infanterie," *AMZ*, 1861. No. 46; W. Bigge *Feldmarschall Graf Moltke. Ein militärisches Lebensbild*, 2 vols. (Munich, 1901), II, pp. 106-107; Hohenloe, II, pp. 282-283, 363-364. Cf. also the enthusiastic report on the French army in the London *Times*, August 26-27, 1861, with the account of the Prussian maneuvers in the *Times* of September 25.

22. "Einige Winke für die Offiziere der unter meinen Befehlen ins Feld rückenden Truppen," Foerster, I, pp. 279ff; Graf von Haeseler, *Zehn Zahre im Stabe des Prinzen Friedrich Karl. Erinnerungen*, 3 vols. (Berlin, 1910-1915), I, pp. 123ff.

23. Hohenloe, *Aus meinem Leben*, III, pp. 31-32. See also Friedrich III, *Tagebücher 1848-1866*, pp. 251-252; and "Die Oestreicher im

Schleswig-holsteinischen Kriege," *Die Grenzboten,* 1864, III, pp. 201-213, 271-276.

24. Theodor Fontane, *Der Schleswig-Holsteinische Krieg im Jahre 1864* (Berlin, 1866), p. 348.

25. *Der Krieg in Schleswig und Jutland im Jahre 1864, Nach authentischen Quellen bearbeitet im K. K. Generalstabs-Bureau für Kriegs-Geschichte durch Friedrich von Fischer* (Vienna, 1870), p. 348, fn. 1.

26. Emil Rothpletz, *Bericht eines schweizerischen Offiziers über seine Mission nach Dänemark (1864),* ed. by Emil Rothpletz (Bern and Leipzig, 1924), p. 35.

27. *Ibid.,* pp. 20ff.

28. Freiherrn von Löe, *Errinnerungen aus meinem Berufsleben 1849 bis 1867* (Stuttgart and Leipzig, 1906), pp. 70-71; Thoumas, II, pp. 97-98. E. Ann Pottinger, *Napoleon III and the German Crisis, 1865-1866* (Cambridge, 1966), pp. 194ff. provides archival documentation for her assertion that their lack of a breechloader did not deter French military leaders from recommending armed mediation in 1866.

29. For the evolution of his thinking see "Wilhelm von Plönnies, Grossherzoglich Hessischen Major a. D.," *Militär-Wochenblatt,* 1889, *Beiheft* 2, pp. 65ff. Compare also Plönnies, *Neue Studien über die gezogene Feuerwaffe der Infanterie,* with the *Supplement-Band, Das Zündnadelgewehr* (Darmstadt and Leipzig, 1865).

30. Cf. J. von Hardegg, *Vorlesungen über Kriegsgeschichte von J. V. H.,* Vol. III (Stuttgart, 1862), pp. 533ff.

31. A. Keim, *Erlebtes und Erstrebtes* (Hanover, 1925), p. 9.

32. Sauer, pp. 294ff.

CHAPTER VII

1. "Notes on the War, No. 1," in the *Manchester Guardian,* June 30, 1866, reprinted in *Engels as Military Critic,* pp. 123-125 *passim.* The relationship of Engels' low evaluation of the Prussian army to his desire for Bismarck's overthrow is discussed in Reinhard Höhn, *Sozialismus und Heer,* 2 vols. (Bad Homburg, Berlin, Zürich, 1959), I, pp. 177ff. But if Engels may have been indulging in wishful thinking, his opinions paralleled those of many professionals. See, for example, "Blicke auf die Armeen der Grossmächte Europas im Jahre 1864," übersetzt aus dem *Moniteur de l'Armée* vom Jahre 1864," *Österreichische Militärische Zeitschrift,* 1864, III, pp. 197-204, and Edmond Favre, *L'Autriche et ses institutions militaires* (Paris and Leipzig, 1866). For similar evaluations in the popular press see the *Fortnightly Review,* June 1, 1866, pp. 231ff; and the excerpt from *La Patrie* printed in

Public Opinion, April 7, 1866.
2. Friedjung, I, p. 376; Johann Christoph Allmayer-Beck, "Der Feldzug der österreichischen Nord-Armee nach Königgrätz," in *Entscheidung 1866*, ed. by Wolfgang von Groote and Ursula von Gersdorff (Stuttgart, 1866), p. 110. For an early favorable analysis of the needle gun see "Die Waffenwirkung in den preussischen Gefechten im Feldzuge 1864, bis nach des Erstürmung der Düppeler Schanzen," *Österreichische Militärische Zeitschrift*, 1864, IV, pp. 126-132.
3. Friedjung, I, pp. 375-376; Oskar Regele, *Feldzeugmeister Benedek: Der Weg nach Königgrätz* (Vienna, 1960), pp. 355ff. Wolfgang von Groote, "Königgrätz im Blick der Militärgeschichte," in Richard Dietrich (ed.), *Europa und der Norddeutsche Bund* (Berlin, 1967), p. 111; and Allmayer-Beck, p. 110, deny that civilian agencies were entirely responsible for Austria's failure to rearm. A detailed study of this issue is badly needed.
4. Cf. Friedjung, I, pp. 376-377; and Allmayer-Beck, p. 111. For a contemporary comparison of the rifles see Andres, "Das neue Füsiliergewehr, Modell 1860, in der königlich-preussischen Armee im Vergleiche mit dem österreichischen Infanteriegewehr," *Österreichische Militärische Zeitschrift*, 1863, IV, pp. 265-273. One version of the Lorenz, issued to the *Jäger*, had an effective range of twelve hundred paces.
5. "Eine Discussion über das Tirailliren in aufgelöster Linie und in Gruppen (Schwärmen) . . ." *Österreichische Militärische Zeitschrift*, 1864, III, pp. 1-21; C. H., "Moderne Taktik," *ibid.*, IV, pp. 198-204; "Über die Ursachen der Misserfolge bei der Österreichischen Nordarmee im Kriege Preussens gegen Deutschland im Jahre 1866," *ibid.*, 1866, II, pp. 349ff; Friedjung, I, pp. 367, 386; Emil Franzel, *1866. Il Mondo Casca*, 2 vols. (Munich and Vienna, 1968), II, pp. 497-498.
6. Cf. for example, W. v. H., *Studien aus dem Manövrier-Reglement für die k. k. Fusstruppen* (Vienna, 1865); "Gedanken über Offensive und Defensive," *Österreichische Militärische Zeitschrift*, 1863, I-II *passim*; "Zur taktischen Offensive und Defensive der Infanterie," *ibid.*, pp. 276-286; "Die Angriffskolonne der Infanterie—speciell die Bechtoldsche Massenkolonne," *ibid.*, 1862, III, pp. 353-358; J. M. A., "Die Feuerwaffen und das Bajonett im ihrem Wesen und ihtrer Wirksamkeit," *ibid.*, 1863, IV, pp. 363-374.
7. Cited in Friedjung, I, pp. 377ff. Cf. "Taktische und Dienst-Instructionen fur die k. k. Nordarmee," printed in *Österreichische Militärische Zeitschrift*, 1866, III, pp. 234-250; IV, pp. 213-222.
8. Jay Luvaas, *The Military Legacy of the Civil War* (Chicago, 1959), pp. 119ff.
9. C. von Bincke-Olbendorf, *Die Reorganization des Preussischen Heerwesens nach dem Schleswig-Holsteinschen Kriege* (Berlin, 1864), pp. 70-71.
10. "Bemerkungen vom Jahre 1865 über den Einfluss der verbesser-

ten Feuerwaffe auf die Taktik," *MMW*, 2, II, pp. 45ff. Cf. also *Instruktion über das Scheibenschiessen der mit Zündnadelgewehren bewaffneten Infanterie-Bataillone, vom 2. Novbr. 1864* (Berlin, 1864); and the analyses of the implementation of this document in A. von Witzleben, *Heerwesen und Infanteriedienst der Königlich Preussischen Armee*, 2 vols., 11th ed. rev. (Berlin, 1869), II, pp. 154-191; and "Die Schiessübungen der königlich preussischen Infanterie," *Österreichische Militarische Zeitschrift*, 1865, III, pp. 19ff.

11. "Einige Winke für die unter meinen Befehlen ins Feld rückenden Truppen," printed in Haeseler, III, pp. 22-32.

12. von Loebell, "Der Patronenverbrauch im Ernstfalle und die Kriegsausrüstung der Infanterie mit Munition," *Archiv für die Offiziere der Königlich Preussische Artillerie-und Ingenieur-Korps*, LXIII (1868), p. 88; Theodor Fontane, *Der Deutsche Krieg von 1866*, 2 vols. (Berlin, 1871-1872), I, p. 157.

13. Though the literature on the campaign of 1866 is overshadowed by that on the Franco-Prussian War, it is nevertheless extremely comprehensive. The operational narrative supporting the following analysis has been largely reconstructed from seven basic works. The respective official histories, *Österreichs Kämpfe im Jahre 1866: Nach Feldakten bearbeitet durch das k. k. Generalstabsbureau für Kriegsgeschichte*, 5 vols. (Vienna, 1868), and *Der Feldzug von 1806 in Deutschland*, ed. by *Grossen Generalstab, Kriegsgeschichtliche Abteilung*, Vol. 1 (Berlin, 1867), were composed immediately after the war and have a contemporary flavor. Fontane's two volumes and Max Jähns, *Die Schlacht von Königgrätz* (Leipzig, 1876), are spirited anecdotal accounts which do not sacrifice essential accuracy for the sake of colorful description. Two studies written at the turn of the century, Heinrich Friedjung's from the Austrian perspective and Oscar von Lettow-Vorbeck, *Geschichte des Krieges von 1866*, 3 vols. (Berlin, 1896-1902), incorporate most of the relevant monographic literature. Finally Gordon Criag, *The Battle of Königgrätz* (Philadelphia and New York, 1964), offers a brief but definitive modern synthesis which is readily available.

14. Fontane, *Krieg 1866*, I, p. 159; Friedjung, II, p. 37.

15. A Prussian corps in 1866 consisted of a *Jäger* battalion and two divisions, each of two brigades of two three-battalion regiments. An Austrian corps had four brigades, each of two three-battalion regiments and a *Jäger* battalion. Austrian brigades were known by their commanders' names. Both formations were approximately 30,000 strong.

16. Alfred von Schlieffen, "Cannae," *Gesammelte Schriften*, Vol. I (Berlin, 1913), p. 101.

17. Albrecht von Stosch, *Denkwürdigkeiten*, ed. by Ulrich von Stosch (Stuttgart, 1904), p. 87; Fred Graf Frankenberg, *Kriegstagebücher von 1866 und 1870/71*, ed. by Heinrich von Pochinger (Stuttgart, 1896), p. 33; Friedjung, II, pp. 60ff.

18. *Armee-Befehl* Nr. 41, printed in *Benedeks nachgelassene Papiere*, ed. by Heinrich Friedjung, 3rd ed. rev. (Dresden, 1904), pp. 369-370.

19. Friedjung, II, pp. 76-77.
20. Cf. *Benedeks nachgelassene Papiere*, pp. 371-372, 375; Craig, pp. 40-41; Eberhard Kaulbach, "Königgrätz nach Hundert Jahren-Zur militärischen Fuhrüng," in *Entscheidung 1866*, pp. 153ff.
21. For details of Benedek's plans and positions see *Österreichs Kämpfe im Jahre 1866*, III, pp. 238ff; Friedjung, II, pp. 215ff; Craig, pp. 88ff.
22. *Der Nebel von Chlum* (Prague, 1867), cited in Jähns, p. 98; Friedjung, II, p. 238.
23. *Österreichs Kämpfe im Jahre 1866*, III, p. 292.
24. Friedjung, II, pp. 251-252; Anton Freiherr von Mollinary, *Sechsundvierzig Jahre im österreich-ungarischen Heere, 1833-1879*, 2 vols. (Zürich, 1905), II, pp. 158ff. Benedek had originally ordered II and IV Corps to occupy the entrenchments along the ridge line running from Chlum to Nedelist. Since this position was dominated by the heights of Maslowed and Horenowes, Festetics advanced on his own initiative to occupy the line Maslowed-Horenowes, and II Corps followed him. By the time the movement was completed, however, the attention of both corps had been focused westward instead of northward; instead of eight brigades, only one was left to screen the Austrian right flank. Cf. Lettow-Vorbeck, II, pp. 426ff; Friedjung, II, p. 249; *Österreichs Kämpfe im Jahre 1866*, III, pp. 266ff; Craig, p. 91.
25. *Österreichs Kämpfe im Jahre 1866*, III, p. 296.
26. *Ibid.*, p. 297.
27. *Ibid.*, pp. 303-304.
28. Fontane, *Krieg 1866*, I, p. 572.
29. This opinion was current at least in Hesse. Zimmerman, *Hessischen Armee-Division*, p. 273.
30. The quotation is from one of the more contemptuous studies of the south German military methods, *Suddeutsches Heerwesen und suddeutsche Politik, von einem Norddeutschen*, pp. 24-25.
31. Cf. Hugo Arnold, *Unter General v. der Tann* (Munich, 1896), pp. 51ff; Pfister, *Zwietracht*, 157 *passim*, for corroboration by a Bavarian captain and a Württemberg lieutenant; Fritz Hoenig, *Die Entscheidungskämpfe des Mainfeldzuges an der Fränkischen Saale* (Berlin, 1898), pp. 1ff., gives the views of a distinguished Prussian authority. Probably the most devastating criticism of south German military institutions was contained in several long memoranda submitted by the Württemberg Lieutenant-Colonel von Suckow, the future General and War Minister. Cf. Albert von Suckow, *Rückschau*, ed. by Wilhelm Busch (Tübingen, 1909); and the analyses in Sauer, pp. 330 ff. and 337ff.
32. Keim, pp. 10-11.

PART III

Chapter VIII

1. For summaries of the work of the APK, cf. the *Kurzgefasste Geschichte der königlich preussischen Artillerie-Prüfungs-Kommission* (Berlin, 1895); C. v. Decker, *Geschichte des Geschützwesens und der Artillerie in Europa von ihrem Ursprunge bis auf die gegenwärtigen Zeiten*, 2nd. ed. rev. (Berlin, 1822), pp. 157 *passim*; and W. H. G. von Müller, *Die Entwickelung der Feldartillerie in Bezug auf Material, Organization und Taktik, von 1815 bis 1892*, 3 vols., 2nd ed. (Berlin, 1893-1894), I, 100ff.

2. For a general discussion of the adoption of shrapnel, see Müller, I, pp. 35 *passim*, and III, pp. 24ff. Representative contemporary analyses include C. von Decker, *Die Shrapnels* (Berlin, 1842); "Ueber Vergleichung der Kartäschwirkung verschiedener Geschütze und verschiedener Kugelsorten," *Archiv für die Offiziere der Königlich Preussische Artillerie-und Ingenieur-Korps*, X (1840), pp. 175-179. (Hereafter cited as *Archiv*); and 'Das Shrapnel," *ibid.*, XLVI (1859), pp. 67-94.

3. Müller, I, pp. 37ff, 59ff; du Vignau, "Der Breithaupts'che Zünder für Granatkartäschen, Granaten, und Bomben in seiner Bedeutung für die allgemeine Lösung der Frage des Hohlgeschossfeuers," *Archiv*, XLII (1857), pp. 87-113.

4. Beutner, *Die königliche preussische Garde-Artillerie*, 2 vols. (Berlin, 1889-1894), I, p. 281.

5. A mobilized army corps had three horse and five 6-pounder batteries, each of six 6-pounders and two 7-pounder howitzers, three 12-pounder batteries of six cannon and two 10-pounder howitzers, and a howitzer battery. The remaining three companies were intended for fortress duty. Each battery was formed and manned by a company. For problems of command, organization, and training in this period see Hamm and Moewes, *Geschichte des 1. Westfälischen Feld-Artillerie-Regiments Nr. 7* (Berlin, 1891), pp. 26ff; Eltester and Schlee, *Geschichte der Rheinischen Feldartillerie bis zu ihrer Teilung in vier Regimenter 1. Oktober 1899* (Berlin, 1910), pp. 67ff; Beutner, I, pp. 269-270; and the general discussion in O. von der Osten-Sacken, *Preussens Heer von seinen Anfängen bis zur Gegenwart*, 3 vols. (Berlin, 1911-1913), II, pp. 186ff.

6. Cf. R. von Bonin, "Ueber die Errichtung, Formation und Ausrüstung der preussischen reitenden Artillerie," *Archiv*, IX (1839), pp. 202-237; von Strotha, *Die Königlich Preussische Reitende Artillerie vom Jahre 1759 bis 1816* (Berlin, 1868), *passim*; Eltester and Schlee, p. 69; von Stumpff, *Geschichte des Feldartillerie-Regiments General-Feldzeugmeister (1. Brandenburgisches) Nr. 3* (Berlin, 1900), pp. 107-108; Müller, I, pp. 15ff, 76ff.

7. Müller, I, pp. 82ff; Decker, *Geschützwesens*, pp. 154ff; "Was leistete die reitende Artillerie seit ihrem Bestehen und was kann und soll sie leisten," *Archiv*, XVI (1844), pp. 207-243.

8. [Ernst Monhaupt], *System der reutende Artillerie* (Leipzig, 1823), esp. pp. 30ff, 41ff; 97 *passim*; offers a good example of his thought.

9. Cf. "Allgemeine Aufsichten über die Taktik, als Einleitung zu einer Taktik der Artillerie," *Allgemeine Militär-Zeitung*, 1829, Nos. 8-9 (Hereafter cited as *AMZ*); Beutner, I, pp. 270-271; Müller, I, pp. 90-91; Osten-Sacken II, pp. 275-276; and Stumpff, pp. 107-108.

10. "Uebersicht der hauptsächlichsten Veränderungen in der Einrichtung bei der Feldartillerie des Systems von Jahre 1842 im Vergleich zu dem vom Jahre 1816," *Archiv*, XX (1846), pp. 28-60; Beutner, I, pp. 267-268; Osten-Sacken, II, pp. 248; Müller, I, pp. 17ff, 53-54. The elimination of the 10-pounder howitzer meant that each 12-pounder battery consisted of eight cannon and no howitzers.

11. Cf. the review of *Die reitende Artillerie im Cavaleriegefecht: Ansichten eines preussischen Artillerieoffiziers*, in *AMZ*, 1838, No. 95; Carl von Decker, *Die Taktik der drei Waffen: Infanterie, Kavallerie, und Artillerie, einzeln und verbunden*, 2 vols., 2nd. ed. (Berlin, 1833), I, p. 129; K. W. G. von Grevenitz, *Organization und Taktik der Artillerie*, 2 vols. (Berlin, 1824), II, p. 20.

12. C. von Decker, *Die Artillerie für alle Waffen*, 3 vols., 2nd ed. (only Vol. 1 published) (Berlin, Posen, Bromberg, 1826), I, pp. 25ff, 122; Muller, I, pp. 115-116.

13. L. von Breithaupt, *Die Artillerie für Offiziere aller Waffen*, 3 vols. (Stuttgart, 1834), I, *passim*; C. F. Borkenstein, *Versuch zu einem Lehrgebäude der theoretisch-praktisch Artillerie-wissenschaft*, 2 vols. (Berlin, 1822), II, pp. 170-171.

14. Borkenstein, II, XXIII.

15. "Betrachtungen über Belagerungsgeschützröhre und über die letzten in Lafére gemachten Versuche mit 24- und 16-pfündigen gusseisernen Röhren," *Archiv*, XIV (1843), pp. 1-24; "Veränderungen in dem Material und in der Organization der Preussischen Artillerie," *ibid.*, X (1840), pp. 243-252; Decker, *Artillerie für alle Waffen*, I, pp. 206ff; "Uber die Verfertigung der Geschütze aus Eisen," *AMZ*, 1828, Nos. 91-93.

16. Norbert Mühlen, *The Incredible Krupps* (New York, 1959), p. 283.

17. The most recent best-selling example of this school is William Manchester, *The Arms of Krupp, 1587-1968* (Boston and Toronto, 1968). Cf. also Peter Batty, *The House of Krupp* (New York, 1968); and Mühlen.

18. In addition to the works of Wilhelm Berdrow cited below, see particularly Gert Klass, *Die Drei Ringe, Lebensgeschichte eines Industrisunternehmens* (Tübingen, 1953), tr. by James Cleugh as *Krupps: The Story of an Industrial Empire* (London, 1954). Footnotes are to the English edition.

19. For the development of steel in the modern era cf. T. S. Ashton, *Iron and Steel in the Industrial Revolution*, 2nd ed. (Manchester, 1951), pp. 54ff; David S. Landes, *The Unbound Prometheus* (Cambridge, 1969), pp. 251ff; and W. H. Dennis, *A Hundred Years of Metallurgy* (Chicago, 1964), pp. 92ff.

20. For other efforts to produce steel in the Napoleonic Era see "Die Walder Gusstahlerfindungsgesellschaft: Ein Kapitel aus 'Johann Abraham Gottlieb Fries und seine Familie' von J. A. G. Fries," introduction and commentary by Ernst Schröder, *Tradition*, IV (1959), pp. 149-173, 223-232.

21. Krupp to *Generalmünzdirektor* Goedeking, October 13, 1826; Krupp to Kopstadt; Widow Krupp to King Frederick William III, March 31, 1830; in *Alfred Krupps Briefe 1826-1887*, ed. by Wilhelm Berdrow (Berlin, 1928), pp. 1, 6-7, and the discussion in Wilhelm Berdrow, *Alfred Krupp*, 2 vols. (Berlin, 1927), I, pp. 37-38.

22. Krupp to Moldenhauer, January 27, 1830, *Alfred Krupps Briefe*, p. 7.

23. The process is briefly described in Dennis, pp. 306ff.

24. Cf. T. S. Hamerow, *Restoration, Revolution, Reaction* (Princeton, 1958), pp. 75ff; Walther Hoffman. "The Take-Off in Germany," in W. W. Rostow (ed.), *The Economics of the Take-Off into Sustained Growth* (New York, 1963), pp. 95-118; and J. A. Schumpeter, *Business Cycles: A Theoretical and Statistical Analysis of the Capitalist Process*, 2 vols. (New York and London, 1939), I, pp. 346ff.

25. Berdrow, *Alfred Krupp*, I, p. 191 *passim*.

26. Krupp to Lt. von Donat, July 16, 1843, *Alfred Krupps Briefe*, pp. 67-68.

27. Krupp to Boyen, March 1, 1844; and Boyen's reply of March 23, in *Alfred Krupps Briefe*, pp. 73-74.

28. Cf. Mühlen, p. 41; Batty, pp. 60-61; Manchester, pp. 65ff; *Krupp und die Hohenzollern in Dokumenten. Krupp-Korrespondenz mit Kaisern, Kabinettschefs und Ministern*, ed. with an introduction by Willi A. Boelcke (Frankfurt, 1970), p. 28.

29. Bernhard Menne, *Krupp-Deutschlands Kanonenkönige* (Zürich, 1936), p. 63.

30. Berdrow, *Alfred Krupp*, I, pp. 195-196.

31. Krupp to Georg Solling, February 18, 1846, *Alfred Krupps Briefe*, pp. 87ff.

32. Krupp to von Rohr, October 23 and December 12, 1847, *ibid.*, pp. 97-99, 102.

CHAPTER IX

1. Berdrow, *Alfred Krupp*, I, p. 242ff; Kraft Karl zu Hohenloe-Ingelfingen, *Aufzeichnungen aus meinem Leben*, 4 vols. (Berlin, 1897-1907), I, pp. 120-121.

2. "Achsen von Gusstahl aus der Gusstahlfabrik von Friedrich Krupp bei Essen in Rheinpreussen," *Archiv*, XXV (1849), pp. 59-62; Berdrow,

Alfred Krupp, I, p. 245; Krupp to G. Jurst, June 16, 1849; Krupp to APK, September 4, 1849, *Alfred Krupps Briefe*, pp. 108-109, 110.

3. Hohenloe, *Aus meinem Leben*, I, pp. 70-71, 224ff; *Militärische Briefe*, III, *Ueber Artillerie*, 2nd ed. (Berlin, 1887), pp. 86-88. Cf. von Stein-Gwiazdowski, "Betrachtungen über die Stellung und das Benehmen der Art.-Offiz. den Führern gemischter Truppen-Detachements gegenüber, usw." *ibid.*, XXIII (1848), pp. 174-184.

4. Cf. Hohenloe, *Aus meinem Leben*, I, pp. xvi, 74, 141, 215ff; Beutner, I, pp. 343ff; Müller, I, pp. 108ff; Eltester and Schlee, p. 71; Capt. Hoffman, "Versuch zur Begründung einer Evolutions-Vorschrift für die Feldartillerie," *Archiv*, XX (1846), pp. 191-237, XXI (1847), pp. 33-69.

5. Müller, I, pp. 194-195; "Ueber den Einfluss der Einführung des verbesserten Infanterie-Gewehrs auf den Gebrauch und die Organisation der Artillerie," *Archiv*, XXXVII (1855), pp. 1-21; "Ueber die praktische Ausbildung und Verwendung des Artillerie-Offiziers," *ibid.*, XXXVIII (1855), pp. 16-25; Eltester and Schlee, pp. 72, 97.

6. Beutner, I, pp. 324ff; Hamm and Moewes, p. 31; "Wünsche und Ansichten über die Friedens-Formation der Preuss. Artillerie," *Archiv*, XXXVII (1855), pp. 145-173.

7. W. Heydenreich, *Das moderne Feldgeschütz*; I. Teil, *1850 bis 1890* (Leipzig, 1906), p. 24; W. H. G. von Müller, *Die Entwickelung der preussischen Festungs-und Belagerungsartillerie von 1815-1875* (Berlin, 1876), pp. 118-119; and *Feldartillerie*, I, pp. 162ff, 172ff; Taubert, "Die historische Entwickelung des preussischen Systems der gezogenen Geschütze," *Archiv*, LXI (1867), pp. 216-246.

8. Cf. such contemporary accounts as *Die gezogenen Geschütze: Kritische Untersuchungen über ihre Vorzüge und Nachtheile, von einem deutschen Artillerie-Offizier* (Darmstadt, 1861); "Die wirkung des verbesserten Infanteriegewehrs und der Einfluss derselben auf die Artillerie," *AMZ*, 1857, Nos. 71-74; "Ueber den Einfluss . . . des verbesserten Infanterie-Gewehrs," pp. 1-21; "Die Anwendbarkeit gezogenen Geschütze," *Archiv*, XXXVIII (1855), pp. 39-46; and the summaries in Müller, *Feldartillerie*, I, pp. 131ff, 181ff.

9. Favorable summaries of Encke's character can be found in Hohenloe, *Aus meinem Leben*, II, pp. 61ff; and *Kurzgefasste Geschichte der königlich preussischen Artillerie-Prüfungs-Kommission*, pp. 10-11. For Hahn see Hohenloe, *Aus meinem Leben*, II, pp. 62-63; and K. von Priesdorff, *Soldatisches Führertum*, 10 vols. (Hamburg, 1936-1945), VI, No. 1865.

10. Cf. Lt. Col. Zoller, "Versuche, die broncenen Geschützröhren gezogen zum Schiessen von Spitzkugeln zu verwenden," *Archiv*, XLIII (1858), pp. 205-209; "Die wesentlichsten Erfahrungen und Versuche der preussischen Artillerie über das gusseiserne Geschütz," *ibid.*, XXXIII (1853), pp. 37-92; Berdrow, *Alfred Krupp*, I, pp. 333-334, 342; Louis Reybaud, *La Fer et la Houille; suivis du canon Krupp et du Familistère de Guise* (Paris, 1874), pp. 380-381; and "Noch ein Wort zur Geschützfabrication," *AMZ*, 1856, Nos. 3-4.

11. Cf. Josef Schmoelzel, *Die gezogene Kanone* (Munich, 1860), pp. 57ff; d-V. "Die ausserordentliche Haltbarkeit der Krupp'schen gusstahlernen Geschütze," *AMZ*, 1857, Nos. 79-80; and the reports on cast steel cannon in *ibid.*, 1858, Nos. 91-92, and 1860, No. 8. For general discussions of rifles in this period, cf. Morton Borden (ed.), "Friedrich Engels on Rifled Cannon," *Military Affairs*, XXI (1957), pp. 75-77, 193-198; Müller, *Feldartillerie*, I, pp. 294-295; E. Terssen, "Gezogene Kanonen," *Archiv*, L (1861), pp. 213-225.

12. Wilhelm Rüstow, *Der Krieg und seine Mittel* (Leipzig, 1856), p. 329.

13. John Anderson, "Iron and Steel as Materials for Rifled Cannon," *Journal of the Royal United Services Institution*, VI (1862), pp. 185-201. The quotation is from p. 200.

14. Hohenloe, *Aus meinem Leben*, II, pp. 63, 91, 207-208; Müller, *Feldartillerie*, I, p. 174; "Ueber gezogene Kanone," *AMZ*, 1861, Nos. 20-21; Taubert, pp. 241-242.

15. Cf. Jac Weller, "The Confederate Use of British Cannon," *Civil War History*, III (1957), pp. 144-145; Taubert, pp. 238-239; "Ueber Bewaffnung und Organization der Feld-Artillerie," *Archiv*, LVI (1864), pp. 13-43.

16. Cf. among many discussions of this issue du Vignau, "Der Einfluss der gezogenen Geschützrohr auf die Kaliber der Feldkanonen und auf die Wahl kurzer oder langer Haubitzen (Granatkanonen)," *Archiv*, XLII (1857), pp. 226-234; "Beschreibung eines Vorderladungs-Geschützes neuer Construction," *ibid.*, LIII (1863), pp. 136-142; "Engels on Rifled Cannon," p. 198; *Die gezogenen Geschütze, passim*; and Schmoelzel, pp. 42ff.

17. Berdrow, *Alfred Krupp*, I, pp. 334ff; Klass, p. 42.

18. Müller, *Feldartillerie*, I, p. 176.

19. Krupp to Meyer, January 18, 1860, *Alfred Krupps Briefe*, p. 175.

20. Krupp to Voigts-Rhetz, October 13, 1859; Krupp to Meyer, January 18, 1860; Krupp to Prince Regent William, March 8, 1860; *ibid.*, pp. 171 *passim*.

21. Voigts-Rhetz to Krupp, March 17, 1860, *Alfred Krupps Briefe*, pp. 178-179; and fn. 1, p. 178; William to Ministry of Commerce, April 25, 1860, in Boelcke, p. 41.

22. Berdrow, *Alfred Krupp*, II, pp. 10-11; Manchester, p. 83; Mühlen, pp. 46-47.

23. Krupp to Roon, June 6, 1860, *Alfred Krupps Briefe*, pp. 180-181; Krupp to Ministry of Commerce, December 12, 1860, and February 15, 1861, in Boelcke, pp. 43ff.

24. Krupp to Meyer, October 13 and November 11, 1860; Krupp to Roon, February 2, 1861; Krupp to Geh. *Staats-und Kabinettsrat* Illaire, May 25, 1861, *ibid.*, pp. 183 *passim*, 190-191; Berdrow, *Alfred Krupp*, II, pp. 28ff.

CHAPTER X

1. "Ueber die Ermittlung von Distanzen," *Archiv*, LIX (1866), pp. 181-187; du Vignau, "Einfluss der gezogenen Geschützrohr," pp. 226 *passim*; "Engels on Rifled Cannon," p. 198; Müller, *Feldartillerie*, I, pp. 176ff, 184-185. For a defense of percussion-fused shrapnel see Col. Neumann, "Der Schrapnellschuss bei zu kurz geschätzter Entfernung," *Archiv*, LVI (1864), pp. 1-13.

2. Müller, *Feldartillerie*, I, pp. 129-130, 160-161, 197ff; *Die Artillerie im Felde. Eine Zusammenstellung von Beispielen aus der Kreigsgeschichte von einem Artillerieoffizier*, 2nd ed. rev. (Dresden, 1863), pp. 35 *passim*; "Einige Worte über reitende Artillerie," *Archiv*, XXXIX (1856), pp. 70-74; d-V, "Der heutige Standpunkt der reitende Artillerie," *AMZ*, 1857, Nos. 19-28.

3. Cf. among many examples Feréol Fourcault, *Le canon rayé prussien: comparison des systèmes francais et prussien* (Paris, 1861); and *Le canon prussien jugé par les allemands* (Paris, 1861); Schmoelzel, *passim; Die gezogene Geschütze*, pp. 88 *passim*; "Engels on Rifled Cannon," pp. 76-77, 195; J. G., "Über den Einfluss der gezogenen Geschütze auf taktische Anordnungen," *Österreichische Militärische Zeitschrift*, 1861, I, pp. 350-356, II, pp. 40-50, 301-309; "Ueber Bewaffnung und Organisation der Feldartillerie," pp. 13-43 *passim*.

4. The deliberations and decisions of the commission are discussed in Müller, *Feldartillerie*, I, pp. 209ff.

5. As finally designed the four-pounder barrel, carriage, and loaded limber, weighed 1572 kilograms, as opposed to the 1835 kilograms of the six-pounder. Cf. Müller, *Feldartillerie*, I. pp. 217ff, 378; and "Ueber Bewaffnung und Organisation der Feld-Artillerie," pp. 13 *passim*.

6. Krupp to Crown Prince, February 27, 1863, *Alfred Krupps Briefe*, pp. 197-198; Berdrow, *Alfred Krupp*, II, p. 52; Müller, *Feldartillerie*, I, pp. 221ff.

7. Cf. Hempe, "Ueber den Werth des gezogenen Feldgeschützes dem glatten und namentlich dem kurzen 12-pfder gegenüber," *Archiv*, LII (1862), pp. 1-37; "Ueber Einführung des gezogenen Vierpfünders in der k. preussischen Artillerie," *AMZ*, 1863, Nos. 16-17; "Ueber die Kaliberfrage in der Feldartillerie," *ibid.*, No. 43; Müller, *Feldartillerie*, I, p. 225.

8. Cf. "Ueber die praktische Ausbildung und Verwendung des Artillerie-Offiziers," *Archiv*, XXXVIII (1855), pp. 16-25; du Vignau, "Die Artillerie-Schulen für Offiziere nach dem Bedürfniss der Gegenwart," *ibid.*, XLIV (1858), pp. 49-85, 205-234; Beutner, I, pp. 339ff; Müller, *Feldartillerie*, I, pp. 268ff; "Wissenschaftlichkeit im Militärwesen und die preussische Artillerie," *AMZ*, 1863, Nos. 1-2; Jesser, "Zur Taktik der Artillerie mit gezogenen Rohren," *Österreichische Militärische Zeitschrift*, 1860, II, pp. 55-67.

9. Beginning in the fall of 1863, the rifle and twelve-pounder batteries of each regiment were reorganized into four six-gun units. The howitzer batteries remained on the old establishment pending a final

decision on the four-pounder rifle. The horse battalion retained its traditional three batteries, each reduced to six guns. A projected wartime expansion to six four-gun batteries was eventually abandoned due to a shortage of qualified commanders.

10. Cf. "Einige Verbesserungvorschläge für die Schiessübungen der Artillerie," *AMZ*, 1863, No. 13; and J. B., "Die gezogene Kanone als Feldgeschütz in der Eintheilung bei den Truppen," *Österreichische Militärische Zeitschrift*, 1861, III, pp. 35-38.

11. Wolfgang Foerster, *Prinz Friedrich Karl von Preussen: Denkwürdigkeiten aus seinem Leben*, 2 vols. (Stuttgart, 1910), I, p. 260.

12. For the artillery's role at Missunde cf. Graf von Haeseler, *Zehn Jahre im Stabe des Prinzen Friedrich Karl. Erinnerungen*, 3 vols. (Berlin, 1910-1915), I, pp. 141ff; Hohenloe, *Aus meinem Leben*, III, pp. 22ff; Stumpff, p. 142; and the Prussian official history, *Der Deutsch-Dänisch Krieg 1864*, pub. by *Grossen Generalstab, Abteilung für Kriegsgeschichte*, 2 vols. (Berlin, 1886), I, pp. 139ff.

13. Cf. "Die deutschen Festungen und das gezogene Geschütz," *AMZ*, 1861, No. 35; "Die Verstärkung des Feuers aus Flankencasematten . . . durch Einführung von rückwarts zu ladender Geschütze," *ibid.*, No. 10; "Ueber den Einfluss der gezogenen Geschütze auf den Festungskrieg," *ibid.*, 1862. Nos. 7-8. These articles are primarily intended to suggest methods of neutralizing the effect of siege rifles.

14. *Deutsch-Dänisch Krieg*, I, pp. 255ff; Haeseler, I, pp. 204ff.

15. H. O. Meisner (ed.), *Kaiser Friedrich III, Tagebücher 1848-1866* (Leipzig, 1929), p. 284; *Deutsch-Dänisch Krieg*, I, p. 298, Appendix 27a.

16. Cf. Friedrich III, *Tagebücher*, p. 299; *Deutsch-Dänisch Krieg*, II, pp. 328 *passim*; Hohenloe, *Aus meinem Leben*, III, pp. 76, 105; and *Militärische Briefe*, III, pp. 33-34.

17. Cf. *Deutsch-Dänisch Krieg*, I, pp. 436ff, 471ff; and the detailed account in R. Neumann, *Ueber den Angriff auf die Düppeler Schanzen in der Zeit vom 15. März zum 18. April 1864* (Berlin, 1865).

18. Friedrich III, *Tagebücher*, pp. 319-320.

19. The best summaries of Hindersin's career and temperament are in Hohenloe. *Aus meinem Leben*, I, xiv-xv, and III, pp. 165-166; and *Militärische Briefe*, III, pp. 141ff. Cf. "Gustav Eduard von Hindersin," Priesdorff, VI, No. 2079.

20. Hohenloe, *Aus meinem Leben*, III, pp. 162ff. In 1860 the artillery regiments had been redesignated brigades, and in June, 1864 separate field and fortress artillery regiments were created under each brigade headquarters. Officers remained interchangeable between field and fortress artillery until 1872.

21. R. Roerdansz, "Das gezogene vierpfündige Feldgeschütz," *Archiv*, LVIII (1865), pp. 1-54; presents a favorable analysis of the four-pounder in the light of the Danish campaign. Cf. "Einige Worte über die reitende Artillerie, mit besonderer Berücksichtigung der k. preussischen Armee," *AMZ*, 1863, No. 27; and Müller, *Feldartillerie*, I, pp. 226-227, 259ff.

22. Roon to Krupp, January 31, 1864; Krupp to Firm, February, 1864;

Krupp to Roon, February 22, 1864; *Alfred Krupps Briefe,* pp. 202-203.
23. Berdrow, *Alfred Krupp,* II, pp. 57-58; Krupp to Firm, end of March, 1864, *Alfred Krupps Briefe,* pp. 204-205. For the Prussian army's continued interest in bronze rifles see Müller, *Feldartillerie,* I, pp. 298ff.
24. The process of elevating the social status of the artillery's officer corps had begun in the previous decade under von Hahn. Karl Demeter, *Das deutsche Offizierkorps in Gesellschaft und Staat 1650-1945,* 2nd. ed. rev. (Frankfurt a/M, 1962), p. 15.
25. Hohenloe, *Aus meinem Leben,* III, p. 217. Cf. D. J., "Über den Einfluss der gezogenen Geschütze auf die Aufstellung der Truppen im Gefecht," *AMZ,* 1863, No. 34; "Einige gedanken über die Taktik der neuen Feldartillerie," *ibid.,* 1864, Nos. 1-3.
26. *Hand-und Taschenbuch für Offiziere der preussischen Feld-Artillerie* (Berlin, 1865). Cf. the war-interrupted "Gedanken über das Wesen der Artillerie," *Österreichische Militärische Zeitschrift,* 1865, III, pp. 347-360, IV, pp. 85-104, 339-356, and 1867, pp. 159-178; where clarity and perception more than compensate for absence of profundity.
27. Hohenloe, *Aus meinem Leben,* III, pp. 195-196.

Chapter XI

1. Frederick Charles's "Einige Winke für die unter meinem Befehlen ins Feld rückenden Truppen," in Haeseler, III, pp. 22ff; E. von Hoffbauer, *Entwickelung des Massengebrachs der Feldartillerie und des Schiessens im grösseren Artillerieverbänden in Preussen* (Berlin, 1900) pp. 30 *passim*; Hohenloe, *Militärische Briefe,* III, pp. 30-31; *Aus meinem Leben,* III, pp. 357ff.
2. For general discussions of the Austrian artillery see Heinrich Friedjung, *Der Kampf um die Vorherrschaft in Deutschland,* 2 vols., 10th ed. (Stuttgart and Berlin, 1916), I, pp. 367, 384-385; *Österreichs Kämpfe im Jahre 1866,* ed. by *Generalstabsbureau für Kriegsgeschichte,* 5 vols. (Vienna, 1867-1868), I, pp. 66-67; Fritz Wiener, "Die österreichische Artillerie im Feldzug von 1866. Organization, Waffen und Gerät, Kampfweise," *Artillerierundschau,* V (1966), pp. 101-110; Hohenloe, *Militärische Briefe,* III, pp. 1-2. For the rearmament see also J. F., "Die österreichischen Feldgeschützbatterien mit gezogenen Röhren," *Österreichische Militärische Zeitschrift,* 1860, I, pp. 47-53; R-y and G-l, "Die gezogenen Feldgeschütze der k. k. österreichischen Schiesswollbatterien," *ibid.,* 1862, III, pp. 1-16, 63-78, 149-158; "Über die Beschaffenheit den Gebrauch und die Ausrüstung der k. k. österreichischen neuen Feldgeschütze im Jahre 1863," *ibid.,* 1864, I, pp. 273-283, 371-384.
3. A. Schmarda, "Über Artillerie-Reserven," *Österreichische Militärische Zeitschrift,* 1861, I, pp. 94-98; "Wahrnehmungen über die Leistungen der k. k. Artillerie und der neuartigen österreichischen

Geschütze im Kriege gegen Dänemark im Jahre 1864," *ibid.*, 1864, I, pp. 404-406, II, pp. 3-6; A. V., "Über Eintheilung und Gebrauch der Artillerie im Felde," *ibid.*, 1865, II, pp. 120-126; C. H., "Moderne Taktik," *ibid.*, I, pp. 218-223, II, pp. 228-242; and "Über die Verwendung der Brigade-und Massen-Artillerie," Part III of "Gedankeń über das Wesen der Artillerie," *ibid.*, IV, pp. 339-356.

4. For the opening battles cf. O. von Lettow-Vorbeck, *Geschichte des Krieges von 1866*, 3 vols. (Berlin, 1896-1902), II, pp. 205ff; *Der Feldzug von 1866 in Deutschland*, ed. by Grossen Generalstab, *Kriegsgeschichtliche Abetilung*, Vol, I, (Berlin, 1866), pp. 115ff; *Österreichs Kämpfe im Jahre 1866*, III, pp. 70ff; Gordon A. Craig, *The Battle of Königgrätz* (Philadelphia and New York, 1964), pp. 43ff; Friedjung, II, pp. 43ff; and Alfred Graf von Schlieffen, *Gesammelte Schriften*, 2 vols. (Berlin, 1913), I, 126 *passim*. The use of sources on the Seven Weeks' War in narrative citation is discussed above in fn. 13, Chapter VIII.

5. Hohenloe, *Militärische Briefe*, III, p. 1.

6. *Ibid.*, pp. 16-17.

7. *Ibid.*, p. 2.

8. Cf. Albrecht von Stosch, *Denkwürdigkeiten*, ed. by Ulrich von Stosch (Stuttgart, 1904), pp. 92-93; Hohenloe, *Aus meinem Leben*, III, pp. 268ff.

9. Benedek to Archduke William, February 22, 1864, in *Benedeks nachgelassene Papiere*, ed. by Heinrich Friedjung, 3rd ed. rev. (Dresden, 1904), pp. 290-291. In the aftermath of Königgrätz, it was the Archduke whom Benedek nominated as the officer best fitted to relieve him in command of the army. E. von Glaise-Horstenau, *Franz Josephs Weggefährte* (Zürich, Leipzig, and Vienna, 1830), pp. 114-115.

10. *Österreichs Kämpfe im Jahre 1866*, III, pp. 271-273; Eberhard Kaulbach, "Königgrätz nach Hundert Jahren-Zur militärischen Führung," in *Entscheidung 1866*, ed. by Wolfgang von Groote and Ursula von Gersdorff (Stuttgart, 1966), pp. 161-162.

11. Adolf Strobl, *Königgrätz* (Vienna, 1903), pp. 72-73.

12. Anton Freiherr von Mollinary, *Sechsundvierzig Jahre im österreich-ungarischen Heere 1833-1879*, 2 vols. (Zürich, 1905). II, pp. 163ff; *Österreichs Kämpfe im Jahre 1866*, III, pp. 292, 299ff; Craig, *Königgrätz*, pp. 110-111.

13. Hohenloe, *Aus meinem Leben*, III, p. 271. For the Crown Prince's decision cf. *Der Feldzug von 1866*, pp. 311-312; Lettow-Vorbeck, II, pp. 457-458.

14. Rudolph Broecker, "Erinnerungen an die Thätigkeit der 11. Infanterie-Division und ihrer Artillerie während des Feldzuges 1866," *Archiv*, LXI (1867), pp. 1-37; *Österreichs Kämpfe im Jahre 1866*, III, pp. 312-313; Max Jähns, *Die Schlacht von Königgrätz* (Leipzig, 1876); pp. 276ff.

15. Hohenloe, *Aus meinem Leben*, IV. p. 282; *Der Feldzug von 1866*, p. 327.

16. Lettow-Vorbeck, II, p. 474.

17. Hohenloe's shame at retiring in the face of an emeny remained vivid for years. In his memoirs he declared that at the age of 19 he knew Clausewitz and had been taught to smile sympathetically at the errors of Napoleon and Frederick the Great, but of what could depend on ammunition, and what colossal difficulties were involved in replacing it during battle, he heard not a syllable, (*Aus meinem Leben*, III, pp. 303-304).

18. Kaulbach, pp. 182, 184; Jähns, pp. 439ff; Lettow-Vorbeck, II, pp. 516ff; and Craig, *Königgrätz*, pp. 160-161 discuss in detail the Prussian failure to pursue.

19. Printed in Theodor Fontane, *Der deutsche Krieg von 1866*, 2 vols. (Berlin, 1871), II, p. 322.

20. Cf. von Zimmerman, *Der Antheil der Grossherzoglich Hessischen Armee-Division am Kriege 1866*, Vols. XXII-XXIII of *Kriegsgeschichtliche Einzelschriften*, ed. Grossen Generalstab (Berlin, 1897), pp. 278-279; Lettow-Vorbeck, I, p. 182; *Österreichs Kämpfe im Jahre 1866*, Appendix I, pp. 23ff; Oskar Bezzel, *Geschichte des Königlich Bayerischen Heeres von 1825 mit 1866*, Vol. VII of *Geschichte des Bayerischen Heeres* (Munich, 1931), p. 29.

21. Fontane, II, pp. 83-84.

22. Cf. among many accounts Fritz Hoenig, *Die Entscheidungskämpfe des Mainfeldzuges an der Fränkischen Saale* (Berlin, 1898), pp. 4-5; W. Loeb, *Das kgl. bayerische 4. Feldartillerie-Regiment König* (Stuttgart, 1909), pp. 23ff; and *Wirkungen und Ursachen der preusssischen Erfolge in Bayern 1866: Eine Erwiderung auf die offizielle Broschüre "Ursachen und Wirkungen."* Vom Verfasser des Bundesfeldzuges in Bayern (Wenengen-Jena, 1866), p. 14.

23. As at Tauberbischofsheim. *Österreichs Kämpfe im Jahre 1866*, V, "Die Kriegsereignisse in Westdeutschland im Jahre 1866," pp. 139-140; Fontane, II, p. 218.

CONCLUSION

PORTENTS

1. Gramont to Drouyn de Lhuys, July 5, 1866; Merlin to Randon, July 6, 1866, *Ministére des Affaires Etrangères, Les Origines diplomatiques de la guerre de 1870-71*, Vol. X (Paris, 1915), pp. 327-328, 339-340.

2. Cf. for example, Wendelin Boeheim, "Die Elementär-Taktik der Infanterie," *Österreichische Militärische Zeitschrift*, 1867, II, pp. 234ff; Carl Morawetz, "Rückblicke auf unsere Taktik auf dem nördlichen Kriegsschauplatze 1866. . . ." *ibid.*, IV, pp. 319ff; and Leopold Auspitz, "Zur Taktik des Hinterladers," *ibid.*, pp. 179ff; with Heinrich Friedjung, *Der Kampf um die Vorherrschaft in Deutschland*, 2 vols., 10th ed. (Stutt-

gart and Berlin, 1916), II, pp. 76ff, 238, 254.

3. In the Manchester *Guardian*. Reprinted in *Engels as Military Critic*, ed. by W. H. Chaloner and W. O. Henderson (Manchester, 1959), pp. 139-140. See also the leters in the London *Times* of July 7 and July 16, which express similar opinions. But on July 9 Engels wrote to Marx that "Prussia has 500,000 needle guns and the rest of the world not 500. No army can be armed with breechloaders in less than 2, 3, perhaps 5 years. Until then Prussia has supremacy." Reinhard Höhn, *Sozialismus und Heer*, 2 vols. (Bad Homburg, Berlin, Zürich, 1959), I, p. 191.

4. Quoted in Max Jähns, *Die Schlacht von Königgrätz* (Leipzig, 1876), p. 189

5. Merlin to Randon, July 17, 1866, *Ministére des Affaires Etrangères, Les Origines diplomatiques de la guerre de 1870-71*, Vol. XI (Paris, 1920), pp. 94-96.

6. Baron Stoffel, *Rapports militaires écrits de Berlin 1866-1870*, 3rd ed. (Paris, 1871), pp. 4-12. In evaluating Stoffel's conclusions, it must be remembered that he was an admirer of universal conscription as opposed to the existing French professional army—a fact which may have influenced his evaluation of the relative importance of men and material.

7. See Moltke's "Verordnungen für die höheren Truppenführer von 24. Juni 1869," in *Moltkes Militärische Werke*, 2 Abt., *Die Thätigkeit als Chef des Generalstabes der Armee im Frieden*, ed. by Grossen Generalstab, Kriegsgeschichtliche Abteilung, 3 vols. (Berlin, 1892-1906), II, p. 195 (Hereafter cited as *MMW*).

8. "Memoire . . . über die bei der Bearbeitung des Feldzuges 1866 hervorgetretenen Erfahrungen," *MMW*, 2, II, pp. 93ff.

9. O. von Lettow-Vorbeck, *Geschichte des Krieges von 1866*, 3 vols. (Berlin, 1892-1902), III, pp. 412-413; O. von der Osten-Sacken, *Preussens Heer von seinen Anfängen bis zur Gegenwart*, 3 vols. (Berlin, 1911-1914), III, pp. 164ff.

10. Cf. G. Schrieber, *Geschichte des Infanterie-Regiments von Borcke (4. Pommerschen) Nr. 21, 1813 bis 1889* (Berlin, 1889), pp. 255-256; Karl Meyer, *Geschichte des Infanterie-Regiments Fürst Leopold von Anhalt-Dessau (1. Magdeburgischen) Nr. 26, 1813-1913* (Magdeburg, 1913), pp. 252-255; F. von der Wülbe, *Das Garde-Füsilier-Regiment* (Berlin, 1876), pp. 212-213.

11. Arkolay [Woldemar Streubel], *Die Taktik der Neuzeit vom Standpunkt des Jahrhunderts und der Wissenschaft* (Darmstadt and Leipzig, 1868), especially pp. 120ff, 185, 211ff.

12. The figures are from the report of February 20, 1868, in Stoffel, pp. 87ff.

13. Krupp to Roon, July 30, 1866, Krupp to Pieper, January 26, 1868, *Alfred Krupps Briefe 1826-1887*, ed. by Wilhelm Berdrow (Berlin, 1928), pp. 224, 233-234.

14. W. H. G. von Müller, *Die Entwickelung der Feldartillerie in Bezug auf Material, Organization und Taktik, von 1815 bis 1892*, 3 vols., 2nd ed. (Berlin, 1893-1894), I, pp. 297-298; Stoffel, pp. 87ff.

15. Müller, pp. 298ff; Wilhelm Berdrow, *Alfred Krupp*, 2 vols. (Berlin, 1927), II, pp. 121-122, 135-136. For a brief discussion of the process of casting and cooling cannon steel see Henry Bessemer, "On the Employment of Cast-Steel for the Manufacture of Ordnance and Projectiles." *Journal of the Royal United Services Institution*, VIII (1864), pp. 302-320.

16. This hyperbolic statement is included in the report of February 20, 1868, in Stoffel, pp. 87ff.

17. Cf. the reports of July 29 and August 31, 1868, and July 5, 1870, in *ibid.*, pp. 210ff, 215-216, and 439ff; Müller, I, pp. 299ff; v. Loebell, "Ueber die Möglichkeit des Springens broncener Geschützröhre," *Archiv für die Offiziere der Königlich Preussische Artillerie-und Ingenieur-Korps*, LXV (1869), pp. 1-18, (Hereafter cited as *Archiv*); "Kritische Gedanken über die Schrift: 'Taktik der Neuzeit von Arcolay'," *ibid.*, LXVI (1869), pp. 1-22; Gustav Lehmann, *Die Mobilmachung von 1870/71* (Berlin, 1905), pp. 14-15.

18. Cf. W. Witte, *Die gezogenen Feldgeschütze nach ihrer Einrichtung, Ausrüstung, usw.*, 3rd ed. (Berlin, 1867), pp. 64ff; Kraft Karl zu Hohenlohe-Ingelfingen, *Militärische Briefe*, III, *Ueber Artillerie*, 2nd ed. (Berlin, 1887), pp. 43-44; and *Aufzeichnungen aus meinem Leben*, 4 vols. (Berlin, 1897-1907), III, pp. 375ff.

19. "Die Ausbildung der preussischen Fussbatterie," *Archiv*, LXVII (1870), pp. 64-79, 95-130, 236-274, and LXVIII (1871), pp. 97-154. Cf. the report of October 25, 1869, in Stoffel, pp. 338ff; and Hohenlohe, *Aus meinem Leben*, III, p. 392. An embarrassing moment occurred when Stoffel discovered that the targets were painted to resemble French soldiers, with blue tunics, red trousers, and pointed beards!

20. Hohenlohe, *Militärische Briefe*, III, pp. 89-90.

21. The development and implementation of these ideas is discussed in Hohenlohe, *Militärische Briefe*, II, *Ueber Infanterie*, 2nd ed. (Berlin, 1886), pp. 82ff; and III, 73 *passim*; and *Aus meinem Leben*, I. xxxvi; and III, 375 *passim*. Cf. also "Verordnungen für die höheren Truppenführer von 24. Juni 1869," *MMW*, 2, II, pp. 203ff; Frederick Charles's army order on artillery of July 31, 1870, in Wilhelm Colmar von der Goltz, *Feldzug 1870-71. Die Operationen der II. Armee. Vom Beginne des Krieges bis zur Capitulation von Metz* (Berlin, 1873), pp. 6-7; du Vignau, "Welches sind die wesentlichsten Eigenschaften . . . welche der neuen Feldartillerie nothtun, damit sie ihre volle Wirksamkeit im Feldkriege entfalten kann," *Archiv*, LXVII (1870), pp. 23-64; and the summary in Osten-Sacken, III, pp. 169ff.

22. "Des chemins de fer, au point des operations," October 4, 1866, Stoffel, pp. 14ff.

23. Cf., for example, Julius von Wickede, *Die Heeresorganization und Kriegführung nach den Berechtigungen der Gegenwart* (Jena, 1867), pp. 163ff; Louis Gregoire, "La Guerre, les telegraphes electriques et les chemins de fer," *Revue des deux mondes*, 1866, V, pp. 213-230; and J. E. Lassmann, *Der Eisenbahnkrieg: Taktische Studien von J. E. Lassmann* (Berlin, 1867).

24. For the Prussian military railway organization after 1866 and its role in 1870-71 see "The Railroad Concentration for the Franco-Prussian War," *The Military Historian and Economist*, III (1918), April-July; E. A. Pratt, *The Rise of Rail Power in War and Conquest, 1833-1914* (London, 1915), pp. 105ff; Lehmann, pp. 58ff; and Conrad von Hugo, "Carl von Brandenstein, Chef des Feldeisenbahnwesens und engster Mitarbeiter Moltkes 1870-71," *Wehrwissenschaftliche Rundschau*, XIV (1964), pp. 676-684.

25. Wolfgang von Groote, "Königgrätz im Blick der Militärgeschichte," in *Europa und der Norddeutsche Bund*, ed. by Richard Dietrich (Berlin, 1968), p. 132.

26. Gordon A. Craig, *The Battle of Königgrätz* (Philadelphia and New York, 1964), p. 177.

27. The quotations are from Otto Pflanze, *Bismarck and the Development of Germany* (Princeton, 1963), pp. 261, 285, 286.

28. Craig, p. xi.

29. Stoffel, pp. 9-12.

30. Craig, p. 137.

31. A statement made by the distinguished war correspondent William Howard Russell in a letter of July 9. J. B. Atkins, *The Life of Sir William Howard Russell*, Vol. II (London, 1911), pp. 140-141.

32. Cf. Gerhard Ritter, *The Schleiffen Plan: Critique of a Myth*, tr. by Andrew and Eva Wilson, foreword by B. H. Liddell-Hart (New York, 1958), esp. pp. 9-10, 51ff; and L. H. Addington, *The Blitzkrieg Era and the German General Staff, 1865-1941* (New Brunswick, N.J., 1971), pp. 1ff. For a clear expression of this view by a distinguished contemporary student of military history see Hans Delbrück, "Ueber die Bedeutung der Erfindungen in der Geschichte," in *Historische und politische Aufsätze* (Berlin, 1887), pp. 339-356.

33. G. C. Wynne, *If Germany Attacks: The Battle in Depth in the West* (London, 1940), p. 130.

34. Erich Ludendorff, *Urkunden des Obersten Heersleitung* (Berlin, 1920), pp. 553ff; contains the full text of the report.

Suggestions for Further Reading

A work proposing to examine the impact of technological development on military thought and practice in the context of the complex economic, social, and political changes taking place in Germany between 1815 and 1870 must acknowledge a massive debt to a century of scholars who have analyzed and interpreted specific aspects of these subjects. A complete listing of the sources examined would, however, have burdened the reference apparatus beyond bearing in this era of high-cost publishing. The footnotes therefore include only a cross-section of the most useful references. These suggestions concentrate on material specifically relevant to the main theme of the book, and assume a basic acquaintance with the works of such authorities as Gerhard Ritter, Gordon Craig, T. S. Hamerow, Otto Pflanze *et. al.* The best general accounts of the organization and equipment of the Prussian army in the nineteenth century remain Curt Jany, *Geschichte der Preussischen Armee vom 15. Jahrhundert bis 1914*, Vol. IV, *Die Königlich Preussische Armee und das deutsche Reichsheer 1807 bis 1914*, 2nd ed. rev. (Osnabrück, 1967); and O. von der Osten-Sacken, *Preussens Heer von seinen Anfängen bis zur Gegenwart* (Berlin, 1911-1914). Joachim Hoffmann, "Wandlungen im Kriegsbild der preussischen Armee zur Zeit der nationalen Einigungskriege," *Militärgeschichtliche Mitteilungen*, 1969, 1, pp. 5-33, offers a recent general summary of the relationship of technology and tactics between the War of Liberation and the mid-1870s. It is marred, however, by inexplicable errors of fact, such as the author's statement on p. 13 that the Austrian and south German artillery was primarily armed with muzzle-loading smoothbores in 1866. Heinz Helmert, *Militärsystem und Streitkräfte im Deutschen Bund am Vorabend des Preussisch-Österreichischen Krieges von 1866* (Berlin, 1964) by a leading East German military historian, incorporates much useful material in a Marxist framework. Wolf D. Gruner, *Das Bayerische Heer 1825 bis 1864. Eine kritische Analyse der bewaffnete Macht Bayerns vom Regierungsantritt Ludwigs I bis zum Vorabend des Deutschen Krieges*, Vol. 14 of *Militärgeschichtliche Studien*, ed. by MGFA (Boppard, 1972); and Paul Sauer, "Das württembergischen Heer in der Zeit des deutschen Bundes," Ph. D. dissertation, University of Freiburg (Freiburg, 1956); are the best of numerous recent analyses of the military systems of south Germany. An edited version of Sauer's dissertation was published as *Das Württembergische Heer in der Zeit des Deutschen und Norddeutschen Bundes*, Vol. V of *Veröffentlichungen der Kommission für Geschichtliche Landeskunde in Baden-Württemberg* (Stuttgart, 1958). Gordon Craig, *The Battle of Königgrätz* (Philadelphia and New York, 1964); and Michael Howard, *The Franco-Prussian War* (New York, 1962); include brief descriptions of the nature of the contending armies. The essays in Wolfgang von Groote and Ursula von Gersdorff, *Entscheidung 1866* (Stuttgart, 1966); are valuable in themselves and for their bibliographies.

Most contemporary treatments in English of nineteenth-century German military technology are incorporated in coffee-table books. Dudley Pope, *Guns* (Verona, Italy, 1964); J. Jobé (ed.), *Guns: An Illustrated History of Artillery* (Greenwich, Conn., 1971); are good representatives of the genre, well-illustrated and with generally accurate texts. W. Eckardt and O. Morawietz, *Die Handwaffen des brandenburgisch-preussisch-deutschen Heeres, 1640-1945* (Hamburg, 1957), is a definitive study. While nothing similar exists for the artillery, W. H. G. von Müller, *Die Entwickelung der Feldartillerie im Bezug auf Material, Organization und Taktik von 1815 bis 1892*, 3 vols. 2nd ed. (Berlin, 1893-1894); remains a useful account. The relationship of soldiers to railroads in Germany before 1870 has been ignored or mishandled by scholars for a half-century. The best interpretations are Bernhard Meinke, "Die ältesten Stimmen über die militarische Bedeutung der Eisenbahnen," *Archiv für Eisenbahnwesen*, XLI (1918), XLII (1919); *Regierungsrat* Wernekke, "Die Mitwirkung der Eisenbahnen an den Kriegen in Mitteleuropa," *Archiv für Eisenbahnwesen*, XXXV (1912); and "Die Entwicklung des Militäreisenbahnwesens vor Moltke," *Militär-Wochenblatt*, 1902, *Beiheft*. E. A. Pratt, *The Rise of Rail Power in War and Conquest, 1833-1914* (London, 1915), is an often-cited work whose chief worth is that it is written in English.

Autobiography has been described as the life story of a hero by one who knows him well. Kraft Karl zu Hohenloe-Ingelfingen, *Aufzeichnungen aus meinem Leben*, 4 vols. (Berlin, 1897-1907), fits this description while simultaneously providing a colorful account of the Prussian army at midcentury by its best artilleryman and one of its brighter intellects. Hohenloe's *Militärische Briefe*, Vol. II, *Ueber Infanterie*, and Vol. III, *Ueber Artillerie*, 2nd eds. (Berlin, 1886-1887); are similarly worthwhile despite a tendency to twenty-twenty hindsight. Of the biographies not discussed in the footnotes, Wilhelm Berdrow, *Alfred Krupp*, 2 vols. (Berlin, 1927); and Wolfgang Foerster, *Prinz Friedrich Karl von Preussen. Denkwürdigkeiten aus seinem Leben*, 2 vols. (Stuttgart, 1910); contain much useful material on their subjects. The numerous German and Austrian regimental histories compiled before 1914 vary widely in quality, but are also a neglected source of information on the soldiers of the German Confederation and their adjustment to new weapons and techniques.

Index